Learning Disability

Physical Therapy Treatment and Management
A Collaborative Approach

Second edition

Edited by
JEANETTE RENNIE BSc. MPhil. MCSP
Self-employed Physiotherapist for People with Learning Disabilities

BICENTENNIAL
1807
WILEY
2007
BICENTENNIAL

John Wiley & Sons, Ltd

Other Wiley Editorial Offices

John Wiley & Sons Inc., 111 River Street, Hoboken, NJ 07030, USA

Jossey-Bass, 989 Market Street, San Francisco, CA 94103-1741, USA

Wiley-VCH Verlag GmbH, Boschstr. 12, D-69469 Weinheim, Germany

John Wiley & Sons Australia Ltd, 42 McDougall Street, Milton, Queensland 4064, Australia

John Wiley & Sons (Asia) Pte Ltd, 2 Clementi Loop #02-01, Jin Xing Distripark, Singapore 129809

John Wiley & Sons Canada Ltd, 6045 Freemont Blvd, Mississauga, ONT, L5R 4J3, Canada

Wiley also publishes its books in a variety of electronic formats. Some content that appears in print may not be available in electronic books.

Anniversary Logo Design: Richard J. Pacifico

Library of Congress Cataloging-in-Publication Data

Learning disability : physical therapy treatment and management : a collaborative approach / edited by Jeanette Rennie. – 2nd ed.
   p. ; cm.
   Includes bibliographical references and index.
   ISBN-13: 978-0-470-01989-4 (pbk. : alk. paper)
   1. Learning disabilities–Treatment.   2. Learning disabilities–Physical therapy.
I. Rennie, Jeanette.
   [DNLM: 1. Learning Disorders–therapy.   2. Physical Therapy Modalities.
WS 110 L4379 2007]
   RC394.L37L4283   2007
   616. 85'88906 – dc22

                                                                       2006038740

A catalogue record for this book is available from the British Library

ISBN   978-0-470-01989-4

Typeset in 10/12pt Times by SNP Best-set Typesetter Ltd, Hong Kong
Printed and bound in Great Britain by TJ International Ltd, Padstow, Cornwall

This book is printed on acid-free paper responsibly manufactured from sustainable forestry in which at least two trees are planted for each one used for paper production.

Contents

Preface

Since the first edition of this book there has been a proliferation of surveys, reports, recommendations and Acts of Parliament around the world relating to people who have learning disabilities.

The expansion of post-graduate diploma and higher degree courses in all the therapies and nursing has also continued.

However, literature relevant to the physical treatment and management of people who have learning disabilities is still very limited. Other professionals who are unfamiliar with the UK usage of the term 'learning disability' such as general medical practitioners (GPs), generic nurses, therapists and social workers continue to have difficulty finding a comprehensive book that sets the presenting physical disability, whether long-term or acute, in the context of learning disability and conditions associated with learning disability.

The new authors included in this second edition have, like the original authors, based their writing on available research and have many years of practical knowledge in the subject matter of their own chapter.

The book has been written as a resource for health professionals working with people (primarily adults) who have learning disabilities, students, social services staff and carers involved in their day-to-day management. It will provide the necessary background on learning disability and allied conditions for therapists working in general and specialist hospitals who occasionally have people with learning disabilities referred for specific short-term treatment. Also addressed are some of the many questions asked or implied by other health, education or social services professionals who are confused by the multiplicity of terms such as 'mental retardation', 'learning difficulty', 'cognitive impairment', 'intellectual disability' and 'learning disability'. The book cannot answer all the questions nor go into detailed treatment methods; it is hoped that the appendices and reference lists will point readers in the direction of further study. It is also hoped that all who work in this area will be constantly alert for further changes in legislation and their own profession's guidelines.

The term 'learning disability', which is used in the UK, is currently preferred by most learning disabled adults and their families. However, even that can be misunderstood by the general public and some health professionals who tend to assume that it is used only to mean 'very low intelligence' and with which there are no other associated conditions. The place of educationalists, occupational therapists and speech and language therapists to assist their intellectual development can easily be accepted but questions are frequently heard regarding the involvement of doctors, nurses and physiotherapists.

Professionals working with people who have learning disabilities are also guilty of using 'verbal shorthand' and failing to mention that clients have one or more disabilities associated with the learning disability, for example physical, psychiatric or behavioural problems, epilepsy, autistic spectrum disorders or speech disorders.

It is worth repeating the following frequently asked questions that were listed in the first edition:

- Why do people with learning disabilities have physical disabilities?
- How do the various problems associated with learning disability affect each other?
- Why do physiotherapists work with people who have learning disabilities?
- How can I talk to a person with learning disability – will they understand me?
- Where does a physiotherapist new to learning disability start?
- How do you encourage learning disabled people to get fit and stay fit?
- Why do fully grown adults need to use special seating and equipment?
- What's the point of surgery for people with learning disabilities?

The once frequently asked question 'Why is it important that a range of professionals and care staff work in conjunction with each other?' is heard less often since flexible working practices were proposed in the 1999 Health Act and followed by the report 'Working Differently' (published by the Department of Health in 2005). It is an area in which learning disability has been one of the leaders of the field.

Since the 1950s when therapists began to work with people who had a combination of physical and learning disabilities four points have emerged. First, there have never been sufficient staff to meet the need; second, consistency of treatment is essential; third, individual therapy sessions cannot succeed without ongoing involvement from day care staff and family or carers; and fourth, people with learning disabilities need to find out for themselves that therapy is fun, creates a sense of achievement and makes them feel better. Now that fewer people with learning disabilities live in NHS long-term accommodation in the UK and most live in family-sized houses therapists have to be capable of delivering treatment and management in a wide range of settings.

No book relating to learning disability can ever be written for one single profession neither can it refer to only one profession's or one country's literature. Although physiotherapists have written many of these chapters each includes involvement by other professionals and agencies.

The book is divided into three sections. Part I describes the theory underlying learning disability and conditions associated with learning disability. This begins with worldwide social policy developments that have influenced attitudes towards learning disability and therefore subsequently affected treatment and management of physical disabilities. It has been extended to include rapidly developing policies emanating from the United Nations, the European Assembly and devolved UK government. Further revised and expanded chapters describe the following: the causes and classification of learning disability, medical treatment of associated conditions, side-effects of medication and their impact on physical ability and orthopaedic procedures. Additional information includes an introduction to Autistic Spectrum Disorder. Part II focuses on assessment. It outlines the multi-professional structure within which assessments are undertaken and describes communication skills, which are a prerequisite of their success. Chapters 7 and 8 in this section are physiotherapy assessments but are applicable to other professions; they include a résumé of the International Classification of Functioning, Disability and Health (ICF) (WHO 2001). Part III describes nine different methods of managing and treating physical disability and improving physical fitness and general health of learning disabled people. Additional sections have been added to two chapters and the importance of health promotion and use of standard facilities are reflected in a completely new chapter.

Apart from the main chapter authors there are many other people I would like to thank in addition to those whose names appear in the first edition. It should be noted that the tables in the revised Chapter 3 are almost entirely the work of Dr Mohamed Megahed MB ChB MRCPsych, formerly a Specialist Registrar in Psychiatry, The Royal London and St. Bartholomew's Scheme, who wrote Chapter 3 for the first edition.

Thanks to the following people are recorded:

- Members of the ACPPLD who responded to the original questionnaire and participated in discussions on assessment.
- Dr Walter Muir, Department of Psychiatry, University of Edinburgh and NHS Lothian, Primary and Community Division Learning Disability Services, who read and discussed sections of Part I.
- Daniel Mold, YOU and ME trainer, lecturer Orchard Hill College of Further Education; Pat Pickering, Casteleigh Day Services Officer, Cheshire YOU and ME practitioner; Lynn Bhania, teacher and YOU and ME practitioner who all contributed case studies in Chapter 17; Karen Leslie, senior 1 Paediatric Physiotherapist and External Moderator for the Students' YOU and ME Foundation Program.
- Stella Giblin and Helen Baggs of the Office of National Statistics Library, for finding and checking references.
- Staff of the library of the Scottish Executive, for finding and checking references.

- Margaret Owens, Senior Physiotherapist and Fiona Wilkie, Community Nurse NHS Lothian, Primary and Community Division Learning Disability Services, who have continued to be a support.

Finally I would again like to thank the children and staff of Oslo Observasjonshjem og Poliklinikk for Åndssvake, Norway who started me on this journey in 1964 and my husband who has patiently continued to encourage me.

Jeanette Rennie

Figures

Tables

Contributors

Anneliese Barrell MCSP
Part time lecturer, City College, Plymonth, Therapy and Rehabilitation Assistants' course; formerly Superintendent Physiotherapist in Learning Disability, Plymouth Teaching Primary Care NHS Trust.

Jane Bruce DipCOT ISPA
Reflexologist and aromatherapist with the elderly and people who have physical disabilities and learning disabilities.

Lucy Clark DipCOT DipJABADAO
Senior Occupational Therapist, Community Mental Health Team, Mold.

Debbi Cook MCSP
Senior physiotherapist, South Derbyshire Community Team.

Michael Craven MCSP
Physiotherapist/Manchester Fighting Fit Co-ordinator.

Libby Davies MCSP
Senior Physiotherapist, NHS Lothian, Primary Care and Community Division, Learning Disability Services.

Ann Findlay MCSP
Lead Physiotherapist NHS Lothian, Primary Care and Community Division, Learning Disability Services.

John Goldsmith
Director, The Helping Hand Company Ledbury Ltd.

Liz Goldsmith MCSP
Senior Physiotherapist, Premier Health Trust Advisor and The Helping Hand Company Ledbury Ltd.

Jonathan Gray Dip RG RT MCSP
Senior Physiotherapist in Mental Health, Kendray Hospital.

Maria Gunstone
Originator of YOU & ME Yoga for people with learning disabilities.

Helen Holme MSc MCSP
Falls Prevention Co-ordinator for Birkenhead and Wallasey PCT; formerly Senior Physiotherapist, Adult Learning Disability Services, Wirral and West Cheshire Community NHS Trust.

Angela Johnson MA MCSP
Formerly Physiotherapy Lecturer, Huddersfield University.

Amanda Leech MCSP
Superintendent Physiotherapist, Learning Disability Physiotherapy Department, Lynebank Hospital, Dunfermline Hospital.

Jane Neil-MacLachlan BPhil MRCSLT
Adults' Autism Co-ordinator, NHS Lothian Primary Care and Community Division, Learning Disability Services.

Patricia Odunmbaku Auty MCSP
Independent physiotherapy consultant in learning disability.

Jeanette Rennie BSc MPhil MCSP
Self-employed physiotherapist working with people with learning disabilities; formerly Senior Physiotherapist, NHS Lothian Primary Care and Community Division, Learning Disability Services.

James E Robb BSc MD FRCS FRCP
Consultant Orthopaedic Surgeon, Royal Hospital for Sick Children, Edinburgh.

Ian Silkstone MCSP
Senior Physiotherapist, The Child Development Centre Dewsbury District Hospital, Mid Yorkshire Trust.

Sally Smith Dip RG RT MCSP
Senior Physiotherapist Learning Disability Services, Nottinghamshire Health Care NHS Trust.

Sue Smith MRCSLT
Principal Speech and Language Therapist for People with Learning Disabilities, Southampton Community NHS Trust.

Sue Standing MSc MCSP
Lead Physiotherapist for Learning Disability, Hampshire Partnership Trust.

Mark Sterrick MSc MB ChB LLB DFM FACLM
Formerly Associate Specialist, Lothian Primary Care NHS Trust, Learning Disability Services

Tanya Thiagarajah MSc MB ChB BaO MRCPsych
Specialist Registrar in Learning Disabilities, NHS Lothian Primary Care and Community Division, Learning Disability Services.

Alys Watson MCSP
Riding for the Disabled Association, Edinburgh.

Sybil Williams MCSP
Project Manager of Pedal Power amd formerly Physiotherapy Manager, Bro Morganwg Trust, Wales.

I Learning Disability and Associated Problems that Affect Physical Ability

1 What is Learning Disability?

JEANETTE RENNIE

INTRODUCTION

In the UK the term 'learning disability' is used to mean mental retardation or intellectual disability (see Table 1.4 and Chapter 2). It is used throughout this book except where it is important to record terminology of a particular period.

A number of writers have described the history of the concept of mental retardation – for example Morris (1969), Scheerenberger (1987), Trent (1994) and Harris (2006). This chapter examines the way in which history has influenced treatment and management of associated physical disabilities. It does not deal in depth with social and educational developments or specify the work of individual voluntary agencies, nor does it detail all legislation that impinges upon learning disability.

The chapter is divided into sections describing:

- the events and attitudes leading to the establishment of institutions and organisational developments within them
- the concept of community care for people with learning disabilities and its development
- the present legal aspects in the UK and recent changes in health and social care

Tables are used to show international influence on policymaking, UK legislation, development of definitions and terminology and evolution of the definition of 'normalisation'.

A MIX OF POLITICS, EDUCATION, SOCIAL POLICIES AND MEDICINE

- Have ideologies, theories and practices benefited or deprived people with learning disabilities with regard to facilities that would assist them to lead a fulfilled life?

Learning Disability: Physical Therapy Treatment and Management. Edited by Jeanette Rennie
© 2007 John Wiley & Sons Ltd

- Have neurological and sensory impairments present in people with mild mental retardation (Fryers 1997) been considered worthy of treatment or ignored as a nonspecific associated clumsiness?
- Does the term 'learning disability', used in the UK to assist integration into normal society, promote misunderstanding amongst generic healthcare professionals who associate 'learning' with 'education'?
- Does the term 'learning disability' hinder research between countries? For example, in the US the term was introduced in 1962 to mean: 'A disorder in one or more of the basic psychological processes involved in the understanding or in using language, spoken or written, which may manifest itself in an incomplete ability to listen, think, speak, read, write or spell, or to do mathematical calculations . . .' It includes 'perceptual handicaps, dyslexia, developmental aphasia, brain injury, mid brain dysfunction'. It does not include motor handicaps or mental retardation (Education for All Handicapped Children Act. Public Law 94–42, 34 C.F.R. 300.5 [b] [9], in Brown and Aylward 1996).

People with learning disabilities have produced many and varied reactions in those around them. They have also caused philanthropists, educationalists, health professionals and sociologists to consider deeply how their needs may be met. The social and economic climate of the time has influenced thinking, which in turn has informed political decision making, sometimes clashing with isolated progressive thought and sometimes reinforcing it. Many caring and progressive attitudes of previous years, interpreted today as selfish and condescending, were the building blocks for present policies. Key developments and interaction between countries in the developed world are listed in Tables 1.1, 1.2 and 1.3.

Before the development of modern medicine the majority of profoundly learning-disabled children died in infancy. In general, therefore, the literature refers to people who would now be regarded as having mild to moderate learning disability.

Writings such as Arthurian legends and Shakespearean plays refer to people 'possessed' or with 'second sight' who influenced everyday occurrences or major battles. Such people were either venerated or locked up and maltreated (Morris 1969, Scheerenberger 1987, Trent 1994). In the early fourteenth century in England, differentiation was made between learning disability (people who were born 'fools') and mental illness (people who became 'mad') on the basis that the former could never become 'normal' but the latter might regain their sanity: 'born fools could not inherit property, the King as *parens patriae* assumed rights over the fool and his property as if he were an infant' (O'Connor and Tizard 1956).

Comparison with infants led to a protective and humane attitude towards the more severely learning disabled. It was also possible, however, for anyone to sue for the guardianship and administration of a 'fool's estate' – 'to beg for

Table 1.1. Key developments worldwide

France	
1801	Itard published his book *The Wild Boy of Aveyron*. It described innovative treatment of a 'mentally defective' boy (Lane 1977).
1806	Pinel published his paper 'Treatise on Alienism'. 'Defectives' had the ability to be trained to their level of intelligence but no further (Trent 1994).
1846	Seguin published 'The psychological treatment, hygiene and education of idiots' a handbook for institutional care (Kanner 1964).
US	
1820–60	The Depression, ideas from Europe and Britain and the Civil War led to end of 'outdoor relief' and development of 'indoor relief'.
1848	Seguin moved to US.
1856	Schools for feebleminded children became residential asylums for training feebleminded adults and idiots. Medically trained superintendents replaced headteachers.
Late 1800s	Wilbur categorised mental defectives (Table 1.4)
1958	Anthony Dexter conceived a 'social system concept' and 'labelling'
1961	President Kennedy appointed a President's Panel on mental retardation.
1969	Concept of normalisation introduced by Bank Mikkelsen and Bengt Nirje (Table 1.5)
1970	The Developmental Disabilities Services and Facilities Construction Act.
1971	International League of Societies for the Mentally Handicapped endorsed philosophy of normalisation
1973	The Rehabilitation Act
1987	The Developmental Disabilities Assistance and Bill of Rights Amendments include persons with mental retardation
1990	Americans with Disabilities Act (ADA) included mental retardation in its category 'mental or psychological disorder'
2001	The President's New Freedom Initiative promoted full inclusion of people with disabilities in all aspects of life and work – included mental retardation
2002	Surgeon General's Conference on Health Disparities and Mental Retardation
Switzerland	
1839	Guggenbuhl established a 'colony' on the Abendberg
Italy	
1870s	Lombroso suggested that inherited factors caused criminal tendencies.
1978	Law passed to replace all institutions with community care
Denmark	
1959	The Government passed an Act concerning Care of the Mentally Retarded and other Exceptionally Retarded Persons (Table 1.5)
Canada	
Early 1970s	Responsibility for people with mental handicap transferred from health to social welfare and educational ministries.
Australia	
1970s	Several states acted upon reports recommending mentally handicapped people transfer to the community
1998	The state of Western Australia proposed 'local area coordination'.

Table 1.1. *Continued*

UN	
1971	Declaration on the Rights of Mentally Retarded Persons
1975	Declaration on the Rights of Disabled People
2004	Reported that disability was beginning to be treated as a broad human rights issue
WHO	
1980	International Classification of Impairments, Disabilities and Handicaps (Table 1.4)
Sweden	
1990	Recommended that all institutions close
European Assembly	
2002	European Social Charter (revised) Article 15: the right of persons with disabilities to independence, social integration and participation in the life of the community
2003	European Year of People with Disabilities

(Compiled in part from Morris 1969, Scheerenberger 1987, Trent 1994)

Table 1.2. UK, key reports and legislation

1713–14	Vagrancy Acts: 'apprehension of those who might be dangerous'
1774	Madhouses Act: 'provision of minimum standards of care and for the control of private madhouses'
1808	County Asylums Act: public asylums in England replaced private madhouses.
1908	Report of Royal Commission on Care and Control of the Feebleminded.
1913	Mental Deficiency Act: people with mental deficiency dealt with as a specific group. Segregation introduced. Mental defectives classified
1914	Mental Deficiency Act: Local authorities to protect mentally defective patients by providing accommodation.
1927	Mental Deficiency Act: Creation of separate institutions for the mentally ill and mentally handicapped.
1946	National Health Service Act: minimum standard of care available for all who needed it.
1948	The National Health Service Act (as amended) standardised mental subnormality hospitals in accordance with general hospitals.
1959	Mental Health Act repealed all previous legislation. Emphasis placed on voluntary instead of compulsory admission to hospital. Civil rights of patients recognised, including access to a Health Service Commissioner.
1961	Minister of Health proposed start of 'running down' mental hospitals.
1971	Better Services for the Mentally Handicapped
1975	The National Development Group and National Development Team for the Mentally Handicapped established
1978	Helping Mentally Handicapped People in Hospital
1978	Warnock Committee Report on special educational needs
1979	Jay Report. Policy based on principles of normalisation. Special help would be required from their communities and the professional services. Advocacy recommended
1979	'A Better Life' (Scotland). Concept of community care endorsed, gradual progress recommended

Table 1.2. *Continued*

1980	SHAPE (Scottish Health Authorities Priorities for the Eighties)
1981	Education Act for Children with Special Education Needs and Education (Scotland) Act. Education should be fitted to the child's requirements as far as possible. Statement of needs and needs assessments proposed.
1983	The All Wales Strategy
1983	Mental Health Act
1984	The Mental Health (Scotland) Act
1986	The Disabled Persons Act (Tom Clarke Bill). Right to representation, assessment, information, consultation. Carers right to ask for assessment of disabled persons' needs and carers' ability to care taken into account.
1987	Report by the Department of Health and Social security: *Mental Handicap: Progress, Problems and Priorities A Review of Mental Handicap Services in England since the 1971 White Paper*
1988	Community Care: Agenda for Action (Griffiths Report)
1988	SHARPEN (Scottish Health Authorities Review of Priorities for the Eighties and Nineties)
1989	White Paper *Caring for People: Community Care in the next Decade and Beyond.*
1990	NHS and Community Care Act. Confirmed proposals in 1989 White Paper.
1995	The Health of the Nation including 'A strategy for people with learning disabilities and their carers'
1998	'Signposts for success'
1998	Health laws for Northern Ireland devolved to Northern Ireland Assembly
1999	Health laws for Scotland devolved to The Scottish Executive
1999	The Health Act to improve coordination of services for everyone
1999	National Assembly for Wales established The Learning Disability Advisory Group
2000	White Paper, The NHS Plan 2000
2000	The Same as You? A Review of Services for People with Learning Disabilities encouraged use of generic services with appropriate support
2000	The Adults with Incapacity (Scotland) Act
2001	Valuing People – A New Strategy for Learning Disability for the Twenty-first Century' refined 1995 definition of learning disability for England and Wales
2001	The Learning Disability Advisory Group reported to the Welsh Assembly *'Fulfilling the Promise'*
2001	Seeking consent: working with people with learning disabilities
2003	Partnership for Care, Scotland's Health White Paper
2003	The Mental Health (Care and Treatment) (Scotland Act) had relevance to people with a dual diagnosis of learning disability and mental disorder by making new arrangements for detention, care and treatment
2004	Improving Mental Health law: towards a New Mental Health Act
2005	The Mental Capacity Act
2006	White Paper, Our health, Our care, Our say; A New Direction for Community Services
2006	Start of three-year strategic plan for assessing and encouraging improvement in the healthcare of adults with learning disabilities

Table 1.3. Development of terminology

Year	Country	Terminology
Late 1890	US	Wilbur's categories of mental defectives (Table 1.4)
Late 1890	UK	Feeble minded, imbecile, idiot
1913	UK	Moral imbecile, feeble minded, imbecile, idiot
1921	US	Mental Retardation
1927	UK	England, moral defective replaced moral imbecile
1959	UK	Legal terminology England and Wales: subnormal, severe subnormal. (Also used 'mental handicap' and 'severe mental handicap') Scotland mental deficiency, severe mental deficiency
1968	WHO	Mental Retardation: mild, moderate, severe, profound
1978	UK	Education terminology England and Wales moderate and severe learning difficulties replaced moderate and severe educationally subnormal
1980	WHO	Mental Retardation – all people with IQ of <70
1981	UK	Education terminology: one category – learning difficulty
1983	UK	England and Wales mental impairment, severe mental impairment. Scotland mental handicap, severe mental handicap
1995	UK	Learning disability accepted terminology. Medically, used in conjunction with more specific definition (Chapter 2 and Table 1.4)
2000	US	Began to use intellectual disability in documents and referred to a wide range of terms used world wide
2003	US	Federal Advisory Committee replaced Mental Retardation with Intellectual Disability – the 'President's Committee for People with Intellectual Disabilities'
2003	US AAMR	Continued the use of mental retardation, 'American Association on Mental Retardation'
2005	Scotland	Learning disability confirmed as legal terminology
2006	WHO ICD 10	The 2006 version continued the use of Mental Retardation

a fool' (see *The Chambers Dictionary*, 1994 edition). In the sixteenth and seventeenth centuries various tests were devised to verify 'fools', both to protect them and to gain their property rights.

Before the Industrial Revolution, however, local people with learning disabilities were an accepted part of life. This probably contributed to the success of outdoor relief given as direct aid to 'worthy' dependants in the US before 1820 (Trent 1994).

Until France produced pioneers such as Itard, Pinel and Seguin in the early nineteenth century, positive treatment or teaching had been deemed impossible. The first steps towards enabling 'defectives' to learn and to grow in self-esteem were Itard's use of warm baths as sensory stimulation to train 'defectives', Pinel's humanitarian, psychological approach and Seguin's 'physiological and moral training' with 10 'idiots' in Paris (Kanner 1964).

Spa treatment was being used throughout Europe for a variety of medical conditions and the term 'hydrotherapy' was an accepted description for specifically medical treatment in England. However, Itard appears to have used baths for training purposes only and not to improve physical abilities in 'mental defectives'.

DEVELOPMENT OF INSTITUTIONS

During the mid-nineteenth century two parallel strands developed:

- an awareness that 'defectives' had an ability to learn and that it was society's duty to provide education and security for them
- the proposal that low intellectual ability was an entirely inherited factor – the 'degeneration' theory, which later gave rise to eugenics

In 1839, Guggenbuhl established a colony for the cure of cretinism on the Abendberg in Switzerland. It was closed 20 years later due to failure to discover a 'cure'. However, the principle of 'colonies' and Guggenbuhl's treatment theories of a sensible diet, massage and physical exercise, spread to other countries in Europe, the UK and the US.

In the UK, philanthropic reformers began to found institutions to replace the asylums where mentally ill and learning-disabled people were kept together, a problem only solved in the early twentieth century. For example Dr and Mrs Brodie (Henderson 1964) founded the Edinburgh Idiot Asylum in 1855. It transferred to Stirlingshire and became The Scottish National Institution for the Education of Imbecile Children and subsequently the Royal Scottish National Institution for Mental Defectives, the first purely for 'mental defectives'.

In the Republic of Ireland, Stewarts Hospital in Dublin was opened in1869. This was a private charitable institution administered on a voluntary basis by a committee of management, supported by the state through revenue allocations and capital grants.

The US responded to pressure from local officials, parents and superintendents by ending outdoor relief and following the UK's government-driven programme of building large centralised hospitals for 'idiots' and 'feebleminded' individuals.

Gradually medically trained superintendents and medical terminology became normal practice in the residential institutions and an increasing number of physicians was employed. Dr John Haydon Langdon-Down, who had been Superintendent of the Asylum for Idiots, Earlswood, since 1858, opened a private home for 'mental defectives' in 1868. There, he recognised and described 'Mongolism' (Down syndrome). The home developed into a community where residents learned life skills and sports and enjoyed various excursions.

Despite this development, all study and research appears to have been directed towards assessing and categorising 'idiots' into different levels by intellectual ability.

CATEGORISATION

Galton (in 1869) and McKeen Cattell (in 1890) were amongst the earliest individuals to attempt categorisation and measurements using new tests of IQ (intelligence quotient). The most notable tests, however, were devised by Binet and Simon. (Savage 1970). The tests were revolutionary but assumed that intelligence could be tested in isolation, without reference to an individual's social and environmental conditions or physical disabilities. They therefore reinforced the theory of hereditary transmission, which inadvertently fostered fear of a further increase in the number of people with learning disability. In the late nineteenth century this fear led to the development of the eugenics movement and custodial care of people with learning disability.

SEGREGATION

In 1908, the first edition of Tredgold's renowned book, *Textbook on Mental Deficiency*, was published. In 1909, in an article in the *Eugenics Review*, he referred to the high inheritance factor in mental deficiency and a relatively high birth rate amongst the poor and the handicapped. It has been suggested that this influenced the addition of a statutory instrument to the Mental Deficiency Act of 1913 in 1927. The 1913 Act had originally been introduced to separate people with learning disabilities from those with mental health problems. The statutory instrument that was added to become part of the 1927 Act introduced the category of 'moral defective', which segregated 'mentally deficient' people from the general population and from the opposite sex to prevent an increase in 'mental deficiency . . . as a protection of society as a whole'.

One of the effects of segregation was to retain children and adults who had a combination of physical disabilities and learning disability in hospitals specialising in learning disability. Staff were not equipped to treat their physical disabilities and were, on the whole, unable to recognise the impact that such disabilities made upon communication, mobility and daily living skills and subsequently to frustration and resulting in aggressive behaviour.

Photographs from large UK and US hospitals, however, showed that active exercise was provided for physically able people with learning disabilities, in the same way as social reformers such as Robert Owen provided 'exercise classes for the moral and physical development of his young workers' (Barclay 1994).

Institutions grew in size and numbers and segregation continued but gradually attitudes towards aims of treatment within the institutions changed. For example, Dr Chislet the first medical superintendent of Lennox Castle Hospital, Glasgow, wrote in 1936 that treatment should consist of 'Custodial care for those who require such for life, i.e. the lower grades of defectives, and an endeavour by treatment and training to render certain defectives fit to take their place in the general community.'

Suggestions and Instructions regarding the developing 'colonies' included the '. . . necessity of a rural setting away from danger . . . adequate classification according to sex, age, ability, medical condition and behavioural problems' (Loudon 1992).

However, isolated institutions were liable to have difficulty attracting specialist staff to deal with medical conditions and behavioural problems. They therefore tended to become self-contained units largely ignored by the rest of the nursing and medical professions, and society as a whole.

The 1948 National Health Service Act (as amended) required

- appointment of appropriately qualified senior doctors
- local authorities to remove 'persons in need of care and attention to suitable premises'
- local authorities to provide temporary accommodation where necessary

This produced rapid expansion of both the number of hospitals for people with learning disability and the patients that they could accommodate.

NEW THOUGHTS ABOUT INSTITUTIONS

The Mental Deficiency Act 1913 had introduced a category of 'moral imbeciles'. People with borderline learning disabilities, angry and frustrated teenagers and sexually promiscuous adults who lacked perception of the consequences of their actions and so appeared to be potential criminals were frequently hospitalised for life. Although this was preferable to life imprisonment in a standard gaol it still grossly restricted their freedom.

During the 1950s, publicity about such hospitalisation led to the Royal Commission on the Law relating to Mental Illness and Mental Deficiency (1957) and the Mental Health Act 1959. This Act introduced informal admission to learning disability hospitals and changed terminology. It created a greater awareness of 'mental handicap' and mental illness, although 50 years later confusion still arises between the two in the mind of the general public.

At this time there was a worldwide search for a more appropriate definition and method of care. The medical model was increasingly considered inappropriate for people with learning disabilities who had no single physical disease that could be cured by medical intervention. Lewis Anthony Dexter proposed a 'social systems concept' in 1958. He viewed the 'cost and trouble' caused by 'mental defectives' in society as a result of both 'society's expectations of the mentally defective and the mental defectives' learned role as to what was expected of them' (in Scheerenberger 1987).

It was gradually acknowledged that only the most severely 'subnormal' people required skilled nursing care and few needed the support of custodial care. However, appropriate nursing care for the most severely 'subnormal' who also had severe physical disabilities was considered to be palliative and protecting, not stimulating, and did not enable patients to achieve their maximum potential.

Access to a range of treatments for children with physical disabilities and normal intelligence was being developing by people like Karl and Bertha Bobath in England in the 1930s (Bobath and Bobath 1975). In Hungary in the 1940s Andreas Peto was developing conductive education (Hari and Akos 1988). Infants with physical disabilities and learning disability were usually excluded on grounds of lack of understanding and short life expectancy. In the UK treatment was made available through special schools such as Trefoil, founded in 1939, Westerlea, founded in 1948 and Craig-y-Park, Drummonds and Thomas de la Rue all founded in 1955. Many paediatric services began to provide preschool treatment either at hospital outpatient departments or on a domiciliary basis.

INTRODUCTION OF THE CONCEPT OF 'COMMUNITY CARE'

Community care was first mentioned in a statutory report of midwives in 1955 but the Danish government's Parliamentary Act acted as the major catalyst for change (see box).

Danish government passes the Act of 'Normalisation', 5 June 1959

The Act profoundly affected the lives of people with learning disabilities throughout the world by:

- permitting children to go to normal schools
- permitting adults to leave their parents' home and be trained, taught and employed

At the time the Danish government was accused of abdicating responsibility for the mentally retarded.

In the US, four alternative methods of care were proposed in the 1960s (Scheerenberger 1987):

- the least restrictive alternative allowed equal protection under law including the right to deny and accept treatment, and requiring informed consent by individuals or their guardians
- the developmental model: mentally retarded children and adults were capable of growth, learning and development
- mainstreaming recommended integration of mentally retarded children into mainstream schools but offered no additional assistance
- normalisation

At about the same time Wolfensberger introduced the concept of 'citizen's advocacy', by which volunteers were able to represent the views of individual institutionalised residents.

In 1961 the President's Panel, set up by President Kennedy to produce recommendations for mental retardation, included ideas for research, preventive health measures and production of a new legal as well as social concept of 'the retarded'. However, the concept of normalisation was not introduced to the US by Nirje until 1969. It was followed in 1970 by an Act that gave Federal authorisation to 'assist States to ensure that people with disabilities were enabled to receive the necessary care treatment and other services to live their lives to the maximum' (Scheerenberger 1987).

Although community care is known to have been mentioned as early as 1955 and was first recommended for people with learning disability in the UK in 1961, partly as a cost-cutting exercise (Scrivens 1986) the number of residents in large institutions peaked at approximately 52000 in the early 1970s (Brown 1992). A number of factors lay behind this statistic including:

- the statutory obligation of the National Health Service (NHS) to meet the care needs of the whole population
- the NHS was supported by central funding, which removed dependence on local rates or charitable donations
- prevailing medical and social opinion was that the most appropriate form of care was sheltered living, offered by hospital services
- people with learning disability were living longer

This was the period in which therapists began to expand their work in hospitals for people with learning disability. For example, occupational therapy started at Gogarburn Hospital, Edinburgh, in 1964, physiotherapy began in 1966, and speech therapy was seconded from the Scottish Council for Spastics (now Capability Scotland) in 1966. Recreation was recognised as an important part of rehabilitation (Luckey and Shapiro 1974) and remedial gymnasts began to organise sporting activities (see Chapter 15). Physiotherapy, occupational therapy, speech therapy and psychology were available for children and young adults in Oslo Observasjonshjem og Poliklinikk for Andssvake, Norway, in the 1950s, physiotherapy and occupational therapy started at St Michael's House in Dublin in 1955 and physiotherapy started in Denmark and Bermuda in the early 1960s. In the former Eastern region of Nigeria, people with learning disabilities were treated in small general hospitals and specialist parts of large general hospitals in the 1970s and day centres and special education centres began to be established.

The first attempts were made to quantify the number of therapists working in this field in the UK in 1970. The numbers at the time were:

England

- occupational therapists 77 (others, for example technicians and assistants 212)
- physiotherapists 37 (others, for example assistants 4)
- speech therapists 18
- chiropodists 20
- other therapists 285 (in 1971)
- psychologists 54 (DHSS 1987)

Scotland

- occupational therapists 0.22 per 100 patients
- physiotherapists 0.17 per 100 patients
- speech therapists 0.06 per 100 patients
- chiropodists 0.06 per 100 patients
- other therapists 0.27 per 100 patients
- psychologists 0.07 per 100 patients (Scottish Home and Health Department 1970)

In many hospitals residents were encouraged and supported to live their lives as fully as possible but this failed to achieve full individual development. In other hospitals, residents lived in restricted and repressive conditions. A series of scandals resulted in the publication of *Better Services for the Mentally Handicapped* (Department of Health and Social Security 1971).

Internationally, in 1971 the United Nations published the Declaration on the Rights of Mentally Retarded Persons. It prescribed that they should have 'to the maximum degree of feasibility the same rights as other human beings' and a right to a qualified guardian.

Central government support for community care in the UK began with publication of *Better Services for the Mentally Handicapped* (DHSS 1971).

- multiprofessional teams encouraged, to support and enable people with 'mental handicap' to live more normal lives in the community
- links encouraged between health authorities and local authorities
- community integration strongly recommended

SEARCH FOR COMMON DEFINITIONS
AND TERMINOLOGY

Wolfensberger's reworded principle of normalisation and his introduction of
the term 'social integration' encouraged worldwide progress towards care in
the community (Loudon 1992).

Social integration

Living as an integrated member of the local community; participating in
local activities.

However, multidisciplinary and interagency work has always been impeded
by variations in terminology both nationally and internationally (Table 1.4 and
see Chapter 2). An attempt to reduce frequency of change in terminology was
made by the American Association on Mental Retardation in 1973. When it
revised its definitions, it also defined aims for future development and standardisation of a common base for classification of terminology.

ACCELERATION OF COMMUNITY CARE

Acceleration towards community care was further assisted by the United
Nations Declaration of the Rights of Disabled People in 1975. It included,
among its 13 statements, the assertion that disabled persons have the inherent
right to respect for human dignity. Whatever the origin, nature and seriousness
of their handicaps and disabilities, they have the same fundamental rights of
their fellow citizens of the same age, which implies first and foremost the right
to enjoy a decent life, as normal and as full as possible (in Mittler 1979).

Progress could be seen by developments in both private and charitably run
facilities and the long-stay hospitals. For example, in the Republic of Ireland,
St Michael's House, Dublin, was extending its services to support learning-
disabled children in integrated education, to provide appropriate further
education through developmental day centres, to give support and training
for clients in open employment and to provide residential services for very
small groups in ordinary homes. Also in Dublin, Stewarts Hospital began to
develop clinical services with family support and respite for children and
adults, courses for sports and leisure, an introduction to parenting and budget-
ing skills and advice on nutrition. Its residential numbers decreased and its
services became more available both on the campus and to clients in the
community.

Table 1.4. Development of definitions

Late 1800 US	Wilbur's categories
	Simulative idiots: could be prepared for ordinary duties and enjoyments of humanity
	Higher grade idiots: would attend common schools to be qualified for civil usefulness and social happiness
	Lower grade idiots: could become decent in their habits, educated in simple occupations, capable of self support under judicious management in their own families, or in public industrial institutions for adult idiots.
	Incurables: aim to achieve some education. (In Trent 1994).
1913 UK Mental	Idiots – people unable to guard themselves from physical danger
	Imbeciles – people incapable of managing themselves or their affairs
Deficiency Act	Feeble-minded persons – people who require care, supervision or control for their own protection or the protection of others. Children who cannot benefit from ordinary schools
	Moral imbeciles – people with a mental defect coupled with strong vicious or criminal propensities on which punishment has no or little deterrent effect
1921 US (AAMR)	American Association on Mental Retardation (AAMR) published first edition of *Manual on terminology and classification in mental retardation*
1973 US (AAMR)	'Mental Retardation refers to significantly subaverage general intellectual functioning existing concurrently with deficits in adaptive behaviour and manifested during the developmental period'
1980 WHO ICD 10	International Classification of Diseases
	Mental retardation
	Mild: IQ: 50–70 individuals who can acquire practical skills and functional reading and arithmetic abilities with special education, and who can be guided towards social conformity
	Moderate: IQ: 35–49 individuals who can learn simple communication, elementary health and safety habits, and simple manual skills, but do not progress in functional reading or arithmetic
	Severe: IQ: 20–34 – individuals who can benefit from systematic habit training
	Profound: IQ < 20 – individuals who may respond to skill training in the use of legs, hands, and jaws
1980 WHO	*International Classification of Impairments, Disabilities and Handicaps*
	Impairment: musculo skeletal abnormality, and organ misfunction.
	Disability: the resultant functional ability
	Handicap: the disadvantage arising from impairment or disability.
	Intellectual Impairments include: intelligence, memory and thought but excluded language and learning
	Impairments of intelligence include: 'disturbances of the rate and degree of development of cognitive functions, such as perception, attention, memory, and thinking, and their deterioration as a result of pathological processes')
1983 US (AAMR)	Definition of Mental Retardation updated (In Scheerenberger 1987)

Table 1.4. *Continued*

1983 UK (England and Wales)	'Mental impairment': 'a state of arrested or incomplete development of mind which includes a significant impairment of intelligence and social functioning and is associated with abnormally aggressive or seriously irresponsible conduct on the part of the person concerned' (Mental Health Act 1983)
1983 UK (Scotland)	Mental handicap replaced mental deficiency but had the same general meaning. (Mental Health (Scotland) Act 1983).
1992 WHO ICD 10	ICD 10 Mental retardation accepted terminology but definition updated
1992 US (AAMR)	Mental retardation: accepted terminology. In 1992 AAMR began to develop a more functional approach by changing its 1973 definition to require 'significant delay in two or more of ten areas of adaptive functioning', which include 'daily living skills, self care and communication'
1994 US (APA)	American Psychiatric Association DSM-IV: Mental retardation: accepted terminology
1995 UK	'Learning disability' accepted terminology. Generally used to mean mental retardation: impaired intelligence and impaired social functioning . . . a reduced ability to understand new or complex information and learn new skills and a reduced ability to cope independently. Learning disability is a condition that starts before adulthood and has a lasting effect on development (DOH 1995). Medically used in conjunction with ICD10, AAMR or DSM-IV
2000 US (APA)	DSM-IV-TR (American Psychiatric Association 2000). Mental retardation accepted terminology, guidelines updated (See current classification in Chapter 2)
2001 UK	In Valuing People' (DOH 2001a) Learning Disability includes the presence of: <ul><li>A significantly reduced ability to understand new or complex information learn new skills (impaired intelligence), with;</li><li>A reduced ability to cope independently (impaired social functioning);</li><li>Which started before adulthood, with a lasting effect on development.</li></ul> It encompasses people with a broad range of disabilities. Many people with learning disabilities also have physical and/or sensory impairments. The definition includes adults with autism and learning disability. It does not include people with 'learning difficulty', which is more broadly defined in education legislation. Medically used in conjunction with ICD10, AAMR or DSM-IV-TR
2002 US AAMR	Revised definition '. . . a disability characterised by significant limitations both in intellectual functioning and in adaptive behaviour as expressed in conceptual, social and practical adaptive skills. This disability originates before the age of 18.' (See current classification in Chapter 2.)
2006 WHO ICD 10 2006 version	Mental retardation accepted terminology but definition updated to include 'Intellectual abilities and social adaptations may change over time, and, however poor, may improve as a result of training and rehabilitation' (see current classification in Chapters 2 and 3)

In the UK the National Development Group and Development Team for the Mentally Handicapped was established to facilitate progress from hospitals to the community. A series of consultation documents have continued to be issued and Parliamentary Bills passed. These are listed in Table 1.2.

Community care was also stimulated by:

- increasing awareness amongst families
- the growth of voluntary organisations
- realignment of funding from central government
- increased involvement of social services departments
- the Warnock Report (Department of Education and Science 1978) on special educational needs
- the introduction of a named 'key worker' to work with and coordinate activities for one or more adults with learning disabilities
- pressure groups, leading to campaigns on related issues for adults

DEVELOPMENT OF HEALTH SERVICES WORKING PRACTICE

The unexpected opportunities given to many people with learning disabilities meant that healthcare staff had to learn how to work closely with people whose background was socially, not medically, orientated. It was essential to find workspace. It was also essential to ensure that social services and voluntary agency staff understood that appropriate equipment supplied by therapists was necessary to enhance quality of life and was not re-enforcement of a disability.

In 1977 the numbers of therapists working with learning disabled people in England had risen to

- occupational therapists 113 (helpers 484)
- physiotherapists 103 (helpers 62)
- speech therapists 32
- chiropodists 23
- other therapists 269 (decrease)
- psychologists 140 (Department of Health and Social Security 1987)

VIEWS OF PEOPLE WITH LEARNING DISABILITIES

While reformers were working hard to integrate people with learning disabilities into normal society they themselves were not necessarily acquiescent of the principle. At a National (American) Conference on Normalisation and Contemporary Practice in Mental retardation in 1980 representatives of the People First International, an organisation of disabled persons, stated that 'consumers need a group identity. They need a culture, a history and their own

Table 1.5. Normalisation and beyond

1959	Danish Act of Parliament: 'Whatever facilities are open to all other citizens must, in principle, also be available to the mentally retarded.'
1969	Bank-Mikkelsen and Bengt Nirje 'making available to the mentally retarded patterns and conditions of everyday life which are as close as possible to the norms and patterns of the mainstream of society.'
1972	Wolfensberger. 'Utilization of means which are as culturally normative as possible, in order to establish and/or maintain personal behaviours and characteristics which are as culturally normal as possible.'
1981	O'Brien – five essential accomplishments for quality of life: community presence, choice, competence, respect and community participation.
1983	Wolfensberger redefined normalisation as Social Role Valorisation (SRV): 'The enablement, establishment, enhancement, maintenance, and/or defence of valued social roles for people – particularly for those at value risk – by using, as much as possible, culturally valued means.'
1987	Kristiansen and Ness additional accomplishments for quality of life: expression of individuality and experience of continuity in one's own life.
1992	Wolfensberger differentiated between valuing a person for themselves and ensuring that that person filled a valued role.

heroes. They need each other so that they're able to develop what the rest of society has . . . Groups give a special meaning and identity.'

They saw themselves as any other minority group in the US and normalisation as a way in which they would become isolated within the 'normal' community (Scheerenberger 1987). Table 1.5 shows how Wolfsenberger, one of the main proponents of normalisation (Wolfensberger and Thomas 1983), attempted to answer their concerns by gradually redefining the concept of normalisation.

PROVISION OF SERVICES IN THE COMMUNITY

Between 1967 and 1982, the number of residents in large institutions in the UK fell by over 40 %. In 1983 the All Wales Strategy was published. This emphasised development of community services underpinned by the principles of normalisation and has been referred to in many studies.

The DHSS (1987) reported that it was recognised that:

- Most people with learning disability lived at home.
- Of the few children not living at home most were older and had profound learning disability.
- Multidisciplinary 'community mental handicap teams' were developing.
- Good community services could improve the quality of life of individuals and their families and could help to ensure that residential care was only for those with greatest need.

- There were concerns regarding the level of help and priority given to people with learning disabilities by generic services.
- There were also concerns regarding respective roles of health and local authority services in service provision.
- Response to concerns had been made by
  - increased requests for specialist staff to support generic staff in the community and work directly with people with learning disability and their families
  - some social services departments employing healthcare staff
  - some learning disability nurses undertaking domiciliary work from a hospital base.

These trends and the first report by the Development Team for the Mentally Handicapped were endorsed by White Papers for England and Scotland in 1988. They also recognised that education of the general public, families of people with learning disability and health service providers would be required and that hospital residents would need to be re-educated. Appropriate community facilities and resources would have to be in place before any changes occurred.

Caring for People (Department of Health 1989) placed responsibility for assessing and providing for people's needs with local authorities. They could provide services themselves or contract or buy in from other agencies. Voluntary organisations and families would assume some responsibilities previously provided by Social Services. Residential care was recommended for people with special medical or nursing needs.

By 1993 a joint meeting of a Forum on Learning Disabilities and the Centre for Physiotherapy Research reported that physiotherapists in England and Wales were starting to join multidisciplinary teams. Five hundred and thirty-three were identified and the survey showed that, of the 427 who responded, approximately one-third were working in a hospital, one-third from a community base and the remainder from day centres or a variety of settings. They tended to be experienced senior clinicians who had additional areas of specialisation. (Partridge 1994).

CONSULTATION

Problems of interpreting views of people with learning disability about their future needs continued to be discussed. The necessity for accurate and acceptable terminology, which did not reflect professional or ideological bias, was highlighted in meetings organised by the British Institute of Mental Handicap and the Department of Health (Harris 1991). Cullen (1991) reflected the dichotomy that can arise and the problems of oversimplification. He suggested that 'Normalisation and social role valorisation had suffered at the hands of those who yearn for a simple approach to life'. Mesibov (1990) indicated a similar attitude when he stated that:

> Some of the commonly held tenets of normalisation are vague and unattainable; inappropriate practices are often carried out in the name of normalisation, for example, discouraging contact between people with disabilities; many advocates of normalisation have been overzealous and this overzealousness has resulted in distrust and antagonism.

Such confusion raised concerns amongst healthcare professionals regarding community facilities for the management and treatment of physical disabilities of residents leaving long-stay hospitals.

These concerns were confirmed by data based on 108 community care plans in 1993/4 throughout England (Turner et al. 1995). Proposed community facilities had not been established and resources were still needed for long-stay hospitals, for example:

- Widespread plans for development of day care provision including: employment, training, respite care, education, leisure and advocacy.
- Only three plans anticipated completion of resettlement by 1993.
- On average there were 3.6 long-stay residents per 10000 population.
- The independent sector had increased provision in at least half of the areas. The provision of nursing homes and hostels together equalled the total of group homes and ordinary houses.

In Scotland, where hospital reprovisioning was progressing more slowly, the report on *The Future of Mental Handicap Hospital Services in Scotland* (Loudon 1992) appeared to provide answers to many of the concerns. These included:

- Facilities with high standards should be available before hospitals closed.
- Individuals and their families should be involved in a pre-transfer assessment of needs.
- Guidelines should be issued for residential care to meet the special clinical needs of people with mental handicap and serious behaviour problems and/or major psychiatric illness and/or multiple handicap.
- All Health Boards should be expected to ensure access to a full range of services.
- The Social Work Department, The Education Department and employers should be expected to provide opportunities for recreation, education and high quality work.

In 1995, the UK Government publicly adopted the term 'learning disabilities' in *The Health of the Nation* (England and Wales). A booklet specifically for people with learning disabilities accompanied this strategy for people with learning disabilities (Department of Health 1995). It defined 'learning disability' (Table 1.4) and listed related problems including obesity and poor cardiovascular fitness, together with behavioural, psychiatric, orthopaedic and mobility problems. This term was not used in legislation until years later, for example in the Mental Health (Care and Treatment) (Scotland Act) 2003.

Restructuring of the NHS in the late 1990s led to concerns about allocation of health service resources for people with learning disabilities. However, it also alerted relevant committees to their needs. *Signposts for Success* (Lindsey, 1998) stated that community learning disability health services should:

- offer a wide range of co-ordinated support and advice for people with learning disabilities, their families and carers
- provide therapeutic services
- offer training for people with learning disabilities, their families, carers and staff of other organisations
- work closely with other agencies
- help the development of good practice in relation to health promotion and healthcare
- facilitate access to general health services

In practice these aims were partially met but coordination of services continued to be the greatest stumbling block:

- the development of multiprofessional teams improved management of physical disabilities in people with learning disabilities (see Chapter 5)
- well planned joint working provided new opportunities for effective treatment and management
- care in the community provided opportunities for training parents and carers individually in handling older people with profound disabilities
- use of community facilities enabled adults with learning disabilities to carry their treatment and management into everyday life

However:

- closure of specifically designed physiotherapy treatment areas and hydrotherapy pools limited the range of treatment offered to adults with profound physical and learning disabilities
- parents and carers of people with profound multiple disabilities had difficulties working with health and social services to find day, respite and future long-term care
- general health services did not always have sufficiently long appointment times to accommodate people with learning disabilities
- the move from day centres to individual packages of care involved time-consuming arrangements for therapy sessions, increased travelling time for therapists and reduced client contact time
- attempts to include people with learning disabilities only in 'normal' community activities tended to deprive them of the opportunity to participate in therapy-led peer group work.

The Health Act 1999 sought to improve coordination of services for everyone in the UK. It gave rise to the 'Partnership in Action' agenda, which encouraged improvement of services through flexible interagency work, a practice of seamless working that had long been attempted on an *ad hoc* basis for the benefit of people with learning disabilities. This Act proposed to support local flexible working practices by allowing agencies working together on specific packages of service to pool their budgets. In some areas of the UK it was suggested that delivery of services for people with learning disabilities might be progressed along the lines of Western Australia's Local Area Coordination. In this model local area coordinators hold a budget from which direct payments can be made to clients and their families to select and pay for their own services (Disability Services Commission – Western Australia 1998).

UNITED KINGDOM DEVOLUTION

UK Devolution

- Laws relating to Health in England continue to be framed by the Department of Health at Westminster.
- In 1998 the Health Department for Northern Ireland was devolved to the Northern Ireland Assembly but from 2002 the Secretary of State and his Ministers have been responsible for Northern Ireland Departments.
- In 1999 the Health Department of the Scottish Office became fully devolved to the Scottish Executive.
- In 1999 Laws relating to Health in Wales remained with the Department of Health at Westminster but more responsibility for their framing and interpreting passed to the National Assembly for Wales and the Welsh Assembly government.

1999/2001

Wales 1999

One of the first actions of the National Assembly for Wales in 1999 was to establish the Learning Disability Advisory Group and commission it to prepare a draft service framework for people with learning disabilities. The group listened to people with learning disabilities, their supporters. and representative groups. Their proposals, *Fulfilling the Promise*, were presented to the Assembly in June 2001.

The United Kingdom 2000/2001

The ideals that developed into the principles of normalisation and inclusion of people with learning disability in everyday activities developed into locally accepted codes of practice and relevant legislative provision with enabling powers but few were translated into laws specifically for the benefit of people with learning disability. However, people with learning disabilities were included as of right in the comprehensive proposals set out in the NHS Plan 2000 (Department of Health 2000), *Partnership for Care – Scotland's Health White Paper* (Scottish Executive 2003) and the Community Care and Health (Scotland) Act 2002. More specifically their comments became the basis for proposals in the two reviews of services *The Same as You? A Review of Services for People with Learning Disabilities* (Scottish Executive 2000) and *Valuing People – A New Strategy for Learning Disability for the Twenty-first Century* (Department of Health 2001d).

Both White Papers reported the achievement of many of the aims of the *Better Services for the Mentally Handicapped* (Department of Health and Social Security 1971).

The most fundamental change in these reports was their emphasis on the decision making that people with learning disabilities could and should engage in to contribute to their own life style. While encouraging inclusion the reports also acknowledged that full participation frequently required extra help and facilities. This was highly relevant to therapists and nurses who needed to ensure that appointments were kept, treatment routines maintained and that medication was taken regularly.

Scotland 2000

The Same As You? (Scottish Executive 2000) included recommendations from the Scottish Consortium for Learning Disabilities, 13 organisations concerned with the care and support of people with learning disabilities, including service users. It based its decisions on seven key principles. People with learning disabilities:

- should be valued and encouraged to contribute to their community
- are individual people
- should be asked about the services they need and involved in making choices
- should be helped and supported to do everything that they are capable of doing
- should be helped to use standard local services wherever possible
- should benefit from specialist social, health and educational services
- should have services that take account of their age, abilities and other needs

It progressed the idea proposed in the 1999 Health Act from local flexible working practices to joint commissioning, in partnership between statutory services and voluntary organisations, and recommended:

- closure of the remaining long-stay hospitals by 2005
- development of health service models in the community to support and assess people with the most complex and challenging needs
- healthcare provision within mainstream services
- further development of advocacy services
- support for people with learning disabilities within their local community and development of local links through Local Area Coordination
- enabling individual flexible support via direct payments

The practical difficulties reported anecdotally following earlier hospital closures and greater inclusion in mainstream facilities were echoed in this review. It acknowledged problems encountered by young adults accessing therapy services after leaving school and inconsistency of physiotherapy, occupational and speech therapy services across the country. Lack of facilities, staff shortages and increased referrals for people with complex needs were cited as the cause. The Health Service employed the most therapists and they were usually linked to community learning disability teams. Schools and social services also employed therapists. Occupational therapists continued to develop joint working practices. Many areas established joint equipment stores.

England and Wales

Valuing People A New Strategy for Learning Disability for the Twenty-first Century (Department of Health 2001d) included consultations with children and adults with learning disabilities their parents, carers and relevant staff.

The strategy refined the 1995 definition of 'learning disability' and estimated the prevalence and future numbers in England (see Chapter 2). Its principles of rights, independence, choice and inclusion were grounded in previous rights legislation and had also evolved from the idea of local flexible working practices proposed in the 1999 Health Act.

Recommendations included:

- Increased funding, within which were
  - the Learning Disability Development Fund resources, only to be used as pooled funds under the Health Act
  - an Implementation Support Fund which would exist for three years following the fund's introduction
  - increased financial support for carers
- Eleven broad objectives:
  - maximising opportunities for disabled children living in the community
  - transition into adult life ensuring continuity of care, support and equal opportunity

- enabling people to increase control over their own lives; improved advocacy and person-centred planning
- supporting carers
- good health; to enable access to individually planned health services with additional support where necessary
- housing; enabling choice and control of where and how people live
- fulfilling lives; enabling full and purposeful lives amongst friends and local community
- moving into employment; giving opportunity for valued and, where possible paid, work
- quality provision of high quality, evidence-based and continuously improving services from all agencies

The first nine points were to be enabled by:

- workforce training and planning; improvement of training and qualifications of all social and healthcare staff
- partnership working; promotion of holistic services through effective working between all relevant local commissioning and service-delivery agencies
- a new role of 'health facilitator'
- 'individual health action plans' as part of person-centred planning

In general, locally accepted codes of practice evolved and an increasing number of service providers began delivering services as individually designed packages. Their success continued to be dependent upon

- good communication between the adult with learning disability and his or her support workers (see Chapter 6)
- continuity of support workers
- willingness of all the support workers of each adult with learning disabilities to participate in that adult's selected activities, especially those that involved a regular and long-term commitment including therapy and general fitness activities (Chapters 15 and 17)

MOVING INTO PUBLIC AWARENESS

The concept of increased independence combined with appropriate assistance to use standard local services, wherever possible, meant that the needs of learning disabled people began to be included within general legislation. Concurrently, the balance between that concept and the requirement of specialist social, health and educational services and access to individually planned health services led to increased consultations with service users and providers. Learning disability reports, published locally, nationally and internationally, became the basis for local guidelines.

UNITED STATES

In the US, the President's New Freedom Initiative in 2001 aimed to promote full inclusion of people with disabilities in all aspects of life as proposed in the Americans with Disabilities Act 1990 (ADA). ADA had developed from the Rehabilitation Act 1973 and stated that approximately 43 000 000 Americans had one or more physical or mental disabilities. Mental retardation was included within the category of 'mental or psychological disorder'. It was recognised that a high level of discrimination occurred throughout all aspects of life against which there was no legal recourse.

Two points highlighted on The White House Web site, 'Empowering through the New Freedom Initiative' (www.whitehouse.gov/infocus/newfreedom), were:

- '... People with severe disabilities considered 'homebound' under the Medicare home health requirements ... should be able to leave home occasionally without losing "Medicare cover".'
- Congress was asked to fund a budget for the New Freedom Initiative, including grants for transport to improve job opportunities and a pilot programme for innovative transport initiatives.

For people with learning disabilities this was progressed by the Surgeon General's Conference on Health Disparities and Mental Retardation. The conference report (US Department of Health and Human Services 2002) indicated that impediments to equality of healthcare included:

- poor communication directly with people with mental retardation and between support systems
- problems progressing through age-related healthcare systems (transition)
- difficulties finding out about, travelling to, and paying for healthcare
- finding insurance coverage for a range of needs
- inadequate training for generic healthcare professionals in treating people with mental retardation

UNITED NATIONS

In 2002, preliminary findings of the study to protect and monitor human rights for people with disabilities emphasised the need to strengthen present legislation while drafting a new, more specific convention for people with 'physical, sensory, mental or intellectual disabilities'. They also stated that

> ... approximately 10 per cent of the world's population have a disability of one form or another. Over two thirds of them live in developing countries. Only 2 per cent of disabled children in the developing world receive any education or rehabilitation. The link between disability and poverty and social exclusion is direct and strong throughout the world. (United Nations 2002)

EUROPE

The European Assembly argued that respect for the human rights, fundamental freedoms and dignity of people with disabilities was a collective responsibility of society as a whole and of each individual member. It anticipated the European Year of People with Disabilities in 2003 as potentially guaranteeing such people access to equal political, social, economic and cultural rights as laid down in The European Convention on Human Rights.

A conference on disability in Romania in 2003 was proposed by the Regional Director for South East Europe of the British Council. Laws for disability access had been passed in Romania in 1999 but, in a country undergoing extreme political change, high unemployment and low pay, their enforcement was minimal. People with physical or learning disabilities continued to be excluded.

THE UK

Despite good intentions and considerable work at all levels of government, the general public were slow to accept participation of people with learning disabilities in mainstream activities.

Wales

In response to the Learning Disability Advisory Group's consultation report *Fulfilling the Promises* to the Welsh Assembly (2001), the Joseph Rowntree Foundation (2002) included in its observations:

- continuing problems with public attitudes and discrimination against people with learning disabilities in general
- additional needs of those from black and minority ethnic families
- problems of transfer from child to adult healthcare provision

They welcomed the importance laid on transition planning but referred to the findings of Heslop et al. (2001), which indicated a need for a variety of future options including types of further education and living accommodation for children leaving school.

Scotland

The National Review of the Contribution of all Nurses and Midwives to the Care and Support of People with Learning Disabilities' (Scottish Executive 2002) indicated a need for children and adults living in the community to be supported by nurses from all specialities working together. It recommended complete assessments to clarify their health needs and ability to access appropriate healthcare provision.

England

New lines of communication were established by the Department of Health in a clarification note as an appendix to 'Care trust application, consultation, assessment and establishment processes' (Department of Health 2002). (Figure 1.1).

Local councils were encouraged to refer to the 1999 Health Act flexibilities which allowed for interagency work to ensure the use of the social model and direct access to necessary services. Care trusts should be promoted only in certain circumstances, primarily when in conjunction with other parts of health and social services (Department of Health 2002a). The person-centred approach and support to use mainstream services had to be applied in all proposals.

Concurrently it was acknowledged that a small number of people with highly complex needs have requirements that fall within the category of 'specialised services'. These national services, resulting from the 'The New NHS' (Department of Health 1997), were established in England for groups with low patient numbers where resources are scarce and specialist staff and high-quality research programmes a necessity. They attract different commissioning agents from other NHS services (Department of Health 2002b).

Complex physical disabilities were not mentioned as a qualifying factor for this type of short-term inpatient assessment, treatment and follow-up although any level of physical disability may well be a contributing factor.

Specialised learning disability services – definition no. 21 of December 2002 (Department of Health 2002b)

People with learning disabilities

- who have severe challenging needs and present major risks to themselves and/or others
- and severe mental health problems who cannot be addressed by general psychiatric services
- and autistic spectrum disorder with severe challenging and/or mental health needs.

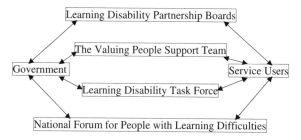

Figure 1.1. Links between government and service users with learning disabilities in England in 2002.

PROGRESS TOWARDS PUTTING WORDS INTO ACTION, 2003–6

2003

It became apparent that adults and children with all types of disabilities were becoming increasingly included in the thoughts and planning of legislatures around the world. It was also clear that large areas of great concern remained.

Middle and Eastern Europe

The Romanian conference took place in 2003. It gathered doctors, therapists, lawyers, teachers and policy makers from Non-Governmental Organisations (NGOs) of Armenia, Azerbaijan, Bulgaria, Croatia, Hungary, Iran, Lithuania, Macedonia, Moldova, Netherlands, Romania, Slovenia, and Uzbekistan both as speakers and delegates. Plenary speakers included lecturers, lawyers, politicians and therapists from Canada, Germany, Romania and the UK. The conference papers, *Linking Globally: Acting Locally* (Wood-Lamont 2004) demonstrated the struggle to implement disability laws without adequate resources, even when there was a sound local knowledge base.

The UK

Progress was made towards implementing the recommendations from *Valuing People* and *The Same as You?* by interviewing people with learning disabilities about their quality of life. Distribution of their time, services accessible to them and their own aims for the future were used as indicators.

England

The Department of Health commissioned a major survey of people with learning difficulties. The Government continued to report progress to the Westminster Parliament through its Annual Report based on *Valuing People*.

2004

United Nations

By 2004 the High Commissioner for human rights at the UN could report that states were beginning to treat disability as a broad human rights issue. However, information, specifically about people with learning disabilities in the most highly populated parts of the world, such as southeast Asia or Africa, was extremely difficult to find. In countries where wars, the AIDS crisis and natural disasters are reported regularly in general news, information tended to occur in conjunction with the crises. For example, the Reuters Web site (www.alertnet.org) on 17 November 2004 reported that 18 % of the Darfurian refugees had mental handicaps. Finance and planning are unlikely to be directed towards apparently less acute problems. Cultural differences were also recognised as playing a large part in hiding and discriminating against people with learning disability. Reports of a few nongovernmental organisations schools and communities for children specifically with learning disabilities in Africa and southeast Asia are available, notably on the Web site of Camphill International Communities (www.camphill.net/index.htm).

THE UK

England and Wales

Delivery of practical and continuous improvements in rights, independence, choice and inclusion was the aim of the Department of Health and the Disability Rights Commission, *Framework for Partnership Action on Disability 2004/5* and the Government's Special Educational Needs Strategy (Department for Education and Skills 2004). The latter included working through Regional Special Educational Needs partnerships, nonprofit agencies and research teams to provide additional learning support and improved transition policies.

Scotland

The Additional Support for Learning (Scotland) Act 2004 similarly made provision for extra support for children who required it to benefit from mainstream education. Multiprofessional Coordinated Support Plans were introduced. Scottish Ministers were allowed to set standards and regulations for special schools. Transition planning was established for all children and young people with recorded needs.

MONITORING PROGRESS IN 2004

England and Wales

Local authority provision was measured against some of the Department of Health's objectives in *Valuing People* (Department of Health 2001). However, the strategy was not a 'National Service Framework' monitored by the NHS because these objectives had not been set as 'national targets'. Complementary monitoring and targets were introduced in Wales. The new Healthcare Inspectorate Wales became responsible for local inspection and investigation of NHS bodies.

Delivery of learning disabilities services was included in the monitoring and auditing of all health service delivery by the Healthcare Commission, established in 2004 under the Health and Social Care (Community Health and Standards) Act 2003.

Scotland

Quality indicators for learning disability that were first published by the Scottish Health Advisory service (SHAS) in 2000 were revised with the introduction of NHS Quality Improvement Scotland (NHS QIS 2004). These included:

- 'Set clinical and non-clinical standards of care to help improve performance and set targets for continuous service improvement . . .'
- 'Review and monitor the performance of NHS Scotland to determine how well NHS services are performing against the targets that we have set.'

Northern Ireland

Northern Ireland announced proposals to introduce a review body, HPSS Regulation and Improvement Authority (HPSSRIA), in April 2005 (Office of Public Sector Information 2003b).

PROGRESSING INCLUSION IN 2004: NEW PROPOSALS MEAN MORE DISCUSSIONS AND CONSULTATIONS

England

Valuing People: Moving Forward Together, the government's annual report on learning disability (Department of Health 2004b) included:

- acknowledgement of concerns of people from black and ethnic minority backgrounds
- implementation of the request to write reports in an accessible way
- gradual increase of people receiving support via direct payment
- acknowledgement that the time scale for closing all long-stay hospitals by 2004 had not been met

Scotland

Implicit inclusion of people with learning disabilities was apparent in the National Health Service reform (Scotland) Act 2004. They would benefit from community health partnerships, which had developed from local healthcare cooperatives and four further aims were particularly pertinent to them and their therapy services:

- ensure patients, carers and the full range of healthcare professionals are involved

- establish a substantive partnership with local authority services
- have greater responsibility in the deployment of Health Board resources
- focus on integrating primary and specialist health services at local level

Despite this potential for improvement in healthcare and the Scottish parliamentary policy of social justice and tackling inequalities, the *Health Needs Assessment Report for People with Learning Disabilities in Scotland* (NHS Scotland 2004) warned that public health policies and practices would widen the health gap for people with learning disabilities. Amongst the assessment's findings were:

- increased incidence of the most severe learning disabilities in each age cohort
- increased life expectancy but one that was lower than the rest of Scotland
- higher level of unmet health needs than the rest of Scotland
- more complex health needs than the rest of Scotland
- there was a barrier to having health needs met

Amongst five proposed areas of action were:

- specific interventions including a health screening programme for people with learning disabilities
- enhancing primary care and specialist community based services for all ages
- education for staff and carers including improved induction in NHS Scotland and both pregraduation and postregistration/postgraduation initiatives
- greater leadership and accountability to include health improvement strategy development

2005

The UN

The Commission on Human Rights produced a draft resolution that urged governments to:

- ensure the full and equal enjoyment by persons with disabilities of all human rights and fundamental freedoms
- prevent and prohibit all forms of discrimination against persons with disabilities
- integrate a gender perspective in all efforts to protect the full and equal enjoyment of all human rights by persons with disabilities
- ensure equal opportunities for full participation of persons with disabilities in all spheres of life

Concern was expressed especially at multiple discriminations. Great concern was shown over the consequences of armed conflict on people with disabilities.

It is clear in all UN papers since 2002 that people with disabilities have been acknowledged increasingly in the area of human rights. The Commission on Human Rights specifically encouraged more rapid progress of the draft convention on the needs of people with 'physical, sensory, mental or intellectual disabilities'.

FOUR KEY REPORTS FOR ENGLAND AND WALES

England

The *Survey of Adults with Learning Difficulties in England 2003/4* (Emerson et al. 2005) was commissioned in 2002 by the Department of Health. This survey used the term 'learning difficulties' at the request of the participants. Participants were interviewed alone or with a support worker or carer. Results from 2 898 participants aged between 16 and 91 years indicated discrepancies between those factors for which legislation can be effective and the more subtle refinements needed for the smooth running of everyday life. For example, the participants were living amongst the general public in urban areas: 38 % in supported living schemes, residential care or long-stay NHS accommodation and 62 % with parents or family. However, as this was not always in their own home town or the area of their previous long-stay hospital, the results showed that companionship with their peer group had decreased:

- 69 % reported some contact with friends 'at least once a year'
- 31 % reported no contact with friends
- 5 % reported that they had no friends and did not see their family
- people living in private households or under a supported living scheme were more likely to live in poor and deprived areas with all the attendant social consequences

Although

- 54 % had an independent advocate
- 63 % indicated that they were happy with the support they received
- 86 % said their health was good or very good
- 99 % were registered with a general practitioner

the general impression was still one of discrimination and lack of independence. Only 19 % received direct payments and 64 % of people in supported accommodation had no choice of where or with whom they lived. Having a job was highly desirable and well promoted in all the literature but of those of 'working age' only 17 % of participants had paid work. Despite that, 47 %

of all participants reported to be very happy and only 9–11 % reportedly felt 'sad', excluded or helpless.

England and Wales

The report *Improving the Life Chances of Disabled People* (Cabinet Office et al. 2005) set out to ensure that 'By 2025, disabled people in Britain should have full opportunities and choices to improve their quality of life and will be respected and included as equal members of society.' It focused on four areas:

- independent living
- early years and family support
- transition to adulthood
- employment

The report *Valuing People the Story So Far* (Greig 2005) – as in the previous report – showed that progress was being made where the relevant service providers and the local community understood the full implications of *Valuing People*. People's lives had improved through, for example, well organised person-centred planning, improved coordination of services and response to requests and suggestions from people with learning disabilities and the increased number of people living independently through the Supporting People programme for independent living. Direct payments improved lifestyle. The continuing need to improve transition from childhood to adult services and the additional problems facing people from minority ethnic backgrounds were highlighted. The report listed priorities that it hoped would be achieved during the period 2005–2010.

The *Draft Three-year Strategic Plan for Assessing and Encouraging Improvement in the Health and Healthcare of Adults with Learning Disabilities 2006–2009* (Commission for Healthcare Audit and Inspection 2005) included input from the Commission for Social Care Inspection, the Department of Health's Valuing People Support Team and the Health Inspectorate for Wales. It was preceded by an extensive consultation and was circulated for further consultation until January 2006. Despite consultation results and recommendations in reports such as *Signposts for Success* (Lindsey 1998) it was still possible for the Healthcare Commission to state in background information to this audit that 'Those with learning disabilities are amongst the most deprived and excluded populations in the UK. Many are unable to have their voice heard in order to exert influence and exert pressure on services to change, which renders them largely invisible and vulnerable.'

To continue the progress towards rectifying this the The Healthcare Commission planned to:

- audit all inpatient care being provided for learning disability service users across the NHS and independent sector, including commissioning arrangements

- investigate the remaining long-stay hospitals for people with learning disabilities – national guidance had recommended that these be closed (Emerson et al. 2005)
- review the care of people with learning disabilities placed outside their local areas, away from family and friends
- increase the accessibility of the Commission's services to enable people with a learning disability to raise complaints and concerns about their care
- establish champions, at their regional offices, responsible for monitoring services for people with disabilities

They proposed joint working with the Commission for Social Care Inspection where appropriate.

One Health Service proposal that appeared to have a positive repercussion for learning disability in England and Wales was the National Service Framework (NSF) for Long-term Conditions (Department of Health 2005). The 11 NSF quality requirements for these conditions were remarkably similar to the recommendations set out in *Valuing People* and the government had set no national targets to be achieved. It was possible that people with learning disabilities and associated neurological conditions (Chapter 2) might become included in this NSF.

2006

The US

Publication of *Intellectual Disability. Understanding Its Development, Causes, Classification, Evaluation and Treatment* (Harris 2006) gave great prominence to the term 'intellectual disability' as a replacement for 'mental retardation'. The term's progress towards gradual adoption was similar to that of the term 'learning disability' in the UK. People formerly known as being 'mentally retarded' preferred to be known as having an 'intellectual disability'. In 2003 the Federal Advisory Committee for Mental Retardation became the President's Committee for People with Intellectual Disabilities. The American Association on Mental Retardation (AAMR) decided to continue using its current title in the meantime, despite recommendations to the contrary by its Board of Governors the previous year.

The UK

Increasing use of mainstream health services and improved coordination between service providers allowed people with learning disabilities to participate as members of the general public in a further consultation paper in England and Wales. This formed the basis for the White Paper *Our Health, Our Care, Our Say: A New Direction for Community Services* (Department of Health 2006). The aims – to transfer more services from general hospitals into local communities – would benefit people with learning disabilities who tend to find both travelling and hospital appointments difficult. For this to work successfully time and resources would be needed to implement reports such as the 2006–2009 strategic plan, (Greig 2005):

- people with learning disabilities would need to be assisted to use the services
- general practitioners would need to be aware of them on their case lists
- Health Service staff and the general public would need to understand that, despite, in many instances, poor social skills, the following statement was still valid: 'People with learning disabilities are individuals. They should be valued for their differences, respected as citizens' (NHS Scotland 2004).

Despite the emphasis on using mainstream services all the reports indicated that people with learning disabilities also needed access to specialist health services. The number of health professionals working in learning disability services, therefore, needed to be maintained or increased. Many universities managed to include an element of learning disability in already overcrowded medical and allied professional degree courses and placement rotas. Those universities ensured a continuing knowledge of the subject. When this was not the case, learning disability services had difficulty recruiting new staff. In some areas staff recruitment improved when rotational links were made with other hospital departments. Increases in the number of peer reviewed papers in journals such as *Physical Therapy: The Journal of American Physical Therapy Association* (Bruckner et al. 2002), features in professional magazines such as *Physiotherapy Frontline* (Hodges 2005) and contributions from the ACPPLD to reports such as *Working Differently* (Department of Health and the Allied Health Professions Federation 2005) served to raise awareness of the service needs.

ETHICS AND THE UK LAW

All professionals are ethically bound by their code of conduct, which includes confidentiality in verbal, written and photographic records (Chartered Society of Physiotherapy 2002; Nursing and Midwifery Council (NMC) 2004; British College of Occupational Therapists 2005). Aspects of these codes are revised regularly, for example Core Standards of Physiotherapy Practice (Chartered Society of Physiotherapy 2005) and Communicating Quality 3 (Royal College of Speech and Language Therapists 2006). All Allied Health Professionals must be registered with the Health Professionals Council and undertake continuing professional development (CPD). The professional respect for all with whom they come in contact is reinforced by the Disability Discrimination Act 1995, 2005, Human Rights Act 1998, Race Relations Act 1998 and Race Relations (Amendment) Act 2000.

It is the responsibility of all staff to be aware of any changes in relevant legislation, for example the results of the Safeguarding Vulnerable Groups Bill and the Adult Support and Protection (Scotland) Bill, being discussed in the respective parliaments in 2006.

DELEGATING TASKS TO ASSISTANTS AND SUPPORT WORKERS

A professional who delegates tasks to a support worker, for example an assistant or technician, has a professional obligation and duty of care to ensure that that member of staff is individually trained (Parry and Vass 1997; Saunders 1997a, and Chartered Society of Physiotherapy (2002b). Carers or support workers should only be requested to undertake specific areas of client treatment or management and should be trained for that task. A written record should be kept of what has been taught and the carer or support worker should not be expected to instruct other care staff. Guidelines for delegation of tasks are published by the relevant professional bodies (Chartered Society of Physiotherapy 2002; NMC 2004; College of Occupational Therapists 2003). The Chartered Society of Physiotherapy and British College of Occupational Therapists published *A National framework for Support Worker Education and Development* in 2005.

MANUAL HANDLING

This should be undertaken in accordance with Manual Handling Operations Regulations 2004 and statutory training for the relevant Health and Social Work Service(s). It should be guided by publications such as Handling Home Care (Health and Safety Executive 2002) and the Chartered Society of Physiotherapy (2002b) guidelines. A risk assessment should be undertaken and written up for individual clients who require any assistance in moving. This should be area specific and take account of the differing skills of carers. The care plan should allow for changes in the client's ability.

RECOGNISING ABUSE

Nurses and physiotherapists, who of necessity see clients unclothed, and speech and language therapists who are in close communication with clients, should be aware of the signs of child and elder abuse and the procedures to take in cases of concern. In respect of Human Rights legislation, if vulnerable people are able to make their own decisions a professional or carer may only recommend services that could be helpful and, if required, assist the individual to access them. Guidelines have been established in many local areas, for example *Protecting Vulnerable Adults: Ensuring Rights and Preventing Abuse* produced in collaboration by the local authorities of East, Mid and West Lothian, Edinburgh and Scottish Borders Councils; NHS Lothian; NHS Borders and Lothian and Borders Police (East, Mid and West Lothian et al., 2003). This arose from the Miss X abuse case in the home of a male carer in the Scottish borders (NHS Scotland 2004).

All professionals should be aware that people with learning disability have a legal right to assistance from an advocate who is not involved with them in a professional capacity and can speak independently on their behalf (Disabled Persons Act 1986), which is reinforced in *Valuing People* (Department of Health 2001d).

All staff working in multiprofessional teams will be indirectly involved with legal aspects such as the holding power, compulsory admission, informal admission, in for example nurse's holding power (Mental Health Act 1983), Adults with Incapacity (Scotland) Act 2000, The Mental Health (Care and Treatment) (Scotland) Act 2003, The Mental Capacity Act (2005), Chronically Sick and Disabled Persons Act 1970, Care Standards Act 2000 and Handling Home Care (Health and Safety Executive) 2002 – see also Department of Health 2004.

Treatment and management of physical disabilities in people with learning disability are most commonly affected by consent to treatment and restraint.

CONSENT TO TREATMENT

The NHS Plan (Department of Health 2000) and Partnership for Care, Scotland's Health White Paper 2003 both committed the National Health Service to improving consent to treatment by actively involving all patients in decision making. In 2002 Northern Ireland produced a consultation document relating to consent. The results were published as a guide for people with learning disabilities (Department of Health, Social Services and Public Safety 2003).

Before commencing treatment with a new client with learning disability it is always wise to consult with medical and nursing staff who have a greater knowledge of the client's ability to give consent and when possible with parents or support workers. Consent to medical treatment by adults with learning disability is only valid if they understand the significance of the consent – that is, if they have capacity. The NHS Plan 2000 gave rise to the Health Service circular *Good Practice in Consent* (Department of Health 2001a) and associated documents including *Seeking Consent: Working with People with Learning Disabilities* (Department of Health 2001c), which stated that the requirements for people to have the capacity to take a particular decision are that they are able to

- Comprehend and retain information material to the decision, especially as to the consequences of having or not having the intervention in question and
- Use and weigh this information in the decision-making process

England and Wales

In England and Wales the health professional undertaking an assessment must also assess for capacity and record the result. National consent forms were introduced as a basis for local documentation in 2002. Relevant law was described in Reference Guide to Consent for Examination and Treatment (Department of Health 2001b).

Scotland

In Scotland incapacity was defined specifically for and within the Adults with Incapacity (Scotland) Act 2000. It specified that capacity was to be assessed for each particular occasion. If incapacity was suspected the adult's medical practitioner was required to assess for capacity and if necessary sign an incapacity certificate.

Adults with Incapacity (Scotland) Act 2000

Assessment should establish whether adults

- are capable of making and communicating their choice
- understand the nature of what is being asked and why
- have memory abilities that allow the retention of information
- are aware of any alternatives
- have knowledge of the risks and benefits involved
- are aware that such information is of personal relevance to them
- are aware of their right to refuse and how to refuse as well as the consequences of refusal
- have ever expressed their wishes relevant to the issue when greater capacity existed
- are expressing views consistent with their previously preferred moral, cultural, family and experiential background

---

Both sets of criteria indicated a change from being an 'outcome-based' or 'status-based' assessment to being 'functionally' based. Understanding, knowledge, skills and abilities were to be related to the specific decision needed at a specific time

- No individual in the UK can give consent on behalf of an adult with learning disability except a welfare guardian in Scotland where financial guardians with powers over property and financial affairs may also be appointed, and for research, when next of kin can be proxy. When an adult lacks capacity the health professional responsible for that person's care is legally responsible for deciding whether a proposed treatment is in the person's best interest. In Scotland this is specifically the medical practitioner who has issued the certificate of incapacity. All the literature recommends that such decisions be taken in conjunction with family and professionals who are most closely involved with the adult.

- Treatment may be given without consent if it is life saving or if it is reversible and immediately necessary to prevent serious deterioration, alleviate serious suffering or prevent the patient from being dangerous to himself or others (Mental Health Act 1983, Mental Health (Scotland) Act 1984). This was retained in subsequent Acts.

The Adults with Incapacity (Scotland) Act (2000), 'Seeking consent: working with people with learning disabilities' (2001) and The Mental Capacity Act 2005 clearly indicated that people should not be denied treatment because of their mental incapacity.

RESTRAINT

'There is an underlying presumption in the law that it is wrong to interfere with the actions of another adult without lawful excuse' (McKay 1998).

The question repeatedly arises as to whether seating harnesses and other positioning equipment used by people with physical and learning disabilities constitute restraint.

There is no specific piece of legislation setting out what is lawful in a care setting and what is not. It would be wise therefore to examine the case for each piece of equipment against the criterion of whether it breaches any statutory provision or any principle of criminal or civil law.

Breaches of criminal law include:

- assault
- cruel and unnatural treatment
- unjust imprisonment

Breaches of civil law include:

- assault
- unlawful detention/wrongful apprehension/wrongful imprisonment
- force and fear

This may be tested by considering the following questions:

- Is the individual's physical condition liable to deteriorate if the equipment is not used?
- Is the individual's general health improved by use of the equipment?
- Does the equipment help to relieve pain?

• Does the equipment enable greater mobility?
• Does the equipment enable greater communication?
• Does the equipment improve overall quality of life?

Seating harnesses are *not* designed to prevent overactive people or people who wander from moving out of a chair.

CONCLUSION

Ideologies, theories and practices have both enhanced and reduced the lives of people with learning disabilities who also have physical disabilities. For example, fear and the desire to protect them led to segregation. This deprived many people of progressive treatments and of recognition of neurological impairments and sensory disabilities in people with mild mental retardation. Normalisation and the term 'learning disability' used in the UK and 'intellectual disability' in the USA and elsewhere have assisted development of self-respect and opportunities for many people. Supported flats and small group homes, which the principle has generated, enable people with such disabilities to live amongst the general public in urban areas but they need careful management to allow opportunity for everyday exercise and freedom of movement. Proponents of inclusion need to recognise the value of therapy-led group work with the clients' own peer group as well as inclusion in local activities with the general population.

Inconsistent terminology still leads to misunderstanding amongst health, educational and social service professionals who are not directly involved in this area and between colleagues internationally. Small groups introducing unique definitions for purposes of apparent clarification can compound this.

Work to enable people with learning disabilities to lead an increasingly full and active life is being progressed by politicians, educationalists, social services and healthcare professionals today. It is presently undertaken through person-centred planning and inclusion, multiprofessional and interagency work and self-advocacy. Management and treatment of physical disability sustained in conjunction with learning disabilities between birth and 16–21 years (Accardo and Capute 1998) or acquired later in life is treated in accordance with the standards laid down by the individual professional bodies. Aims of treatment are achieved while working in a variety of socially accepted settings and while encouraging all people with learning disabilities to enjoy a healthy lifestyle. Treatment and management of their physical disabilities will continue to develop in conjunction with the increased life expectancy of people who have learning disabilities (Fryers 1997; Herge and Campbell 1998; Department of Health 2001d).

In Scotland, Professor Kerr's consultation report *A National Framework for Service Change in the NHS in Scotland* led to reconfiguration of administrative bodies, and delivery of services in partnership with other support and care providers.

REFERENCES

United Kingdom Acts of Parliament are listed in Appendix C.

Accardo, P.J. and Capute, A.J. (1998) Mental retardations. *Mental Retardation and Developmental Disabilities Research Reviews*, **4**, 2–5.

American Association on Mental Retardation (1973) *Mental Retardation: Definition, Classification and Systems of Support*, American Association on Mental Retardation, Washington DC.

Barclay J. (1994) *In Good Hands*, Butterworth-Heinemann, Oxford.

Bobath, K. and Bobath, B. (1975) *Motor Development in the Different Types of Cerebral Palsy*, Heinemann, London.

British College of Occupational Therapists (2005) *Code of Ethics and Professional Conduct for Occupational Therapists*. British College of Occupational Therapists, London.

Brown III, F.R. and Aylward, E.H. (1996) Introduction, in *Diagnosis and Management of Learning Disability* (eds F.R. Brown III, E.H. Aylward and B.K. Keogh), Singular, San Diego and London, p. 2.

Brown, J. (1992) The residential setting in mental handicap: an overview of selected policy initiatives, in *Standards and Mental Handicap* (eds T. Thompson and P. Mathias), Bailliere Tindall, London, pp. 106–22.

Bruckner, J.S., Herge, E.A. and Ogunkua, B. (2002) A modified timed up and go test to assess risk of falls in community-based elders with mental retardation and developmental disabilities. *Journal of the American Physical Therapy Association*, June, 5–8.

Cabinet Office, Prime Minister's Strategy Unit, Department of Work and Pensions, Department of Health, Department for Education and Skills, Office of the Deputy Prime Minister (2005) Improving the life chances of disabled people. Prime Minister's Strategy Unit, London. Available at http://www.strategy.gov.uk/downloads/work_areas/disability/disability_report/pdf/disability.pdf (accessed 12 December 2006).

Chartered Society of Physiotherapy (2002a) *Assistants' Code of Conduct*, Chartered Society of Physiotherapy, London.

Chartered Society of Physiotherapy (2002b) *Guidance in Manual Handling for Chartered Physiotherapists*, Chartered Society of Physiotherapy, London.

Chartered Society of Physiotherapy (2002c) *Rules of Professional Conduct*, 2nd edition, Chartered Society of Physiotherapy, London.

Chartered Society of Physiotherapy (2005) *Core Standards of Physiotherapy Practice*, Chartered Society of Physiotherapy, London.

Chartered Society of Physiotherapy (2005) *Service Standards of Physiotherapy Practice*, Chartered Society of Physiotherapy, London.

Chartered Society of Physiotherapy and British College of Occupational Therapists (2005) *A National Framework for Support Worker Education and Development*. Chartered Society of Physiotherapy and British College of Occupational Therapists, London.

Commission for Healthcare Audit and Inspection (2005) *Draft Three-year Strategic Plan for Assessing and Encouraging Improvement in the Health and Healthcare of Adults with Learning Disabilities 2006–2009*, Commission for Healthcare Audit and Inspection, London. Available at http://www.healthcarecommission.org.uk/_db/_documents/04021628.pdf (accessed 12 December 2006).

Cullen, C. (1991) Bridging the gap between the treatment techniques and service philosophy, in *Service Responses to People with Learning Difficulties and Challenging Behaviour* (ed. J. Harris), British Institute of Mental Handicap, Kidderminster, pp. 55–7.

Department of Education and Science (1978) *Special Educational Needs (Warnock Report)*, Stationery Office, London.

Department for Education and Skills (2004) *Removing Barriers to Achievement: The Government's Strategy for SEN*, DfES Publications, Nottingham.

Department of Health (1989) *Caring for People: Community Care in the Next Decade and Beyond*, Stationery Office, London.

Department of Health (1995) *The Health of the Nation – A Strategy for People with Learning Disabilities*. The Stationery Office, Oldham.

Department of Health (1997) *The New NHS: Modern, Dependable*. The Stationery Office, London.

Department of Health (2000) *The NHS Plan 2000: A Plan for Investment, A Plan for Reform*, Stationery Office, London.

Department of Health (2001a) *Good Practice in Consent Implementation Guide: Consent to Examination or Treatment*, Department of Health Publications, London.

Department of Health (2001b) *Reference Guide to Consent for Examination and Treatment*, Department of Health Publications, London.

Department of Health (2001c) *Seeking Consent: Working with People with Learning Disabilities*, Department of Health Publications, London.

Department of Health (2001d) *Valuing People – A New Strategy for Learning Disability for the Twenty-first Century*, Stationery Office, London.

Department of Health (2002a) *Care Trust Application, Consultation, Assessment and Establishment Processes Appendix B Clarification Note: Learning Disability*. Available at http://www.dh.gov.uk/PolicyAndGuidance/OrganisationPolicy/IntegratedCare/CareTrusts/fs/en.

Department of Health (2002b) *Specialised Services National Definition Set*, 2nd edn, Department of Health Publications, London.

Department of Health (2004a) *Improving Mental Health Law: Towards a New Mental Health Act*, Department of Health Publications, London.

Department of Health (2004b) *Valuing People: Moving Forward Together The Government's Annual Report on Learning Disability*, Department of Health Publications, London.

Department of Health (2005) *The National Service Framework for Long-term Conditions*, Department of Health Publications Orderline, London.

Department of Health (2006) *Our Health, Our Care Our Say: A New Direction for Community Service*, Stationery Office, London.

Department of Health and Allied Health Professions (2005) *Working Differently: The Role of Allied Health Professions*, Allied Health Professions Federation, London.

Department of Health and Social Security (1971) *Better Services for the Mentally Handicapped*, Stationery Office, London.

Department of Health and Social Security (1987) *Mental Handicap: Progress, Problems and Priorities A Review of Mental Handicap Services in England since the 1971 White Paper 'Better Services for the Mentally Handicapped'*, Stationery Office, London.

Department of Health and the Disability Rights Commission (2004) *Department of Health/Disability Rights Commission Framework for Partnership Action on Disability 2004/5*. Available at http://www.dh.gov.uk/assetRoot/04/08/35/05/04083505.pdf.

Department of Health, Social Services and Public Safety (2003) *Consent. What You Have a Right to Expect: A Guide for People with Learning Disabilities*, Department of Health, Social Services and Public Safety, Belfast.

Disability Services Commission – Western Australia (1998) *Local Area Co-ordination – A New Approach to Service Delivery for People with Disabilities and their Families*, submission for the 'Service Design – Delivery' category of 1998 Premier's Awards, Australia.

East, Mid, West Lothian Councils, City of Edinburgh Council, NHS Lothian, NHS Borders, Lothian and Borders Police, Scottish Borders Council (2003) *Protecting Vulnerable Adults: Ensuring Rights and Preventing Abuse, Interagency Guidelines for People Working in Health and Social Care Settings*. www.midlothian.gov.uk/services/webinfo/webinfopdf.asp?blobid=4597

Emerson, E., Malam, S., Davies I. and Spencer, K. for the Department of Health (2005) *Survey of Adults with Learning Difficulties in England 2003/4: Final Report*, Department of Health Publications, London.

Fryers, T. (1997) Impairment, disability and handicap: categories and classifications, in *The Psychiatry of Learning Disabilities* (ed. O. Russell), Royal College of Psychiatrists, London, pp. 16–30.

Fryers, T. and Russell, O. (1997) Applied epidemiology, in *The Psychiatry of Learning Disabilities*, (ed. O. Russell), Royal College of Psychiatrists, London, pp. 31–47.

Goffman, E. (1968) *Asylums*, Penguin Books, Harmondsworth.

Greig R (2005) *Valuing People. The Story so Far . . . A New Strategy for Learning Disability for the Twenty-first Century*, Department of Health Publications, London.

Hari, M. and Akos, K. (1988) *Conductive Education*, Routledge, London.

Harris, J. (ed.) (1991) *Service Responses to People with Learning Difficulties and Challenging Behaviour*, British Institute of Mental Handicap, Kidderminster.

Harris, J. (2006) *Intellectual Disability. Understanding its Development, Causes, Classification, Evaluation and Treatment*, Oxford University Press, New York.

Health and Safety Executive (2002) *Handling Home Care: Achieving Safe, Efficient and Practical Outcomes for Care Workers and Clients*, HSE Books, Sudbury.

Health and Safety Executive (2004) *Manual Handling. Manual Handling Operations Regulations 1992 (as amended). Guidance on Regulations L23*, 3rd edn, HSE Books, Sudbury.

Health Services Council (1970) *The Staffing of Mental Deficiency Hospitals*, HMSO, Edinburgh.

Henderson, Sir D.K. (1964) *The Evolution of Psychiatry in Scotland*. E and S Livingstone, Edinburgh.

Herge, E.A. and Campbell, J.E. (1998) The role of the occupational and physical therapist in the rehabilitation of the older adult with mental retardation. *Topics in Geriatric Rehabilitation*, **13** (4), 12–21.

Heslop, P., Muller, R., Simons, K. and Ward, L. (2001) *Bridging the Divide: The Experiences of Young People with Learning Difficulties and their Families at Transition*, Norah Fry Research Centre, University of Bristol, Bristol.

Hodges, C. (2005) Getting to grips with learning disabilities. *Physiotherapy Frontline*, 15 June, 21–3.

Joseph Rowntree Foundation (2002) *Fulfilling The Promises: A Response From The Joseph Rowntree Foundation to the Proposed Framework for Services for People With Learning Disabilities in Wales*, Joseph Rowntree Foundation, York.

Kanner, L. (1964) *A History of the Care and Study of the Mentally Retarded*, Charles C Thomas, Springfield IL.

Kristiansen, K. and Ness, N.E. (1987) *Hjelpesystenet: Igar, I dag I morgan*, Occupational Therapy Department, Sör-Tröndelage University, Trondheim.

Lane, H. (1977) *The Wild Boy of Aveyron*, George Allen & Unwin, London.

Learning Disability Advisory Group (2002) *Fulfilling the Promises. Report to the National Assembly for Wales*, Welsh Assembly, Cardiff.

Lindsey, M. (1998) *Signposts for Success: In Commissioning and Providing Health Services for People with Learning Disabilities*, Department of Health, Stationery Office, London.

Loudon, J.B. (1992) *The Future of Mental Handicap Hospital Services in Scotland*, Stationery Office, Edinburgh.

Luckey, R.E. and Shapiro, I.G. (1974) Recreation: an essential aspect of habilitative programming. *Mental Retardation*, October, 33–5.

McKay, C. (1998) *Appendix to Restraint of Residents with Mental Impairment in Care Homes and Hospitals*, Mental Welfare Commission for Scotland, Edinburgh.

Mesibov, G. (1990) Normalisation and its relevance today, *Journal of Autism and Developmental Disorder* **20**, 379–90.

Mittler, P. (1979) *People Not Patients: Problems and Policies in Mental Handicap*, Methuen and Co Ltd, Cambridge.

Morris P (1969) *Put Away*, Routledge & Keegan Paul, London.

Muir, W.J. (2004) Learning disability, in *Companion to Psychiatric Studies* (eds C.P.L. Freeman, A. Zealley and E.C. Johnstone), Churchill Livingstone, Edinburgh, pp. 527–78.

NHS Quality Improvement Scotland (2004) *Quality Indicators Learning Disabilities*, NHS QIS, Edinburgh.

NHS Scotland (2004) *Health Needs Assessment Report for People with Learning Disabilities in Scotland*, Public Health Institute of Scotland, Glasgow.

Nirje, B. (1969) The normalisation principle and its human management implications, in *Changing Patterns in Residential Services for the Mentally Retarded* (eds R. Kugel and W. Wolfensberger), President's Committee on Mental Retardation, Washington, pp. 179–95.

Nursing and Midwifery Council (2004) *Code of Professional Conduct*, NMC, London.

O'Connor, N. and Tizard, J. (1956) *The Social Problem of Mental Deficiency*, Pergamon Press, London.

Office of Public Sector Information (OPSI) (2003) *The Health and Personal Social Services (Quality Improvement and Regulations) Northern Ireland Order 2003*, Stationery Office, London.

Parry, R. and Vass, C. (1997) Training and Assessment of Physiotherapy Assistants. *Physiotherapy*, **83**, 1, 33–40.

Partridge, C. (1994) Meeting physical needs of adults with learning disabilities and their carers: a neglected area. *Journal of the Royal Society of Medicine*, **87**, 365–66.

Royal College of Speech and Language Therapists (2006) *Communicating Quality 3.* Royal College of Speech and Language Therapists, London.

Saunders, L. (1997a) Issues involved in delegation to assistants, *Physiotherapy*, **83** (3), 141–6.

Saunders, L. (1997b) A systematic approach to delegation in out-patient physiotherapy, *Physiotherapy*, **83** (11), 582–9.

Savage, D.R. (1970) Intellectual assessment, in *The Psychological Assessment of Mental and Physical Handicaps* (ed. P. Mitler), Methuen, London.

Scheerenberger, R.C. (1987) *A History of Mental Retardation.* Paul H. Brooks, Baltimore.

Scottish Executive (2000) *The Same as You? A Review of Services for People with Learning Disabilities*, Scottish Executive Health Department, Edinburgh.

Scottish Executive (2002) *Promoting Health, Supporting Inclusion: The National Review of the Contribution of all Nurses and Midwives to the Care and Support of People with Learning Disabilities*, Scottish Executive Health Department, Edinburgh.

Scottish Executive (2003) *Partnership for Care, Scotland's Health White Paper*, Scottish Executive Health Department, Edinburgh.

Scottish Executive (2006) *A National Framework for Service Change in the NHS in Scotland, Building a Health Service Fit for the Future*, Scottish Executive Health Department, Edinburgh.

Scottish Health Advisory Service (2000) *Learning Disability Quality Indicators*, Scottish Health Advisory Service, Edinburgh.

Scrivens E (1986) The National Health Service: Origins and Issues; in *Sociology as Applied to Medicine* (eds D.L. Patrick and G. Scambler), Bailliere Tindall, London, pp. 204–10.

Tredgold, A.F. (1908) *Textbook on Mental Deficiency*, Tindall and Cox, London.

Tredgold, A.F. (1909) The feeble-minded: a social danger. *Eugenics Review*, **1** (3) (October), 155.

Trent, J.W. (1994) *Inventing the Feeble Mind – A History of Mental Retardation in the United States*, University of California Press, Berkeley, Los Angeles, London.

Turner. S., Sweeney, D. and Hayes, L. (1995) *Developments in Community Care for Adults with Learning Disabilities A Review of 1993/94 Community Care Plans*, Hester Adrian Research Centre, University of Manchester, Stationery office, London.

United Nations (2002) *Convention on the Rights of Persons with Disabilities*, United Nations Secretariat for the Convention on the Rights of Persons with Disability, New York.

United Nations (2005) *Convention on the Rights of Persons with Disabilities*, United Nations Secretariat for the Convention on the Rights of Persons with Disability, New York.

US Department of Health and Human Services (2002) *Report of the Surgeon General's Conference on Health Disparities and Mental Retardation. Closing the Gap: A National Blueprint to Improve the Health of Persons with Mental Retardation*, MD Office of the Surgeon General, Rockville.

US Department of Labor (1990) *The Americans with Disabilities Act of 1990*, Employment Standards Administration, Washington.

WHO (1980) *The International Classification of Impairments, Disabilities and Handicaps*, World Health Organization, Geneva.

WHO (1992) *The ICD 10 Classification of Mental and Behavioural Disorders, Clinical Descriptions and Diagnostic Guidelines*, World Health Organization, Geneva.

WHO (1993) *The ICD 10 Classification of Mental and Behavioural Disorders. Diagnostic Criteria for Research*, World Health Organization, Geneva.

WHO (2000) *Ageing and Intellectual Disabilities – Improving Longevity and Promoting Healthy Ageing: Summative Report*, World Health Organization, Geneva.

WHO (2001) *The International Classification of Functioning, Disability and Health*, World Health Organization, Geneva.

WHO (2006) *The ICD 10 Classification of Mental and Behavioural Disorders. Clinical Descriptions and Diagnostic Guidelines 1994/2006 Version*, World Health Organization, Geneva.

Wolfensberger, W. and Thomas, S. (1983) *PASSING (Programme Analysis of Service Systems' Implementation of Normalisation Goals): Normalisation and Ratings Manual*, 2nd edn, National Institute on Mental Retardation, Toronto.

Wood-Lamont, S. (2004) *Linking Globally: Acting Locally, Working with the Disabled Community Towards a More Inclusive Society*, Gedo, Cluj-Napoca, Romania.

2 Learning Disability: Classification and Associated Conditions

JEANETTE RENNIE, MARK STERRICK AND JANE NEIL-MACLACHLAN

INTRODUCTION

This chapter describes classification of learning disability and gives a brief overview of neurological conditions that are associated with it and which present with physical disabilities or impinge upon physical ability. These include cerebral palsy, motor delay, epilepsy and autistic spectrum disorder. This chapter does not include normal development or neuroanatomy.

The three internationally recognised methods of classification are described because reference is made to them throughout clients' medical records and team meetings and in the relevant literature.

In the UK, the term 'learning disability' (Department of Health 1995) is used to mean 'mental handicap', 'mental retardation', 'cognitive disability' (see American Psychiatric Association 1994; WHO 2001, 2006; American Association on Mental Retardation 2002) or 'intellectual disability' (Harris 2006).

It should not be confused with the definition of learning disability used in, amongst other countries, the US and described by DSM–IV-TR as being a problem in processing auditory or visual information. In the UK these are known as 'specific learning difficulties' or 'specific learning disabilities' and include problems such as dyslexia.

PREVALENCE AND ESTIMATED NUMBERS

Studies show that prevalence can vary from year to year, by age, socio-economic groups and by country (Murphy et al. 1998). Records for mild 'mental retardation' vary greatly between populations largely because of cultural differences, which preclude standardisation of data collection (Fryers 1997). Wide variations of prevalence have been recorded worldwide across the range of learning disability (Muir 2004). Recent research relating to England

Learning Disability: Physical Therapy Treatment and Management. Edited by Jeanette Rennie
© 2007 John Wiley & Sons Ltd

and published in 2001 reported the lower estimate for prevalence ratios for people with mild/moderate learning disability as 25 in every 1000 (1.2 million people). The estimated number with severe and profound learning disability was 210 000. The population was classified by children and young people, adults of working age and older people; the largest cohort was in the 'adults of working age' group (120 000). It was estimated that numbers would increase by 1 % in each of the next 15 years. Reasons for the increase included increased life expectancy, increased survival into adulthood for people with complex needs, improved recognition of children with autistic spectrum disorders who also had learning disabilities and greater prevalence among some minority ethnic populations. Mild to moderate learning disability was also linked to poverty (Department of Health 2001).

CLASSIFICATION

The problem of defining the concept of learning disability has frequently caused misunderstanding between professionals from different theoretical backgrounds. Some social services, education authorities and voluntary agencies in the UK aim to dispense with any definition or classification, regarding it as a form of labelling and causing stigma. However, a definition and criteria are necessary to guard against incorrect assumptions and to ensure that appropriate treatment and management can be offered to the individual and research can be undertaken for the benefit of all people with learning disability. It should not be used as a label that assumes that a child or adult cannot develop further. In fact ICD 10 states that: 'Intellectual abilities and social adaptation may change over time, and, however poor, may improve as a result of training and rehabilitation.'

Current methods of classification go a long way to clarifying the complex heterogeneous group of conditions causing and associated with learning disability.

The criteria for 'mental retardation' used in three internationally recognised classifications ICD10 (WHO 2006), AAMR (American Association on Mental Retardation 2002), DSM-IV and DSM–IV–TR guidelines (American Psychiatric Association 2000) are:

- intellectual impairment (IQ < 70) (AAMR 70–75)
- diminished social adaptive functioning
- onset during the developmental period (usually regarded as no later than 18 years)

Level of severity is broadly classified by ICD 10 and DSM-IV-TR as IQ < 70 mild, <50 moderate, <30 severe or profound (see, for example, Muir 2004). The AAMR does not refer to levels of severity (American Association on Mental Retardation 2002).

The ICD 10 states that 'mental retardation is a condition of arrested or incomplete development of the mind, which is especially characterised by impairment of skills manifested during the developmental period, skills that contribute to the overall level of intelligence – i.e. cognitive, language, motor and social abilities. Retardation can occur with or without other mental or physical disorders.'

They comment that it is customary to measure mental retardation levels by standardised intelligence tests but that these can be 'supplemented by scales assessing social adaptation in a given environment':

- ICD can be used in conjunction with the functional assessment approach of the International classification of functioning, disability and health (ICF) (World Health Organization 2001) (see Chapter 8)
- ICD 10 has been used, and is expanded upon in Chapter 3
- both AAMR and DSM-IV-TR use a multiaxial method of classification.
- DSM-IV-TR is best defined by use of its guidelines
  - Axis I: major mental disorders, developmental disorders and learning disabilities (UK: specific learning difficulty)
  - Axis II: underlying pervasive or personality conditions as well as mental retardation (UK: learning disability)
  - Axis III: any non-psychiatric medical condition ('somatic')
  - Axis IV: social functioning and impact of symptoms
  - Axis V: global assessment of functioning (on a scale of 100–0) (American Psychiatric Association 2000)

The AAMR has developed into an almost entirely functional classification based on the needs of the individual (Harris 2006). In 2002 it revised its definition of learning disability to '. . . a disability characterised by significant limitations both in intellectual functioning and in adaptive behaviour as expressed in conceptual, social and practical adaptive skills. This disability originates before the age of 18' (American Association on Mental Retardation 2002).

It changed to using a functional classification based on the premise that mental retardation refers to a particular way of functioning that started in childhood. This model is not static and is multidimensional. It includes the way in which individuals interact with their whole environment and the result of that interaction in relation to independence, relationships, social skills, participation in school and community, and personal wellbeing. A more positive result is achieved when a range of 'supports' specific to the individual being assessed are used. The AAMR describe 'supports' as 'the resources and individual strategies necessary to promote the development, education, interests, and personal well-being of a person with mental retardation.'

Families or friends or any professional working with the individual can provide support. They are the basis of the person-centred approach (Chapter 7).

In research DSM-IV-TR is used at least as frequently throughout the UK as is ICD 10.

REASONS FOR LEARNING DISABILITY

Learning disability is caused by a heterogeneous group of disorders. Although it is frequently of unknown aetiology it also includes organic causes such as genetic and chromosomal abnormality, infection, trauma and environmental toxins such as lead, which affect the developing brain (Fryers and Russell 1997; Murphy et al. 1998; Muir 2004). Mild to moderate learning disability is also known to be linked to poverty and social exclusion (Department of Health 2001; United Nations 2002).

Until recently people with an IQ of 50–70 and no recognised organic cause for their learning disability tended to be offered fewer investigations than any other group of people with learning disability. However, more recent studies, reviewed and reported in Accardo and Capute (1998), Murphy et al. (1998) and Muir (2004), suggested that an increasing number of organic factors could also be present in this group. This caused Accardo and Capute to recommend careful investigations for children with developmental delay and mild as well as severe learning disability.

CONDITIONS ASSOCIATED WITH LEARNING DISABILITY

Conditions associated with learning disability include developmental delay, cerebral palsy, epilepsy, behavioural and psychiatric disorders and autistic spectrum disorder. Many of the syndromes and associated conditions require direct physiotherapy intervention and multiprofessional management for physical disability. Epilepsy, psychiatric and behavioural disorders and autistic spectrum disorder can impinge upon that treatment and management. Conditions relating to old age may be apparent as early as mid- to late forties (Herge and Campbell 1998) and people with learning disabilities are known to be living longer into old age (Department of Health 2001; NHS Scotland 2004).

Motor delay, developmental coordination disorder and cerebral palsy are described only briefly in this chapter as a considerable amount of literature is easily accessible to therapists and nurses elsewhere – for example, Levitt (1977), Bobath and Bobath (1987), Illingworth (1987) and Cogher et al. (1992).

Epilepsy and autistic spectrum disorder are described in more detail as they are rarely studied by therapists or nurses during their general training.

Epilepsy is the most common serious neurological condition in the general population with a prevalence of between 0.5 % and 1 % (Goodridge and Shorvon 1983); Muir (2004) considered it to be around 2 %. However, in the learning disabled population a higher proportion of people have epilepsy and often their condition is of a severe and intractable nature. Therefore, in learning disability, epilepsy has a prevalence of 21 % in those who do not have a concomitant cerebral palsy and 50 % in those who do (Richardson et al. 1979; Kerr et al. 1996). As such, epilepsy has an important impact on the physical, social and emotional wellbeing of people with learning disability as a whole. Moreover, it has important repercussions for carers and families of sufferers at a 'local' level and communities and society itself at a more general level. Yet, epilepsy is often 'hidden from sight' because of the perceived and actual stigma that has a habit of accompanying it. It is important, therefore, for health professionals to realise that they have an essential role in supporting individuals with epilepsy, their families and their carers, as well as in educating the wider public.

The estimated prevalence for autistic spectrum disorder is 91 : 10 000. This is made up of 20 : 10 000 people with ASD and learning disability and 71 : 10 000 with an IQ above 70 (NAS 2005). Thus the estimated incidence in the UK is 535 000. Autism is not rare. The sex ratio is currently thought to be 4 : 1 males to females but there is evidence that the female presentation is slightly different and may be harder to discern.

'Autism isn't something a person has, or a "shell" that the person is trapped inside. It is pervasive, it colours every experience, every sensation, perception, thought, emotion, and encounter, every aspect of existence. It is not possible to separate the autism from the person.' (Personal view of an adult with autism.)

As such it is necessary for health professionals to understand that ASD can have a marked impact on their aims and implementation of treatment.

Genetic and chromosomal causes; behavioural and psychiatric disorders; specific developmental delays and their treatments are described in Chapter 3.

MOTOR DELAY

Simple motor delay is delayed attainment of motor milestones such as sitting, standing and walking. Muscle tone is low and there may be associated congenital heart defects and chronic respiratory conditions. It can be caused by the organic and 'sociocultural' causes of learning disability or by sensory and perceptual defects and apraxias. It is most easily recognised in people with Down syndrome.

DEVELOPMENTAL COORDINATION DISORDER

The term has been used synonymously with motor delay, perceptuo-motor dysfunction and developmental dyspraxia. One school of thought suggests that it is caused by motor delay. More commonly it is thought to result from damage to the sensory system either vestibular, visual or proprioceptive or a combination of two or more (Willoughby and Polatajko 1995). It is not thought to be caused by any other physical disability. It manifests itself as delayed motor coordination, which is below the intellectual ability of the child or young adult. Although it is usually seen in children with average or higher than average intellectual ability it can also be present in people with learning disability.

CEREBRAL PALSY (CP)

Cerebral palsy due to brain damage around the time of birth is subclassified as follows

- spastic
- dyskinetic
- choreoathetoid or dystonic
- ataxic
- mixed

These subclassifications relate to the area of brain most severely damaged. The distribution of spasticity may be diplegic (when lower limbs are more involved than upper limbs), quadriplegic (when all four limbs are equally involved), double hemiplegic (when upper limbs are more involved than lower limbs) or hemiplegic (when one side of the body is affected). More rarely, a paraplegic (both lower limbs only), triplegic (three limbs only) or monoplegic (one limb only) distribution may occur (Ingram 1964; Levitt 1977; Gage 1991).

It is a nonprogressive condition that affects normal developmental reactions, postural reflexes, muscle tone and motor development. These in turn affect growth and structure of muscle and bone (O'Dwyer et al. 1989; Gage 1991), which recent studies suggest leads to muscle fibre atrophy and changes in muscular contractile ability. Symptoms of the condition change as:

- the injured brain grows
- the individual grows in height and weight
- external forces react upon the body
- living and working conditions change and individuals wish to participate in the same activities as their non-CP peer group.

There is a very high potential for contractures and deformity in spastic or mixed CP, which frequently require special equipment, orthosis and orthopaedic intervention (see Chapters 4, 9 and 10). Studies are being continued to validate findings that neuromuscular electrical stimulation (NMES) is effective in strengthening hypotrophic muscle and therefore assisting prevention of deformity and reduced mobility (Dali et al. 2002). In conjunction with physiotherapy and increasingly with orthopaedic surgery, botulinum toxin A (BTA) has been used to treat cervical dystonia and is being used in carefully monitored cases to reduce muscle tone (Jankovic 2004).

The potential for deformity and abnormal muscle tone means that eating and drinking disorders are closely associated with CP.

Research is continuing into the area of sensory experiences but it is known that sensory sensitivities can be present in all these conditions. Whilst practitioners should be aware of this when assessing individuals and planning treatment it is also necessary to understand that Sensory Integration and the Sensory Hypersensitivities theories stem from different bodies of work. Reference should be made to studies that outline the differences, treatment and outcomes, for example Bogdashina (2003).

EPILEPSY

Epilepsy may be simply defined as a tendency to recurrent seizures. It is not a disease in itself but merely a symptom of some underlying problem with the brain's ability to regulate its electrical discharge processes on an intermittent, brief and usually spontaneous basis.

Given the right stimulus, everyone is capable of having a seizure but this does not mean that everyone has epilepsy. Approximately one person in 20 will have a single, non-febrile, seizure at some time in his or her life but only half of these will go on to have another seizure (Goodridge and Shorvon 1983). To be epilepsy, there must be recurrent seizures. Someone withdrawing quickly from a chronic and excessive consumption of alcohol may have several withdrawal seizures over time but this does not warrant a diagnosis of epilepsy because there is no intrinsic brain disturbance conferring an automatic tendency to recurrent seizures. The seizures are provoked by the withdrawal of alcohol and will settle when the person's body has adjusted to the change. In comparison, recurrent seizures arising from a damaged area of the brain as a consequence of low oxygen concentration at birth will be regarded as epilepsy because the cause is intrinsic to the brain and not external to it. The problem arises, however, when iatrogenic factors lead to brain damage.

In general, in 61 % of people with epilepsy, the underlying cause of the tendency to recurrent seizures is not identifiable and this situation is often referred to as cryptogenic (or sometimes, and erroneously, idiopathic) epilepsy (Sander et al. 1990). However, in epilepsy specifically affecting people with learning disability, in only about 25 % is the underlying problem unknown (Muir 2004) and it is usually more readily identifiable because it often arises as part of a neurological disorder. This is referred to as symptomatic epilepsy. For example, epilepsy often accompanies cerebral palsy in the context of learning disability. Table 2.1 reveals the causes of epilepsy from a learning disability perspective. It will be noted that genetic conditions play an important part in the aetiology

Table 2.1. Causes of epileptic seizures from a learning disability perspective

Causes	Examples and subdivisions
1 Genetic causes	a) Metabolic disorders e.g. phenylketonuria b) 'Structural' e.g. tuberous sclerosis c) Some primary generalised epilepsies d) Mitochondrial disorders
2 Developmental disorders	For example, arteriovenous malformations
3 Intrauterine and perinatal injury including anoxia	
4 Infection	For example, encephalitis
5 Trauma	
6 Vascular	
7 Tumour	
8 Dementia and neurodegenerative disorder	
9 Metabolic	For example, hypoglycaemia
10 Toxic	For example, alcohol

(abridged from Betts 1998)

of learning disability epilepsy and certain syndromes are almost invariably associated with learning disability – for example West syndrome, Lennox-Gastaut syndrome and severe myoclonic epilepsy in infancy.

The International League Against Epilepsy is undergoing a review of its classification of seizures but in 2006 it was using the 1981 classification. This divides seizures principally into generalised and partial. Generalised attacks essentially involve the whole of the cerebrum in the epileptic discharge whereas partial attacks involve an area that is somewhere short of this. When the electrical discharge of a partial seizure remains relatively well circumscribed to one lobe, the person is likely to retain consciousness and this is classified as a simple partial seizure. However, where the discharge has begun to spread, perhaps to involve the whole of one lobe, or even two, the consciousness becomes impaired (but not necessarily lost) and this is classified as a complex partial seizure (one form being what is referred to as 'temporal lobe epilepsy'). Partial seizures can take many forms depending on the lobes of the brain that are affected, for example a frontal lobe discharge may give some form of 'motor' seizure incorporating a series of jerks affecting one arm. A partial seizure can spread so widely that it may ultimately affect the whole cerebrum and this is then referred to as a secondarily generalised seizure. However, generalised seizures may begin *de novo* and do not always appear to be dependent on spread of discharge from a partial focus. These attacks are therefore known as primary generalised seizures. Generalised seizures are further classified into absence (typical and atypical); myoclonic; clonic; tonic; tonic-clonic; and atonic seizures. The hallmark distinction between a partial and generalised seizure is the loss of consciousness, which is usually sudden. All seizures types usually begin spontaneously and end equally spontaneously but occasionally an episode may develop into a situation involving the onset of serial seizures and status epilepticus. The latter is a medical emergency and people with learning disability and epilepsy have a higher tendency to this type of progression.

People who have epilepsy within the context of learning disability are especially likely to suffer from complex partial seizures. However, it can be difficult to recognise these because of the presence of concomitant neuropsychological problems in people with severe learning disabilities and developmental disorders. In addition, behavioural difficulties and mood disturbances may be genuinely associated with seizure episodes but may be mistaken for separate psychiatric conditions and treated erroneously. Therefore, in order to achieve an accurate diagnosis, it is essential to have a suitably detailed eyewitness account of the attacks under question. However, it is also important for carers and health professionals to have an appreciation of the effects that seizures may have on people's lifestyles as well as the effects that their lifestyles may have on their seizures.

Seizures can be physically, socially and emotionally disabling for the sufferer, both acutely and chronically, but it should not be forgotten that parents, spouses and carers may also be similarly affected due to the impact of caring for someone with intractable epilepsy on top of a learning disability. In addition, the effects of medication may interfere with an individual's ability to concentrate and to learn and perform certain tasks. Some medications such as phenobarbitone, carbamazepine and the diazepam-type drugs have sedative properties and close monitoring and adjustment of doses may be necessary, especially during initial titration of these drugs, if an individual is not to be further handicapped by adverse drug effects. On the other hand, lamotrigine may have a mood-lifting effect and may help to increase concentration and learning ability. Occasionally, these medications may cause significant mood and behavioural disturbances in people with learning disabilities. It is therefore important for doctors to adopt a philosophy of 'start low – go slow', which ensures that drugs are introduced at the lowest practicable dose and are increased in small increments. This seems to be especially important in some people with Down syndrome who appear to be more sensitive to these medications.

Often, combinations of medications are necessary to increase the chances of control but these must be carefully monitored as an additional drug load may exacerbate toxicity with little further to offer by way of seizure control. Therefore, assessment of side-effects from medication is very important especially where there is the use of polypharmacy. However, it is occasionally difficult to assess the efficacy of medications because the recording of seizure frequency and type can be inadequate given the difficulties that some people with learning disabilities have with communication and expression (see

Chapter 6). Further, nonepileptic seizures are common in learning disability and can cause protracted difficulties in the diagnostic and management processes.

A person's lifestyle circumstances may also have an effect on his/her epilepsy control. Thus, alcohol, 'late nights' and stress may have significant adverse effects. Physical stresses by way of infections and other medical diseases may have a drastic but short-lived effect on the seizure rate. However, emotional stress is also significant. Some activities that might be expected to be pleasurable, such as attendance at a party or even going on holiday, may be stressful enough to provoke extra seizures. In addition, being pushed 'to the limit' either physically, emotionally, or educationally by well-meaning but overzealous parents, carers or professionals may have a triggering effect on seizures for people with a learning disability. The concomitant use of psychotropic medication for a variety of psychological and psychiatric conditions (common in learning disability) may also lower the seizure threshold, as may a lack of compliance with medication, for whatever reason.

As far as prognosis is concerned, generally speaking, up to 80 % of people with epilepsy will become seizure free on medication (Betts 1998). The other 20 % will continue to display seizures despite medication but will probably have had some benefit from it by way of a reduction in seizure frequency and/or a reduction in the intensity of individual seizures. Unfortunately, many people with epilepsy within the context of learning disability will fall into this continuing seizure group. Although they do achieve benefits from their anti-epileptic medications, many will never be totally free from seizures despite best efforts at medication manipulation. In turn, these people appear to be at an increased risk for disorders of cognitive function such as memory impairments or attentional difficulties although significant problems appear to affect only a small minority. There are, in addition, techniques that can help to reduce the impact of a weak memory on daily functioning. In recent times, there has been a rekindling of interest in the use of neurosurgery for intractable epilepsies and every two years or so sees the introduction of new, and sometimes better, antiepileptic drugs. Also of importance is the increase in death rate amongst people with epilepsy. Most deaths in epilepsy are due to the underlying cause (Klenerman et al. 1993). Some deaths may be due to trauma sustained during a seizure or due to accidental drowning in the bath at the time of a seizure. However, a small number of people with epilepsy are found to have died unexpectedly. The mechanism of death in these cases is uncertain and post mortems often fail to demonstrate a clear cause. It has been postulated that these deaths may have been due to arrhythmia produced by the effects of intra-ictal anoxia on the heart although this is an area that is yet to be fully researched.

Much can be done to improve the physical, emotional and social wellbeing and status of people with learning disability and ongoing epilepsy. Healthcare professionals do not have a monopoly in this area but they do have an important role, and their actions and attitudes towards people with epilepsy and their carers will often inform the perceptions and reactions of the wider community.

AN INTRODUCTION TO THE AUTISM SPECTRUM

Since the mid-1960s considerable research has been carried out in the field of autism. It is now known that it is a complex, lifelong condition that manifests in many ways. The current concept is broad, recognising that it can manifest as profoundly severe disabilities or as more subtle problems of social understanding and social functioning. It may exist comorbidly with learning disabilities or other developmental disorders and can occur with other physical or psychological conditions. Some people will be severely affected whereas others will have more subtle problems and may not present to services for support.

The concept of a spectrum has evolved and has been widely accepted as a way to collate the variety of behaviours observed. People on the spectrum may be referred to as having an autistic spectrum disorder (ASD), autism or, in the absence of a learning disability, high-functioning autism (HFA) or Asperger syndrome (AS). There are variations in presentation between HFA and AS but both are considered to be on the spectrum.

The triad of impairments

Wing proposed this triad of key impairments that affect all people on the autism spectrum to a greater or lesser degree irrespective of their cognitive ability.

- *Communication.* Language impairment across all modes of communication: speech, intonation, gesture, facial expression and other body language.
- *Imagination.* Rigidity and inflexibility of thought process: resistance to change, obsessional and ritualistic behaviour.
- *Socialisation.* Difficulties with social relationships, poor social timing, lack of social empathy, rejection of normal body contact, inappropriate eye contact. (Wing and Gould 1979)

A number of other aspects of this condition are also becoming more evident. Of these, *sensory sensitivities* appear to be the most significant and to have considerable implications for practitioners and carers in the day-to-day care of adults on the spectrum.

Adults with ASD may be sensorily hypersensitive or hyposensitive on an individual basis. There is considerable variation from person to person and within each person there may be variability depending on time of day, physical state, mental state, location and other factors. Some of the senses affected include auditory, visual, olfactory, tactile, gustatory, vestibular and proprioceptive (Bogdashina 2003).

MENTAL HEALTH

The risk of psychiatric disorders is increased in persons on the autistic spectrum. The reasons are unclear but may relate to genetic and environmental factors. This is an area of much previous and ongoing study. Clearly the presence of autism does not confer immunity to any psychiatric disorders.

Anxiety is the most common stated problem for people with ASD. They appear to experience very high levels of anxiety that may not be apparent to practitioners and carers. Anxiety may be behind many of the behaviour problems of people with ASD and LD and who are not able to express it in more conventional ways. Anxiety appears to interrelate with sensory hypersensitivities and can magnify the effects of both.

Other disorders found include affective disorder, depression, tic disorders, ADHD, and schizophrenia. Recently an apparently different presentation of catatonia found only in those with ASD has been described by Wing and Shah (2000).

PHYSICAL HEALTH

People on the spectrum are as likely as anyone else to develop a variety of illnesses but a few are worth specific mention. Epilepsy is more common in autism than in the general population. It is estimated that as many as 30 % of people with ASD known to services will develop epilepsy by adult life (Mills and Wing 2005).

As previously mentioned, autism can exist comorbidly with almost any other condition. This includes, for example, Down syndrome. Cerebral palsy and other physical disabilities may mask the underlying autism. Many people on the spectrum and their carers report dietary problems and food intolerance. Some literature to date supports this and is included in Lathe (2006) but this is currently a contentious area and research continues into a possible link between gastrointestinal differences and ASD.

SLEEP DISORDERS

These are becoming increasingly apparent as a problem for people on the spectrum. They manifest in a number of ways but a relatively common pattern is for the sleep-wake cycle to gradually slip and can result in a person being awake all night and therefore very sleepy all day.

People with learning disabilities and ASD may present for treatment of other associated conditions such as cerebral palsy or for acute or chronic musculoskeletal conditions. They may also present for treatment of aspects of the ASD, for example to improve social interaction while improving general fitness through exercise classes or individual work with children on sensory integration. Sensory integration work is not recommended for adults with ASD. In all cases it is essential to be aware of strategies to facilitate effective treatment by, for example, providing a safe environment, paying close attention to sensory problems and maintaining a clear sense of structure. A relaxed atmosphere is facilitated when the therapist is sufficiently aware of the family circumstances and history to respond appropriately to repeated phrases. A quiet confident approach using a structured routine is essential for the achievement of treatment progress and improved quality of life of anyone with autistic spectrum disorder.

CONCLUSION

Learning disability can only be identified when the criteria of intellectual impairment, diminished social adaptive functioning and onset before the age of 18 years are met.

The cause may be organic or unknown but recent studies indicate that organic factors are present more frequently than had previously been realised. Where the cause is of an organic nature it is likely that associated conditions will be present. There can also be a link to poverty and social exclusion.

The associated neurological conditions described in this chapter may present with physical disabilities as in motor delay, developmental coordination disorder and cerebral palsy or, like the learning disability itself, may impinge upon the treatment and management of a physical disability, as in epilepsy or autistic spectrum disorder.

Prevalence ratios show that the number of people with learning disability is not large, compared with those without learning disability. However, the numbers are still substantial and people with learning disabilities are living longer than previously. The criteria and associated conditions show that an individual with learning disability is liable to need considerable support throughout life and that this will include all the additional supports required for old age. People with complex needs will require treatment and management from a range of healthcare professionals.

REFERENCES

Accardo, P.J. and Capute, A.J. (1998) Mental retardations. *Mental Retardation and Developmental Disabilities Research Reviews,* **4**, 2–5.

American Association on Mental Retardation (2002) *Mental Retardation: Definition, Classification and Systems of Support,* American Association on Mental Retardation, Washington DC.

American Psychiatric Association (2000*) DSM–IV-TR Diagnostic and Statistical Manual of Mental Disorders,* 4th edn, American Psychiatric Association, Washington DC.

Betts, T. (1998) *Epilepsy, Psychiatry and Learning Difficulty,* Martin Dunitz, London.

Bobath, K. and Bobath, B. (1975) *Motor Development in the Different Types of Cerebral Palsy,* Heinemann, London.

Bogdashina, O. (2003) *Sensory Perceptual Issues in Autism and Asperger Syndrome,* Jessica Kingsley, London.

Cogher, L.. Savage, E. and Smith M.F. (eds) (1992) *Cerebral Palsy – The Child and Young Person,* Chapman & Hall Medical, London.

Dali, C., Henderson, F.J., Pedersen, S.A., Shou, L., Hilden, J., Bjornskov, I., Standberg, C., Christensen, J., Hangsted, U. and Herbst, G. (2002) Threshold Electrical Stimulation (TES) in ambulant children with cerebral palsy: a randomised double blind placebo-controlled clinical trial. *Developmental Medicine and Child Neurology,* **44** (6), 385–90.

Department of Health (1995) *The Health of the Nation – A Strategy for People with Learning Disabilities*. The Stationery Office, Oldham.

Department of Health (2001) *Valuing People – A New Strategy for Learning Disability for the Twenty-first Century,* Stationery Office, London.

Fisher, A.G., Murray, E.A. and Bundy, A.C. (eds) (1991) *Sensory Integration Theory and Practice,* F.A. Davis Company, Philadelphia.

Fryers, T. (1997) Impairment, disability and handicap: categories and classifications, in *The Psychiatry of Learning Disabilities* (ed. O.Russell), Royal College of Psychiatrists, London, pp. 16–30.

Fryers, T. and Russell, O. (1997) Applied epidemiology, in *The Psychiatry of Learning Disabilities* (ed. O.Russell), Royal College of Psychiatrists, London, pp. 31–47.

Gage, J. (1991) *Gait Analysis in Cerebral Palsy*, MacKeith Press, London.

Goodridge D. and Shorvon, S. (1983) Epileptic seizures in a population of 6000. (1) Demography, diagnosis and classification and the role of the hospital services. (2) Treatment and prognosis. *British Medical Journal,* **287**, 641–7.

Harris, J. (2006) *Intellectual Disability. Understanding Its Development, Causes, Classification, Evaluation and Treatment,* Oxford University Press, New York.

Herge, E.A., Campbell, J.E. (1998) The role of the occupational and physical therapist in the rehabilitation of the older adult with mental retardation. *Topics in Geriatric Rehabilitation,* **13** (4), 12–21.

Illingworth, R.S. (1987) *The Development of the Infant and Young Child, Normal and Abnormal,* 9th edn, Churchill Livingstone, Edinburgh.

Ingram, T.T.S. (1964) *Paediatric Aspects of Cerbral Palsy,* Livingstone, Edinburgh.

International League Against Epilepsy (1981) Commission on Classification and Terminology. A proposal for a revised seizure classification. *Epilepsia,* **22**, 489–501.

Jankovic, J. (2004) Botulinum toxin in clinical practice. *Journal of Neurology Neurosurgery and Psychiatry,* **75**, 951–7.

Kerr, M., Fraser, W., Felce, D. (1996) Primary health care for people with a learning disability; a keynote review. *British Journal of Learning Disabilities,* **24**, 2–8.

Klenerman, P., Sander, J. and Shorvon, S. (1993). Mortality in patients with epilepsy: a study of patients in long-term residential care. *Journal of Neurology, Neurosurgery and Psychiatry,* **52**, 659–62.

Lathe, R. (2006) *Autism, Brain and Environment,* Jessica Kingsley, London.

Levitt, S. (1977) *Treatment of Cerebral Palsy and Motor Delay,* Blackwell, Oxford.

Mills, R. and Wing, L. (2005) *Researching Interventions in ASD and Priorities for Research: Surveying the Membership of the NAS,* London, National Autistic Society.

Muir, W.J. (2004) Learning Disability, in *Companion to Psychiatric Studies* (eds C.P.L. Freeman, A. Zealley and E.C. Johnstone), Churchill Livingstone, Edinburgh, pp. 527–78.

Murphy, C., Boyle, C., Schendel, D., Decoufle, P., Yeargin-Allsopp, M. (1998) Epidemiology of mental retardation in children. *Mental Retardation and Developmental Disabilities Research Reviews,* **4**, 6–13.

NAS (2005). www.nas.org.uk.

NHS Scotland (2004) *Health Needs Assessment Report for People with Learning Disabilities in Scotland,* Public Health Institute of Scotland, Glasgow.

O'Dwyer, N.J., Nelson, P.D. and Nash, J. (1989) Mechanism of muscle growth related to muscle contracture in cerebral palsy. *Development Medicine and Child Neurology,* **31**, 543–52.

Richardson, S., Katz, M., Koller, H., McLaren, J., Rubenstine, B. (1979) Some characteristics of a population of mentally retarded young adults in a British city. *Journal of Mental Deficiency Research,* **23**, 275–87.

Sander, J., Hart, Y., Johnston, A. and Shorvon S.D. (1990) National General Practice Study of Epilepsy: newly diagnosed epilepsy seizures in the general population. *Lancet* **336**, 1267–1271

United Nations (2002) *Economic and Social Council Commission on Human Rights of Persons with Disabilities.* E/CN.4/2002/18/Add 1, New York, United Nations.

WHO (2001) *The International Classification of Impairments, Disabilities and Handicaps Second Edition,* World Health Organization, Geneva.

WHO (2006) *The ICD 10 Classification of Mental and Behavioural Disorders. Clinical Descriptions and Diagnostic Guidelines.* World Health Organization, Geneva.

Willoughby, C. and Polatajko, H. (1995) Motor problems in children with developmental co-ordination disorder: review of literature. *The American Jounal Occupational Therapy,* **49** (8), 787–93.

Wing, L. and Gould, J. (1979) Severe impairments of social interaction and associated abnormalities in children: epidemiology and classification. *Journal of Childhood Autism and Childhood Schizophrenia,* **9**, 11–29.

Wing, L. and Shah, A. (2000) Catatonia in autistic spectrum disorders. *British Journal of Psychiatry,* **176**, 357–62.

3 Psychiatric and Behavioural Disorders in People with Learning Disabilities

TANYA THIAGARAJAH

INTRODUCTION

Learning disability affects at least 1 % of the population; some studies have set its prevalence at 3 % in developed countries. The definition and labelling of an individual with an intellectual impairment (IQ < 70) has changed over the years. Severely pejorative terms, such as 'imbecile' and 'idiot' were used officially but these have since been replaced by 'learning disability' (UK) and 'mental retardation' (US). Other terms such as 'cognitive or intellectual disability' and 'cognitive incapacity' are also expressed frequently.

There was little distinction in the UK between learning disability and mental illness until the reigns of Edward I (1272–1307) and Edward II (1307–1327). Unlike mental illness, which caused fluctuations in mental health, recognition that mental retardation was a continuous state of incapacity led to the creation of legislation to provide care for the 'imbecile and his estate' (Penrose 1963).

The first 'asylum for idiots' opened in England in 1847, followed by a flourish of similar institutions thereafter in Britain. The two main reasons were a fear of 'national degeneracy' (born out of psychiatric and eugenic thinking in the late nineteenth century) and, therefore, segregation was encouraged but it was also seen as the duty of society to provide care for these individuals who could not be looked after at home. When the NHS was introduced in 1948, these institutions were given the status of hospitals, and it was not until the revisions of the Mental Health Acts at the end of the 1950s that voluntary admissions were permitted.

Around 1960, services gradually shifted to the needs of these individuals rather than the perceived needs of society. Overcrowding was reduced, occupational activities extended and specialist staff, who now form the core of the multidisciplinary team, were recruited to work in hospitals.

Learning Disability: Physical Therapy Treatment and Management. Edited by Jeanette Rennie
© 2007 John Wiley & Sons Ltd

From the 1980s, UK national policy has dictated the permanent transfer of this population from hospitals to community settings. This meant closure of large hospitals with the provision of a smaller number of beds reserved for inpatient assessments but also for those who were more impaired, requiring long-term care in a health-care setting.

PREVALENCE AND AETIOLOGY

Until fairly recently, it was believed that learning-disabled individuals lacked the cognitive capacity to experience complex emotions and express intricate psychiatric symptoms that define mental disorders. It is now widely accepted that learning disability and mental illness (dual diagnosis) clearly coexist and this is a focus of growing research interest. In fact, the prevalence of psychiatric and behavioural disorders is at least three to four times greater in people with learning disabilities compared with the general population (WHO 1992). Surveys of psychiatric disorders in representative populations indicate a total prevalence (including challenging behaviour) of 30–40 % in adults with learning disability. However, as seen in Table 3.1, the prevalence is wide-ranging due to the diagnostic criteria used: the nature of disorders and samples used, the method used to identify the psychiatric illness severity and definition of learning disability, data used, source of information and the age and gender distributions of the sample.

The increased prevalence of psychiatric disorders in people with learning disability has been attributed to a combination of biological and psychosocial factors. Organic brain damage and dysfunction occur more commonly in those with learning disability and therefore may also account for psychiatric symptoms and signs. This explanation is supported by the degree of specificity of certain psychiatric and behavioural presentations in a number of syndromes that have learning disability as a cognitive outcome. Table 3.2 outlines the common psychiatric and behavioural disorders in some of these syndromes. Many syndromes have a genetic base and so inheritance may also be a major contributory factor. Psychosocial factors such as limited psychological coping resources, consequences of psychological abnormalities such as impaired attention and lack of social skills, and increased exposure to psychosocial stressors including stigmatisation, isolation, unemployment, poverty and abuse also tend to precipitate and perpetuate mental illness.

ASSESSMENT AND DIAGNOSIS

Symptoms that characterise psychiatric disorders in the normal population, particularly schizophrenia, may be poorly expressed in individuals with learning disability as the diagnosis often requires fairly sophisticated communication.

Table 3.1. Prevalence of psychiatric disorders in people with learning disabilities

Study	Age (years)	Method and sample	Percentage of psychiatric disorders among cases	Percentage of psychiatric disorders among controls
Rutter et al. 1976	9–11	Comparative assessment of the entire age cohort in the Isle of Wight	30–42	6–7
Gillberg et al. 1986	13–17	Comprehensive assessment representative cohort	57 mild, 64 severe	5
Lund 1985	over 20	Comprehensive assessment sample from Danish register for learning disabilities	27	noncomparative
Gostason 1985	20–60	Comprehensive assessment sample from Swedish register	33 mild, 71 severe	23
Patel et al. 1994	Over 50	Comprehensive assessment Community cohort South Wales	21 (11.4 dementia)	noncomparative
Deb et al. 2001	16–64		14 (childhood onset disorders, behaviour disorders, personality disorders and dementia excluded)	noncomparative
Clay and Thomas 2005		Marion County, Oregon Only included those receiving support	31 (dementia and personality disorder excluded)	noncomparative

Table 3.2. Syndromes of learning disability, their associated intellectual impairment, behavioural phenotypes and psychiatric vulnerabilities

Syndrome	Aetiology	Learning disability	Behavioural phenotype and psychiatric vulnerabilities
Aicardi syndrome	Possibly X-linked inheritance	Majority die in infancy, rest develop learning disability	Aggression, self-injurious behaviour, lethargy
Angelman syndrome	Chromosomal abnormality (ch.15 *q*)	Present	Laughing at minimal provocation, inquisitiveness
Brachmann-de Lange (also known as Cornelia-de Lange) syndrome	A possible locus is on chromosome 3	Usually moderate to severe learning disability	Explosive outbursts, stereotypic movements and self injurious behaviour
Cerebral palsy	Perinatal brain damage	Majority of below average intelligence, athetoid type more commonly associated with an average IQ	Various forms of challenging behaviour depending on the level of intellectual impairment
Cretinism	Iodine deficiency, thyroid atrophy	Usually present, altered by early diagnosis and thyroxine treatment	Lethargy, psychomotor retardation, challenging behaviour
Down syndrome	Trisomy 21	The mean IQ is 50, most individuals performing at moderately retarded range	Mood disorders, Alzheimer's disease, challenging behaviour
Foetal alcohol syndrome	Excessive alcohol consumption during pregnancy	The mean IQ is 70	Hyperactivity, poor attention span, giving the impression of hyperkinetic disorder
Fragile X syndrome	FMR-1 gene (X linked inheritance)	Usually mild to moderate, accounts for 4% of cases with mild learning disability in males, usually severe	Features of avoidant personality, some features of autism, schizotypal disorder, hyperkinetic disorder
Joubert syndrome	Autosomal recessive inheritance, genetic locus has not yet been identified	Mild to severe	Abnormal breathing sound, autistic features, self injurious behaviour
Klinefelter syndrome	XXY karyotype	The mean IQ is 90 but there is a slight increase in mild learning disability	Passive compliant during childhood, may show aggressive behaviour in adult life

Table 3.2. *Continued*

Syndrome	Aetiology	Learning disability	Behavioural phenotype and psychiatric vulnerabilities
Lesch–Nyhan syndrome	X-linked recessive inheritance leading to error of purine metabolism	Severe learning disability	Self mutilation, in over 85% some form of aggressive behaviour
Neurofibromatosis	Autosomal dominant inheritance	Learning disability in minority	Symptoms depend on site of neurofibromas
Noonan syndrome	Some cases autosomal dominant. Some familial cases have found a gene on the long arm of chromosome 12. Phenotypically related to Turner syndrome (XO genotype) but occurs in both sexes.	Present	Challenging behaviour, stubbornness, problems in peer relations, preservation
Phenylketonuria	Autosomal recessive inheritance leading to an error of metabolism	Present (neonatal diagnosis and dietary management alter the course of illness)	Hyperactivity, impulse control problems, features of bipolar illness
Prader–Willi syndrome	Microdeletion of the long arm of chromosome 15	Variable, some have normal IQ, majority have mild to moderate learning disability	Impulse control problems, mood symptoms, obsessional and compulsive symptoms, sleep problems, self-injury (spot picking)
Rett syndrome	May be an X-linked dominant disorder	Initial period of normal cognitive development followed by intellectual retardation	Language impairment, autistic features, stereotyped movements and self injurious behaviour
Smith–Magenis syndrome	Microdeletion in chromosome 17	Moderate learning disability	Hyperactivity, autistic features, aggressive behaviour, self injurious behaviour, sleep disturbance
Tuberous sclerosis	Autosomal dominant	Learning disability in 70 % of cases	Autistic features and hyperactivity
Velo-cardio-facial	Microdeletion of chromosome 22	Present (can be mild)	Features of schizophrenia, challenging behaviour
Williams syndrome	Microdeletion of chromosome 7	Present	Symptoms of hyperkinetic disorder and anxiety

The more severe the intellectual impairment (particularly with an IQ of less than 50), the more difficult it becomes to diagnose psychiatric illness. Table 3.3 outlines some of the differences between the various IQ ranges and the associated behavioural and psychiatric disorders. The more severely disabled tend to demonstrate nonspecific behavioural changes as manifestations of psychiatric disorders, compared to those with a milder learning disability who are more able to express symptoms similar to those of the general population. Detailed (including developmental) history and prolonged observation from carers and clinical assessment are required to establish diagnosis.

Factors complicating the assessment, and thus diagnosis of mental health disorders in individuals with learning disability include:

- intellectual distortion (concrete thinking and impaired communication skills regarding the person's own experiences)

Table 3.3. IQ ranges and associated behavioural patterns

IQ range	ICD 10 code and diagnosis	Obsolete terms	Associated behavioural patterns and psychiatric morbidity
50–69	F 70: Mild mental retardation	Feeble minded Moron Mild oligophrenia High grade defect	More closely akin to those found in general population. All psychiatric disorders are diagnosed in this IQ range.
35–49	F 71: Moderate mental retardation	Imbecile Moderate oligophrenia	Limited conceptual capacity and poor language development render the diagnosis of psychiatric disorders difficult, increase in challenging behaviour, sometimes serving communicative function. Associated epilepsy.
20–34	F 72: Severe mental retardation	Severe oligophrenia	Marked motor impairment renders the quality of challenging behaviour different compared with the above groups. Associated epilepsy. Formal psychiatric disorders extremely difficult to diagnose.
Less than 20	F 73: Profound mental retardation	Profound oligophrenia Idiocy	IQ is difficult to measure. Formal psychiatric disorders extremely difficult to diagnose.

- psychosocial masking (impoverished social skills/life experiences that lead to 'misdiagnosis' or 'missed diagnosis')
- cognitive disintegration (stress-induced disruption of information process-ing presenting as bizarre behaviour and psychotic symptoms)
- baseline exaggeration (preexisting cognitive deficits and maladaptive behav-iours that distort symptoms and signs, making interpretation difficult)
- overshadowing (where the existence of intellectual disability masks psycho-pathology) and
- developmentally appropriate phenomena (talking to oneself, solitary fantasy play and so forth) (White et al. 2005)

In view of these difficulties, a plethora of validated screening/assessment tools have been developed since the mid-1980s in order to diagnose psychiatric disorders more accurately. The gold standard of ICD-10 (WHO 1992) and DSM-IV (American Psychiatric Association 1994) used to diagnose psychiat-ric illness in the general population does not account for the differences in presentation such as language and intellectual concepts in those with more severe intellectual impairment. For this reason, the Royal College of Psychia-trists (2001) published the Diagnostic Criteria for psychiatric disorders for use in adults with learning disabilities/mental retardation.

SCHIZOPHRENIA

The prevalence of schizophrenic people with learning disabilities is about 3 % compared to 1 % of the general adult population (Turner 1989). Schizophrenic disorders involve fundamental and characteristic distortions of thinking and perception associated with inappropriate affect (WHO 1992). Schizophrenia in people with mild learning disability is closely akin to that found in people of normal intelligence but is more difficult to diagnose in individuals with an IQ of less than 40 (Reid 1983). Hallucinations and delusions may be simpler, less systematised and less sustained (Reid 1989).

Clinical features of schizophrenia are:

- disorders of thought content
- disorder of the form of thought and language
- hallucinations
- catatonia
- negative symptoms

DISORDERS OF THOUGHT CONTENT

These reflect abnormal thought processes and include delusions. Delusions are defined as fixed, false beliefs not correctable by reasoning and not consistent with the prevailing culture. Paranoid ideas and delusions of control (thoughts of being controlled by an external force) are main features. In learning disability, delusions are usually poorly formulated or, instead, are florid with a grandiose wish-fulfilling component. The content of delusions is developmentally appropriate to the person's overall ability level; therefore, witches, monsters, ghosts and pop stars can feature prominently, so differentiation from fantasies is crucial but sometimes difficult. Unexplained agitation, avoidance, altered behaviour and situation-related anxiety can also indicate the presence of delusional thoughts. Delusions may be more apparent in visual material such as drawings and input from the art therapist can be helpful in the interpretation of the material.

DISORDER OF THE FORM OF THOUGHT AND LANGUAGE

Disorders of the form of thought and language reflect disturbed thinking patterns which are manifested in speech. This speech is observed by the outsider to be abnormal. Observed abnormalities of speech include acceleration (constantly changing the topic of speech with some connection between the topics but the goal of thinking is not maintained as the patient is easily distracted), retardation (thoughts are slowed so that there is a long pause before responding to questions), interruption (no order of thinking so that there is no understandable connection between thoughts) and changes to the flow of thought (patient retains ideas long after they cease to be contextually appropriate). In schizophrenia, interruptions and varying degrees of disorganisation of speech resulting in no understandable connection between thoughts are known as 'formal thought disorder'. Other ways that disorders of thinking and language may manifest are disturbance of judgement, belief in interference with the control of thinking (the idea that people can insert/withdraw patient's thoughts) and speech disturbances such as echolalia, unintelligible speech or made-up words (neologisms). Again, these features can be difficult to diagnose in people with moderate to profound learning disabilities who may show an unusual intermixture or disruption of thought process without suffering from schizophrenic formal thought disorder.

HALLUCINATIONS

A hallucination is a false sensory perception in the absence of a real external stimulus. Hallucinations occur in about three-quarters of people with acute schizophrenia, most commonly in the auditory modality and frequently in the third person. Visual hallucinations appear to be commoner in individuals with learning disability than in the general population. In those with moderate to profound learning disability, any abnormal perceptual experience can pass unrecognised due to the limited ability to express morbid experience.

CATATONIA

Catatonia is defined as a state of increased muscle tone at rest, resulting in immobilisation in a particular position; this is abolished by voluntary activities. Catatonia is a relatively rare psychiatric syndrome caused by a large variety of disease processes not specific to schizophrenia and includes complication of treatment with some psychotropic medication. However, catatonic phenomena, more prominent in individuals with learning disability, are described as alternating states of excitement and stupor. In the main, these episodes have a clear onset, and where refractory to medication show a good response to electroconvulsive therapy.

Motor mannerisms (odd, stilted movements) seen in people with learning disabilities can be misinterpreted as catatonic symptoms, but the former usually run a continuous course and may respond to behavioural interventions. The motor side effects of medication are another confounder and may, of course, coexist with catatonia and mannerisms.

NEGATIVE SYMPTOMS

These are characterised by apathy, lack of drive, slowness and social withdrawal and varying degrees of personal neglect that follow an acute episode or present between episodes of illness. These symptoms are usually progressive and can develop early in the course of illness and are relatively refractory to standard therapies. As it is a cause of chronic morbidity, it is important to distinguish between an intellectually disabled person with a longstanding pattern of social withdrawal, poverty of thought and constricted affect and an individual suffering from a schizophrenic illness with negative symptoms.

Bouras et al. (2004) reported that, overall, individuals with intellectual disability demonstrate higher observable psychopathology, more negative symptoms and greater functional disabilities. The ten most common symptoms of acute schizophrenia in the general population are shown in Table 3.4.

Table 3.4. The 10 most frequent symptoms of schizophrenia in the general population

Symptom	Frequency (%)
Lack of insight	97
Auditory hallucinations	74
Ideas of reference	70
Suspiciousness	66
Flat affect	66
Second person hallucinations	65
Delusional mood	64
Delusions of persecution	64
Thoughts spoken aloud	50
Thought alienation	42

AFFECTIVE (MOOD) DISORDERS

Categories of mood disorders include:

- depressive episode
- recurrent depressive disorder (previously known as 'endogenous depression' or 'melancholia')
- cyclothymia
- manic episodes (include hypomania and mania)
- bipolar affective disorder (previously termed 'manic depressive illness')
- rapid cycling disorder
- persistent mood disorder

DEPRESSIVE DISORDER

The prevalence of major depressive disorder among people with learning disabilities is 1–5 %. The principles of diagnosis follow closely with schizophrenia although it may be easier to diagnose on the basis that many of the features are observable, thereby reducing reliance on communication of symptoms by the individual. Observable features include diurnal mood variation, tearfulness, appetite and sleep changes (including early morning awakening), reduced energy and activity levels, social withdrawal, reduced communication and hypochondriacal symptoms. Behavioural concomitants of mood changes are more noticeable, including agitation, withdrawal, aggression, deterioration in problem behaviours, increase in self-injurious behaviour and regression to increased dependency. Cognitive symptoms such as ideas of hopelessness, helplessness, worthlessness and guilt are more difficult to detect; they depend on the level of ability of the individual to express these symptoms. Suicide may be less common in people with learning disabilities (Vitiello and Behar 1992) and attempted or actual suicide may be poorly planned.

Psychotic symptoms such as catatonia and visual hallucinations are more commonly present compared with the general population.

BIPOLAR DISORDER – MANIA AND HYPOMANIA

Cyclical changes in behaviour and mood to varying degrees have been recorded in 4 % of adults with learning disability (Deb and Hunter 1991). Changes are characterised by episodic excitement/ irritability, hyperactivity and distractibility, sleep disturbance, loss of usual social inhibition (leading to sexual disinhibition and overfamiliarity), impaired judgement and pressured speech. Cyclothymia is the least severe form (and may not come to the attention of professionals) followed by hypomania, rapid cycling disorder and mania. They are differentiated by the severity of symptoms and the time course.

In hypomania, and similarly mania and rapid cycling disorder, the changes described above are severe and persistent, causing interference with the person's quality of life.

Mania is distinguished from hypomania by the presence of mood-congruent delusions and hallucinatory experience.

Rapid cycling disorder can be as severe as mania and is differentiated by an increased number of episodes of 'highs and lows' within a given period of time.

Mania and depression can also be precipitated by physical conditions such as frontal lobe tumours and endocrine disorders and medication.

ANXIETY, STRESS-RELATED DISORDERS AND THE 'NEUROSES'

These are a set of disorders that are characterised by anxiety and sometimes fear, and are related to stress. Common neurotic and stress-related disorders are

- phobic anxiety disorders
- generalised anxiety and panic disorders
- obsessive-compulsive disorder
- reaction to severe stress
- adjustment disorders

NEUROTIC (ANXIETY) DISORDERS

These are defined as psychiatric conditions that arise in the absence of gross brain abnormalities and are not associated with delusions, hallucinations or reality distortion. They are clinically significant, unpleasant emotions that have the quality of fear, dread and alarm in the presence or absence of an identifiable psychosocial stressor or stresses. They are accompanied by a physiological arousal resulting in a 'fight or flight' response. In learning disability, behavioural manifestations are wide and bear no consistent relationship to the disorder. These disorders, similar to other psychiatric disorders are overlooked in learning disability. One study identified 27 % of people with learning disability as suffering from anxiety disorders (Stavrakaki and Mintsioulis 1997). Anxiety disorders should be distinguished from the high levels of free-floating anxiety that occur in schizophrenia and autism spectrum disorders.

PHOBIC ANXIETY

This is a group of disorders in which anxiety is precipitated by, or in anticipation of feared situations, resulting in characteristic avoidance behaviour of that situation. It includes agoraphobia (fear of crowds, public places, public transport, leaving home), social phobias (fear of social situations) and specific phobias (such as fear of heights). There is some evidence that specific phobias are especially common in people with learning disability.

Table 3.5. Symptoms and signs of anxiety

Organ System	Symptoms	Signs
Cardiovascular	Palpitations	Increased heart rate
		Chest tightness
		Increased blood pressure
Pulmonary	Difficulty breathing	Facial flushing
	Sense of suffocation	Hyperventilation
Gastrointestinal	Dry mouth	
	Nausea	
	Abdominal pain	
	Belching	
	Altered bowel habit	
	Altered eating pattern	
Nervous	Tension	Stereotypic behaviour
	Poor concentration	Cold/clammy hands
	Dizziness	Pacing/restlessness
	Irritability	
	Hot flushes/cold chills	
	Tremor	
	Sleep disturbance	
	Fatigue	
	Ill-defined fear	
	Headaches	
	Trembling/sweating	
	Numbness/Tingling	
	Depersonalisation/derealisation	

GENERALISED ANXIETY AND PANIC DISORDERS

In comparison to other anxiety and stress-related disorders, generalised anxiety disorder is usually free-floating and not related to any circumstances. The person worries about everyday events and may exhibit fear frequently to a degree that impairs psychosocial functioning. Symptoms and signs are described in Table 3.5. Anxiety may manifest as physical aggression and even self-injurious behaviour as a coping strategy, particularly in learning disability.

Panic attacks are recurrent, discrete episodes of severe anxiety. Typically, they have an abrupt onset and are at their worst in the first few minutes. Malloy (1998) argued that in assessing people with learning disabilities for psychiatric disorders, clinicians should also consider the diagnosis of panic disorder in patients who report vague somatic complaints.

OBSESSIVE-COMPULSIVE DISORDER (OCD)

Believed to be more common in individuals with severe-to-profound learning disability (perhaps due to prevalence of stereotyped behaviours) compared to mild intellectual disability, recognition that unpleasant, intrusive thoughts or compulsive behaviours are internally controlled is a key criterion in diagnosis. Compulsive thoughts or behaviours are usually accompanied by unsuccessful attempts at resistance by the person. These repeated rituals are perceived by the sufferer as a senseless symbolic attempt to avert a perceived danger or other unpleasant feeling. In learning disability, compulsive rituals are more readily diagnosed than obsessional thoughts. For example, stereotyped movements, compulsive self-injurious behaviour, compulsive checking and touching may occur. Features of obsessive compulsive disorders are frequently found in a variety of syndromes, including Rett and Prader–Willi syndromes and tuberous sclerosis.

STRESS-RELATED DISORDERS

Reactions to stressful life events form three main groups: acute stress reaction, adjustment disorder and post-traumatic stress disorder (PTSD). Individuals with learning disability are more vulnerable to physical, sexual and emotional abuse and are therefore more likely to suffer from stress-related disorders. Unsurprisingly, the severity of the stressor, onset and reaction pattern varies. The precipitating stressful event can fall within the range of normal experience (for example, moving to a new social environment). In learning disability, common symptoms observed in adjustment disorder include aggression, agitation, and distractibility, physical and verbal abuse, self-mutilation and sleep and appetite disturbances. Bereavement reaction (a type of adjustment disorder) in learning disability tends to present with irritability, lethargy, hyperactivity, stereotypy and inappropriate speech (Hollins and Esterhuizen 1997), unlike the general population, where numbness, pining for the deceased and depression are the most common symptoms.

Acute stress reaction and PTSD arise as a reaction to an exceptionally threatening or catastrophic life event (for example, rape, serious accident or witnessing a crime). The onset of symptoms varies from within a few hours of the stressor in acute stress reaction, to within six months in post-traumatic stress disorder. PTSD is characterised by repeated reliving of the threatening event in intrusive memories and dreams. This is accompanied by an autonomic response such as hypervigilance and enhanced startle reaction. Violent and disruptive behaviours (Ryan 1994) and self-mutilation are more commonly observed in learning disabled individuals with PTSD than in the general population. Evidence would suggest that PTSD be routinely considered in differential diagnosis when such symptoms are reported (Szymanski and King 1999).

PERSONALITY DISORDERS

A personality disorder is an enduring pattern of inner experience and behaviour that deviates markedly from the expectations of the individual's culture, is pervasive and inflexible, has an onset in adolescence or early adulthood, is stable over time and leads to distress and impairment (American Psychiatric Association 1994). Diagnosis is based on a longstanding pattern of disharmonious attitudes and behaviour that affect the individual in various spheres of life. Thus, the detection of personality disorder relies heavily on subjective information about thoughts – often difficult to elicit in intellectual disability. Additionally, extensive history should be obtained over a period of time from different informants; however its usefulness in moderate to severe learning disability is questionable if diagnosed.

Prevalence of personality disorder in intellectual disability has varied from 1 % to 91 % in the community and 22 % to 92 % in hospitals (Alexander and Cooray 2003). The use of schizoid, dependent and anxious (avoidant) personality disorder is not recommended for use in learning disability as some of the features that characterise LD (such as passiveness, dependence) are difficult to separate from features of personality disorders (DC-LD). However, they will be described below briefly to demonstrate their similarities to aspects of learning disability. On the other hand, there is reluctance to diagnose other personality disorders on the grounds that they may be excluded from services and thus result in lack of access to appropriate therapies.

Types of specific personality disorders are:

- paranoid personality disorder
- schizoid personality disorder
- schizotypal personality disorder (categorised in schizophrenia category in ICD-10)
- anankastic (obsessive-compulsive) personality disorder
- dissocial (antisocial) personality disorder
- emotionally unstable personality disorder (impulsive and borderline type)
- histrionic personality disorder
- dependent personality disorder
- anxious (avoidant) personality disorder
- narcissistic personality disorder

PARANOID PERSONALITY DISORDER

This is characterised by suspiciousness, reluctance to confide in others and conspiratorial explanation of events. It accounts for approximately 15 % of all cases of personality disorder amongst people with learning disabilities.

SCHIZOID PERSONALITY AND SCHIZOTYPAL DISORDER

Both conditions have some common features that overlap with negative symptoms of schizophrenia and autistic spectrum disorders. They are all characterised by emotional coldness, detachment, flat affect and a tendency to solitary activities. The differentiating features that would suggest schizotypal disorder are odd beliefs, magical thoughts and unusual perceptual experiences, whereas schizoid personality disorder is distinguished by a pattern of emotional indifference and excessive preoccupation with fantasy.

ANANKASTIC (OBSESSIVE-COMPULSIVE) PERSONALITY DISORDER

Preoccupation with details, rigidity, stubbornness and excessive doubts are the hallmark of this disorder. This pattern of symptoms is also manifest, however, in people with autistic spectrum disorders and fragile X syndrome.

DISSOCIAL (ANTISOCIAL) PERSONALITY DISORDER

Defined by failure to conform to social norms, aggression and callous unconcern of others, dissocial personality disorder places a heavy burden on psychiatric resources and the criminal justice system. It is usually preceded by conduct problems in childhood and adolescence and is known to be associated with specific reading and hyperkinetic disorders. Like all personality disorders, diagnosis should be made with particular care as it can result in repercussions, such as social exclusion.

EMOTIONALLY UNSTABLE (IMPULSIVE AND BORDERLINE TYPE) PERSONALITY DISORDER

Self-injurious behaviour, impulsivity and affective lability that occur commonly in learning disability can often be mistaken for borderline personality disorder (Mavromatis 2000). Therefore, diagnosis should be made with certainty not least because of the implications on psychiatric resources, where these individuals pose considerable management difficulties.

HISTRIONIC PERSONALITY DISORDER

This is characterised by exaggerated expression of emotions, continual seeking of appreciation by others, overconcern with physical attractiveness and inappropriate sexual seductiveness.

DEPENDENT PERSONALITY DISORDER

It is difficult to distinguish between the dependent state as a result of the disability and a truly dependent personality, so this disorder is rarely diagnosed in this population. Features include difficulty in making decisions, feelings of inferiority to others and constant need for nurturance and support.

ANXIOUS (AVOIDANT) PERSONALITY DISORDER

This group often describe preoccupation with being criticised or rejected in social situations and avoiding interpersonal contact. Similar features are observed in cases of fragile X syndrome.

NARCISSISTIC PERSONALITY DISORDER

Pervasive pattern of grandiosity and preoccupation with fantasies of unlimited success characterise this personality type. It is uncommon, with virtually no research into its association with learning disabilities.

DEMENTIA

Dementia is an irreversible condition that results in deterioration of cognitive functioning (memory, thinking, orientation, comprehension, calculation, learning capacity, language and judgement). Parallel deterioration of emotional control, social behaviour, functional skills and motivation is also commonly observed. Indeed, decline in functional skills, personality/behavioural changes, or psychiatric disturbances may be presenting signs. Gait deterioration, myoclonus, and seizures may be early findings in severe learning disability.

Onset is insidious, and usually non-specific, making it difficult to detect early in those with a pre-existing intellectual impairment. Cognitive testing and imaging investigations (CT scan) are useful as part of a diagnostic workup. However, the alerting factor, arousing suspicion of the condition, is the change from the person's usual behaviour in the older population.

With the exception of Down syndrome, the prevalence of dementia, age of onset and progression in learning disability seems similar to that in the general population over the age of 65. In Down syndrome dementia occurs at an earlier age and has a far higher prevalence (Coppus et al. 2006).

DEMENTIA IN ALZHEIMER'S DISEASE

This is the commonest type, as it is in the general population. Clinical presentation is as described above, with progressive deterioration. Terminal dementia results in total immobility, in loss of communicative functioning, and in seizures. Down syndrome is associated with Alzheimer's disease partially explained genetically by the role of beta amyloid precursor protein gene on chromosome 21.

CORTICAL LEWY BODY DISEASE

Presentation is similar to that seen in Alzheimer's disease but is distinguished by the development of motor disorders of Parkinson's disease and marked visual hallucinations.

VASCULAR DEMENTIA

This type occurs following a stroke or as a gradual progression from small asymptomatic infarcts. Onset is often acute with personality and emotional changes occurring before memory decline. Depression occurs in about 20 % of the sufferers.

OTHER PSYCHIATRIC/NEUROPSYCHIATRIC DISORDERS THAT CAN BE ASSOCIATED WITH LEARNING DISABILITY

HYPERKINETIC DISORDERS

Hyperkinetic disorders typically present within the first five years of life. Core features are overactivity, inattention and impulsivity that persist across different situations. Associated features include lack of perception of danger, social disinhibition, recklessness and poor sleep. Hyperkinetic disorders can coexist with anxiety, conduct disorder, and oppositional and defiant behaviour. They are also prevalent in Williams, fragile X and foetal alcohol syndromes. In learning disability, the diagnosis should only be made when the symptoms of the disorder are in excess of those which might be expected of the individual's degree of learning disability (DC-LD). A higher prevalence in both children and adults with cognitive impairment has been demonstrated (Rutter et al. 1970; Epstein et al. 1986).

GILLES DE LA TOURETTE'S SYNDROME

This syndrome, more common in males is characterised by multiple motor and vocal tics, usually developing in childhood. These are sudden, rapid, involuntary, recurrent and nonrhythmic motor movements or vocalisations. A proportion of these are transient, but more commonly, they persist into adulthood. Other features of Gilles de la Tourette's syndrome include coprolalia (repetitive obscene utterances), distractibility, impulsivity and depressed mood. There is an association with pervasive developmental and hyperkinetic disorders.

OTHER BEHAVIOURAL OUTCOMES OF LEARNING DISABILITY

CHALLENGING BEHAVIOUR IN PEOPLE
WITH LEARNING DISABILITIES

Challenging behaviour is the commonest reason for referral to a psychiatrist in learning disability (Day 1985) although only a minority will have an underlying psychiatric illness. It is defined as 'culturally abnormal behaviour of such intensity, frequency or duration that the physical safety of the person or others is likely to be placed in serious jeopardy which is likely to seriously limit use of, or result in the person being denied access to, ordinary community facilities' (Emerson 1995). There is a strong social element to this definition as well as incorporating a huge swathe of different behaviours. However, a prevalence of between 20% and 44% is consistently reported. The underlying behaviour reflects a variety of causes that relate to psychological, neurobiological, neuropsychiatric, and sociocommunicative factors. Whatever the reasons for the behaviours, they serve an important communicative function, particularly in individuals with impaired language development.

Challenging behaviour includes:

- mannerisms, rocking and other apparently purposeless activities.
- self-injurious behaviour
- violence to others, including hitting, biting, property damage and tantrums
- challenging behaviour of sexual nature, including public masturbation and exposure
- unusual eating behaviour and excretion habits
- production of unusual noises

Behaviours that create the biggest impact for care include aggression, wandering away, disturbing noises, temper tantrums and sexual delinquency (Lowe and Felce 1995). The DC-LD classifies types of challenging behaviour.

Certain chromosomal disorders and syndromes are associated with challenging behaviour (Table 3.2) and sometimes these are of a relatively specific type and clinical course (for example those with Smith-Magenis syndrome). However, no specific relationship has been established between the latter and psychiatric disorders.

MANAGEMENT

The management of psychiatric disorders in individuals with learning disability follows that of the general population. A lack of ability to give full informed consent for research and diagnostic uncertainties still hinder progress in this area, so much has to be extrapolated from the population that is not learning disabled.

Table 3.6 describes the different classes of medications used in psychiatric practice. Surveys have estimated that 30% to 40% of those with learning disability are on psychotropic medication with higher usage in hospitals than in the community (Fraser and Kerr 2003).

The main differences in medication issues in learning disability compared to the general population are as follows:

Table 3.6. Classification of psychiatric medications used
in the field of learning disabilities

Class of medications	Examples	Uses
Older generation antipsychotics (neuroleptics, first generation antipsychotics, typical)	Haloperidol (Serenace) Trifluoperazine (Stelazine) Chlorpromazine (Largactil) Perphenazine (Trilafon) Fluphenazine (Modecate) Pipothiazine (Piportil)	Schizophrenia/psychosis Mania and hypomania Rapid tranquillisation in cases of severe psychomotor agitation Challenging behaviour
Newer generation antipsychotics (Second and third generation)	Sulpiride (Dogmatil) Olanzapine (Zyprexa) Risperidone (Resperdal) Quetiapine (Seroquel)	Schizophrenia (positive and negative symptoms) Anxiety states (in small doses, mainly Risperidone)
Atypical antipsychotic	Clozapine (Clozaril)	Treatment resistant schizophrenia
Antidepressants	Imipramine (Tofranil) Clomipramine (Anafranil) Amitriptyline (Tryptizol) Fluoxetine (Prozac) Paroxetine (Seroxat) Venlafaxine (Efexor)	Depressive disorders (acute treatment and prophylaxis) Anxiety disorders Obsessive compulsive disorder Self-injurious behaviour Autistic rituals
Mood Stabilisers	Lithium salts Carbamazepine (Tegretol) Valproate (Epilim)	Acute treatment of mania and prophylaxis of manic depressive disorders Treatment resistant depression Aggressive behaviour
Anxiolytics	Diazepam (Valium) Lorazepam (Ativan) Chlordiazepoxide (Librium) Buspirone (Buspar)	Anxiety disorders Alcohol withdrawal symptoms Rapid tranquillisation in cases of psychomotor agitation
Hypnotics	Temazepam Zopiclone (Zimovane) Zolpidem (Stilnoct)	Insomnia
Psychostimulants	Dexamfetamine (Dexedrine) Methylphenidate (Ritalin)	Hyperkinetic disorders Narcolepsy
Beta Blockers	Propranolol (Inderal) Atenolol (Tenormin)	Anxiety Impulsivity and rage outbursts Akathisia
Opiate antagonists	Naloxone Naltrexone	Self-injurious behaviour
Anticholinergic antiparkinsonian	Procyclidine	Pseudoparkinsonism Dystonia

Table 3.6. *Continued*

Class of medications	Examples	Uses
Cholinesterase inhibitors	Donepezil	Dementia (Alzheimer's)
	Galantamine	Dementia (Alzheimer's or mixed)
	Rivastigmine	Dementia (Alzheimer's and dementia with Lewy bodies)
Antilibidinal	Cyproterone	Hypersexuality
	Benperidol	Inappropriate sexual behaviour not responsive to psychological interventions

Table 3.7. Behavioural and psychiatric side effects of psychotropic medications used in learning disability

Side effect	Medications precipitating the side effect
Agitation	Anxiolytic (benzodiazepine) withdrawal
	Fluoxetine (possibly occurs in 9 % of those treated with fluoxetine)
	Other SSRIs (reported with paroxetine and citalopram)
Aggression	Psychostimulants (dexamfetamine, methylphenidate)
	Benzodiazepines (paradoxical effect)
	Withdrawal of SSRIs (case reports)
Confusion	Antipsychotics
Depressed mood	Antipsychotics
	β blockers
	Benzodiazepines
Hallucinations	Psychostimulants
	Benzodiazepine withdrawal
	Tricyclic antidepressants (rarely reported)
	Zopiclone
Delusions	Psychostimulants
Manic features	Antidepressants
	Psychostimulants
Delusional thoughts	Psychostimulants
Tics	Psychostimulants

SSRIs, serotonin specific reuptake inhibitors

- drug dosage needed to treat similar disorders is lower than in the general psychiatric population
- compliance of medication is better due to administration by carers
- monitoring of side effects is poor largely due to communication difficulties.

Table 3.7 outlines the most common behavioural side effects in people receiving psychotropic medication.

Extra caution is required when prescribing for people with learning disabilities who have higher rates of epilepsy and movement disorders. Many psychotropic medications are known to lower seizure threshold and are therefore more likely to precipitate fits in those who are predisposed to them.

In psychiatry, the principles of treatment are aimed at symptom relief, restoration of psychosocial functioning and relapse prevention by biological and psychosocial interventions.

BIOLOGICAL INTERVENTION

Medication

- Antipsychotics (refer to Table 3.5 for indications for use). Older, newer generation and atypical drugs exert their effects via dopamine and other receptors resulting in symptom relief and also accounting for side effects. Apart from clozapine, which has specific efficacy on negative symptoms, the main differences between the groups of drugs lie in their side-effect profiles.
- Antidepressants. The two main groups of commonly prescribed antidepressants are selective serotonin reuptake inhibitors (SSRI) and tricyclic antidepressants (TCA). By blocking serotonin and noradrenalin receptors, increased availability of these neurotransmitters in the brain lead to enhanced mood, reduction of anxiety levels and to alleviation of OCD symptoms. Certain antidepressants, such as clomipramine are more effective in treating phobic and obsessional states than others.
- Mood stabilisers. Lithium and antiepileptic medication, such as carbamazepine and sodium valproate are examples. They are used for acute treatment and prophylaxis of mania (bipolar illness) and treatment resistant depression. Whilst lithium remains the mainstay of bipolar disorder mood stabilisation, rapid cycling bipolar disorder is more effectively controlled by carbamazepine and sodium valproate.
- Benzodiazepines. These are helpful in many psychiatric disorders due to relaxant and sedative properties but short-term use is recommended due to the possibility of physiological dependence. They also have antiepileptic effects.
- Opiate antagonists. This group of opioid antagonists may be useful in attenuation self-injurious behaviour, based on the principle that endogenous opioids underlie self-injurious behaviour.

Extrapyramidal (Neuromuscular) Side Effects of Psychotropic Medications

These particular side effects are emphasised as they may be life-threatening or debilitating if not detected and managed appropriately. Movement disorders can also impact on the ability to cooperate with physiotherapy exercises and occupational therapy. Clozapine is the least likely psychotropic to induce extrapyramidal side effects.

Extrapyramidal side effects can be grouped as follows:

- Acute dystonia presents as sustained, involuntary muscular rigidity resulting in twisting of the neck, limbs and trunk. It develops within hours to weeks of treatment. It is reported in 5 % to 20 % of those receiving antipsychotics and is treated with an anticholinergic drug such as procyclidine.
- Akathisia is defined as a subjective motor restlessness resulting in an inability to sit still, observed as constant pacing or shifting posture in the individual. It occurs within hours to weeks of treatment initiation and can be confused with agitation or psychosis. The treatment of akathisia is difficult; where reducing or changing the antipsychotic does alleviate it, beta blockers (such as propranolol) and benzodiazepines have been tried.
- Pseudoparkinsonism occurs in 15 % to 50 % of patients who are not learning disabled and who receive antipsychotic medications. It results from blockade of the dopamine receptors of the nigro-striatal pathway of the brain, implicated in movement control. Symptoms include muscular rigidity, resting tremor and bradykinesia. These symptoms usually occur within days to weeks and are dose related. Management includes reducing the dose or switching antipsychotic medications prior to a trial of anticholinergic agents.
- Tardive dyskinesia develops in 30 % to 45 % of individuals with learning disability following long-term treatment with typical antipsychotic medications. It is characterised by involuntary choreo-athetoid movements of the face, limbs or trunk. Often seen in elderly patients as lingual and masticatory dyskinesia, severe forms can lead to swallowing and speech difficulties. Individuals with gross brain morphological abnormalities are also particularly susceptible to tardive dyskinesia. Treatment is, unfortunately, empirical and is irreversible in 50 % of cases despite cessation of the offending drug (which can sometimes worsen the dyskinesia).
- Neuroleptic malignant syndrome. This idiosyncratic, life-threatening complication of antipsychotic treatment, believed to be more prevalent in learning disability, usually occurs within two weeks of treatment initiation. Muscular rigidity, altered consciousness and hyperpyrexia are main features. The mainstay of treatment is supportive and includes withdrawal of the offending drug, administration of antipyretics and muscle relaxants. It has a mortality rate of approximately 20 %.

Electroconvulsive Therapy (ECT)

Electroconvulsive therapy is the application of electrical stimulus to the brain via scalp electrodes to induce a seizure. The patient receives a short duration anaesthetic and muscle relaxant to prevent any injury ('modified' ECT). The seizure is demonstrable via observable seizure activity on an EEG or direct patient observation. The mechanism involved in symptom improvement is unclear but modulation of the monoamine and dopamine pathways in the brain is implicated.

Indications for ECT include depressive stupor or inanition, psychotic depression, suicidality compelling continuous observation, not responding to medication and as maintenance therapy to prevent relapse of depression.

The side effects of ECT are particularly relevant to learning disability as loss of short- and long-term memory may be significant in these individuals with less functional reserve. The success of ECT depends on activity of generalised cerebral seizure activity. This can be hindered in learning disability where a large proportion of these individuals are on anti-epileptic medication.

Other physical therapies used with mixed evidence in depression include repetitive transcranial magnetic stimulation (rTMS) and left vagus nerve stimulation (VNS).

PSYCHOSOCIAL INTERVENTIONS

Psychological therapy includes:

- Counselling and crisis intervention. This is of benefit to individuals with less severe emotional problems and adjusting to stressful situations.
- Cognitive behaviour therapy (CBT). Cognitive behaviour therapy assesses and modifies dysfunctional cognitive processes in order to improve symptoms and reduce problematic behaviour. It is recommended as first line of therapy in mild to moderate depression, and is also effective in generalised anxiety disorder, panic disorders, OCD and PTSD. In general, combination of medication and cognitive therapy is more effective than either treatment on its own.

Kroese et al. (1997) highlighted that the level of comprehension and expression, the ability to self-report and self-regulation skills were some of the factors to consider when assessing the suitability for CBT in intellectual impairment. This in turn relates to the ability to link emotions, behaviour, physical reactions and thoughts in order to mediate change. Modifications are essential to account for individual cognitive and developmental deficits (for example, slowed thinking and difficulty with abstract thinking). These include roleplay and use of visual material. Furthermore, the reinforcement of skills transferred from therapy to real life situations needs to be reinforced by the wider community teams and carers.

- Cognitive analytic therapy (CAT). This is derived from cognitive therapy techniques with a framework of psychodynamic understanding.
- Behavioural therapy. This encompasses a variety of techniques. Examples include relaxation therapy (used in anxiety and stress-related disorders), exposure, desensitisation and flooding techniques (used in specific phobias),

social skills training (used in anger management and assertiveness training) and specific behaviour applied interventions (see challenging behaviour).

- Dialectic behaviour therapy (DBT). Highly structured and intensive, it is used mainly in borderline personality disorder focussing on social skills and problem-solving techniques.
- Interpersonal therapy (IPT). Initially used in depression, IPT addresses bereavement and loss, role disputes and transitions and 'interpersonal deficits' such as loneliness.
- Psychodynamic therapy. This kind of psychotherapy reconstructs the origins of a psychiatric disorder in the early life experience of the patient, and seeks unconscious factors that account for abnormal thinking, emotions and behaviour.

The above interventions can also be employed in group settings or family therapy. Other interventions in maintaining health and reducing relapses are:

- reducing negative life events
- social supports
- exercise and diet
- rehabilitation

This last concept encompasses a variety of elements to help patients reach and maintain their best level of functioning. This includes sheltered employment programmes/restoration or development of skills using, for example, occupational therapy.

SCHIZOPHRENIA

Biological Intervention

- Antipsychotic medication. Clozapine is prescribed for individuals who have failed to respond to at least two other neuroleptics in adequate doses after between six and eight weeks and requires monitoring of full blood count.
- Electroconvulsive therapy is also used in non-responders to medication or in catatonic states.

Psychosocial Intervention

- Cognitive behaviour therapy is a useful adjunct to medication in alleviating individual symptoms such as hallucinations and reducing the stressors that may exacerbate psychosis.
- Family therapy and carer education has a clear effect on prevention of psychotic relapse and hospitalisation by encouraging medication compliance and reduction of hostility and critical comments.
- Social skills training breaks complex, social repertoires into simpler steps.
- Rehabilitation.

The prognosis for schizophrenia varies from episodic remittent illness, with good response to antipsychotic medication and psychosocial interventions, to a more continuous disorganised illness.

MOOD DISORDERS, NEUROTIC AND STRESS-RELATED DISORDERS

Biological Intervention

- Antidepressants are effective in 65 % to 75 % of people with depression. In addition to depression, this group of drugs is also effective in anxiety states and stress-related disorders.
- Electroconvulsive therapy.
- Augmentation with other drugs such as lithium has been effective in treating resistant depression.
- Antipsychotics in low doses are prescribed to alleviate anxiety symptoms and depression with psychotic features.

Psychosocial Intervention

- Psychological therapies, particularly CBT, are effective in depression, anxiety states and stress-related disorders.

MANIA AND HYPOMANIA

Biological Intervention

- Mood stabilisers and antipsychotics are effective in controlling persistent elevation of mood, irritability, pressure of speech, increased tempo of thinking, distractibility, delusions and hallucinations.
- Benzodiazepines are helpful in acute management by reducing overall activity and insomnia of mania.
- Electroconvulsive therapy is effective in manic stupor.

Psychosocial Intervention

- Cognitive behaviour therapy is aimed at early recognition of symptoms, need for medication, management of psychosocial stressors and interpersonal problems, to prevent a relapse.

PERSONALITY DISORDERS

In general, this group of disorders is difficult to manage. Principles of therapy encompass assessment and circumstances of behaviour over a period of time before appropriate therapy is instituted. Dialectic behaviour therapy and CAT are used particularly in borderline PD. Medication can be useful for comorbid illness, particularly mood disorders and substance misuse.

DEMENTIA

Management is aimed at delaying cognitive decline using cholinesterase inhibitors (Table 3.6), treating associated illnesses such as depression and optimising quality of life for the patient and carer. Antidepressants and antipsychotics (for agitation, hallucinations) can be useful where appropriate. Nonpharmacological interventions include behaviour management, cognitive and multisensory stimulation, recreational and physical activities and reality orientation therapy (SIGN guidelines).

HYPERKINETIC DISORDERS

Treatment consists of a combination of drugs and psychosocial interventions. Stimulants (methylphenidate and dexamfetamine), clonidine, haloperidol and antidepressants treat the core symptoms of hyperactivity disorder.

Nonpharmacological interventions include family-based behavioural interventions, individual behavioural and academic interventions in children.

CHALLENGING BEHAVIOUR

Defining the target behaviour (frequency, intensity, duration), examining the physiological and environmental variables that may relate to the behavioural problems, in addition to identifying the function or reinforcers for the behaviours constitutes the initial approach to treatment. Physical disorders and medication as a cause should also be excluded. Once external factors have been identified, psychological interventions tailored to the individual are applied to reduce target behaviour and to develop the use of alternative, acceptable behaviours. These include applied behaviour interventions (based on classical and operant conditioning) and skill building (for example, alternative strategies for anxiety and anger expression, development of interpersonal skills).

Pharmacological interventions are prescribed for between 5 % and 35 % of this group (Fraser and Kerr 2003) but evidence of effectiveness is generally weak.

Different groups of psychotropic medication have been tried with limited success including drugs prescribed for discrete behavioural components of challenging behaviour such as impulsive behaviour and anxiety.

INAPPROPRIATE SEXUAL BEHAVIOUR

Neuroleptic medications are also used alongside antilibidinal medications in the management of inappropriate sexual behaviour in individuals with learning disability.

CONCLUSION

With the acceptance of dual diagnosis in recent years, research has demonstrated the increased prevalence of psychiatric disorders in learning disability in comparison to the general population. Despite the development of tools to improve diagnostic accuracy, many individuals remain under- or incorrectly diagnosed. This has obvious treatment implications.

Management of psychiatric disorders follows that of the general population, but side effects of medication, particularly movement disorders are commoner, necessitating careful monitoring. It can be difficult to disentangle pre-existing movement disorder from that caused by medication.

Although still in infancy, psychological treatments are being used increasingly with modifications to improve self-awareness and cognitive alteration. Furthermore, input from the multidisciplinary team including speech and language, occupational, art, complementary and physiotherapy is of benefit.

Finally, compared to the general population, healthcare professionals are heavily reliant on carers and family for information as well as administration of medication and interventions. In turn, these individuals are vulnerable and are dependent on carers, not just to seek help on their behalf but also to institute necessary changes in order to improve and maintain the quality of life of the learning disabled individual.

REFERENCES

Alexander, R. and Cooray, S. (2003) Diagnosis of personality disorders in learning disability, *The BVP*, **182**, 528–31.

American Psychiatric Association (1994) *DSM -IV Diagnostic and Statistical Manual of Mental Disorders,* 4th edn. American Psychiatric Association, Washington DC.

Bouras, N., Martin, G., Leese, M. Vanstraelen, M., Holt, G., Thomas, C., Hindler, C. and Boardman, J. (2004) Schizophrenia-spectrum psychosis in people with and without intellectual disability. *Journal of Intellectual Disability Research*, **48**, 548–55.

Clay, J. and Thomas, J.C. (2005) Prevalence of Axis I psychopathology in an intellectual disabled population: type of pathology and residential supports. *Journal of Developmental and Physical Disabilities,* **17** (1), 75–84.

Coppus, A., Evenhuis, H., Verberne, G.-J., Visser, F., Van Gool, P., Eikelenboom, P. and Van Duijin, C. (2006) Dementia and mortality in persons with Down's syndrome. *Journal of Intellectual Disability Research,* **50** (10), 768–77.

Day, K. (1985) Psychiatric disorder in the middle-aged and the mentally handicapped. *British Journal of Psychiatry,* **147**, 660–7.

Deb, S. and Hunter, D. (1991) Psychopathology of people with mental handicap and epilepsy. II: psychiatric illness. *Journal of Psychiatry,* **159**, 830–4.

Deb, S., Thomas, M. and Bright, C. (2001) Mental disorders in adult with intellectual disability. 1. Prevalence of functional psychiatric illness among a community – based population aged between 16–64 years. *Journal of Intellectual Disability Research,* **45** (6), 495–505.

Emerson, E. (1995) *Challenging Behaviour: Analysis and Intervention in People with Learning Difficulties,* Cambridge University Press, Cambridge.

Epstein, M.H. (1986) Teacher ratings of hyperactivity in learning disabled emotionally disturbed and mentally retarded children, *Journal of Special Education,* **22**, 219–29.

Fraser, W.I. and Nolan, M. (1994) Psychiatric disorders in mental retardation, in *Mental Health in Mental Retardation: Recent Advances and Practices* (ed. N. Bouras), Cambridge University Press, Cambridge.

Fraser, W., Kerr, M. (2003) *Seminars in the psychiatry of learning disabilities,* second edition. Gaskell, London.

Gostason, R. (1985) Psychiatric illness among mentally retarded, a Swedish population study. *Acta Psychiatrica Scandinavica,* **318**, supplementum 711–117.

Gillberg, C. (1986) Psychiatric disorders in mildly and severely mentally retarded urban children and adolescents. *British Journal of Psychiatry,* **149**, 68–74.

Hollins, S., Esterhuyzen, A. (1997) Bereavement and grief in adults with learning disabilities. *British Journal of Psychiatry,* **170**, 497–501.

Kaplan, H.I. and Sadock, B.J. (1993) *Psychotropic Drug Treatment,* Williams & Wilkins, Baltimore.

Kroese, B S, Dagnan D. and Lowndis, K. (eds) (1997) *Cognitive Behaviour Therapy for People with Learning Disabilities,* Routledge, London.

Lowe, K. and Felce, D. (1995) The definition of challenging behaviour in practice. *British Journal of Mental Disability,* **23** (3), 118–23.

Lund, J. (1985a) Epilepsy and psychiatric disorder in the mentally retarded adult. *Acta Psychiatrica Scandinavica,* **72**, 557.

Lund J (1985b) The prevalence of morbidity in the mentally retarded adult. *Acta Psychiatrica Scandinavica,* **72**, 563.

Malloy E. (1998) A patient with mental retardation and possible panic disorder. *Psychiatric Services,* **49** (1), 105–6.

Mavromatis, M. (2000) The diagnosis and treatment of borderline personality disorder in persons with developmental disability – three case reports. *Mental Health Aspects of Developmental Disabilities,* **3**, 89–97.

Novosel, S. (1984) Psychiatric disorder in adults admitted to a hospital for the mentally handicapped over a six month period. *British Journal of Mental Subnormality,* **30**, 54–58

Patel, P., Goldberg, D. and Mass, S. (1994) Psychiatric morbidity in older people with moderate and severe learning disability: II The prevalence study. *British Journal of Psychiatry,* **163**, 481–91.

Penrose, L.S. (1963) *Biology of Mental Defect.* Sidgwick and Jackson Limited, London.

Reid, A. (1983) Psychiatry of mental handicap: a review. *Journal of the Royal Society of Medicine,* **76**, 587–92.

Reid, A. (1989) Schizophrenia in mental retardation: clinical features. *Research in Developmental Disabilities,* **10**, 241–9.

Royal College of Psychiatrists (2001) *Diagnostic Criteria for Psychiatric Disorders for Use with Adults with Learning Disabilities/Mental Retardation,* Gaskell Books, London.

Rutter, M., Graham, P. and Yule, W. (1970) *A Neuropsychiatric Study in Childhood,* Spastics International Medical Publications, Heinemann, London.

Rutter, M., Tizard, J., Yule, W., Graham, P. and Whitmore, K. (1976) Isle of Wight studies 1964–1974. *Psychological Medicine,* **6**, 313–23.

Ryan R (1994) Post traumatic stress disorders in persons with developmental disabilities. *Community Mental Health Journal,* **30** (1), 45–54.

Stavrakaki, C. and Mintsioulis, G. (1997) Implications of clinical study of anxiety disorders in persons with mental retardation. *Psychiatric Annals,* **27**, 182–9.

Szymanski, L.S. and King, B.H. (1999) Practice parameters for the assessment and treatment of children, adolescents and adults with mental retardation and co morbid mental disorders. *Journal of the American Academy of Child and Adolescent Psychiatry,* **38**, 5S–31S.

Turner, T.H. (1989) Schizophrenia and mental handicap: an historical review, with implications for further research. *Psychological Medicine,* **19**, 301–14.

Vitiello, B., Behar, D. (1992) Mental retardation and psychiatric illness. *Hospital and Community Psychiatry,* **43** (5), 494.

White, P., Chant, D., Edwards, N., Townsend, C., Waghorn, G. (2005): Prevalence of intellectual disability and comorbid mental illness in an Australian community sample. *Australian and New Zealand Journal of Psychiatry,* **39**, 395–400.

WHO (1992) *The ICD 10 Classification of Mental and Behavioural Disorders. Clinical Descriptions and Diagnostic Guidelines,* World Health Organization, Geneva.

WHO (1993) *The ICD 10 Classification of Mental and Behavioural Disorders. Diagnostic Criteria for Research,* World Health Organization, Geneva.

WHO (2006) *The ICD 10 Classification of Mental and Behavioural Disorders. Clinical Descriptions and Diagnostic Guidelines 1994/2006 Version,* World Health Organization, Geneva.

4 Orthopaedic Aspects of Learning Disability

JAMES E. ROBB

INTRODUCTION

There is a wide spectrum of orthopaedic disorders associated with learning disability, some as a consequence of the underlying condition and others incidental to it. There is little information available on the orthopaedic aspects in the literature and so the information that is to be discussed is based on conditions encountered over a period of 10 years in an orthopaedic clinic devoted to problems in adults with learning disabilities.

ASSESSMENT

Patients with learning disability may not be able to explain their particular problem and may rely on their relatives or carers to give this information. Explanations of the condition and its possible treatment may not be as easily achieved as for the individual who is not learning disabled. It may not be possible for the clinician to present information about the benefits and risks of a particular line of management in a form that is readily understood. See Chapter 1 for a more detailed discussion of the issues of consent.

It is preferable to see patients in surroundings that they find familiar so as to minimise any distress. This also has the advantage that patients can be accompanied by their physiotherapist and carers, and one can thus obtain a better perspective of their functional difficulties. However, there is the logistical problem of holding a clinic in an environment where there is no ready access to radiography, which may necessitate another hospital visit for the patient and carer. When hospital admission is required, communication between the patient's usual carers and hospital staff is invaluable. We have found it extremely helpful to have a member of their care team to assist in their ward care and subsequent rehabilitation. This requires a good working relationship between hospitals and the various disciplines involved. It may

Learning Disability: Physical Therapy Treatment and Management. Edited by Jeanette Rennie
© 2007 John Wiley & Sons Ltd

also help in the early transfer of patients back to their more familiar surroundings.

As many of these patients may have multiple problems, it is helpful to identify the principal area of concern to the patient, relative or carer. These may not always coincide and it is important that decisions are not taken from a 'snapshot' view of the patient. For example, a patient with cerebral palsy who is able to walk may be concerned about the posture of their feet. This could result from excessive internal femoral torsion rather than a problem within the feet themselves. Equally, the tendency to walk by holding the foot in an equinus position could result from a limb length inequality or a hip flexion contracture rather than shortening of the calf muscles. Similarly a patient could have severe windsweeping at the hips, but this might be irrelevant to that particular consultation as the functional problem might be, for example, severe equinus precluding the fitting of footwear.

It also helps to define specific aims of management. For example, the presence of severe knee flexion contractures in nonwalking cerebral-palsied patients may not have an adverse effect on their ability to sit and for this reason they would not necessarily require treatment. But if the aim of the patient's management programme were to include the use of a standing frame there could be justification in surgical treatment of the knee contractures if they precluded its use.

Pain in patients who have learning disability is often difficult to quantify or localise. In severe cerebral palsy, gastro-oesophageal reflux, constipation and hip dislocation can coexist. All may produce 'abdominal' pain. Carers may confirm that the pain is worse when moving the legs at pad changing time thus implicating the hip as the probable source of pain. Abdominal examination may help in determining whether or not the patient is constipated and further investigations such as X-rays or an upper gastrointestinal endoscopy may help further.

Requests for treatment of what initially appears to be a cosmetic problem are also made. For example, in severe hemiplegic cerebral palsy, patients may have concerns about their hemiplegic hand, compare it to the sound side and request surgical treatment. Closer questioning often establishes that the problem is not just one of cosmesis but also of difficulties with volar skin crease hygiene and clothing. Under these circumstances it is justifiable to offer surgical correction of that particular deformity, which does not usually have any functional gain.

REVIEW OF PATIENTS

The following information derives from a clinic that has been held at Gogarburn Hospital for people with learning disabilities. From an organisational point of view it had been traditional for an orthopaedic surgeon to visit the hospital over the years to provide a consultation service for inpatients and outpatients associated with the hospital. Originally, the majority of patients seen were residents of the hospital either because of severe motor and physical disability or because of significant psychiatric morbidity. More recently, because of political changes, a larger number of patients who might have formerly been residents now live in the community. This has resulted in fewer residents attending the clinic but a greater number of outpatients. It could now be argued that as the majority has to travel to the clinic they might be better seen in a conventional hospital setting where ancillary investigations are readily available.

The cases of the most recent 117 patients with learning disabilities aged between 19 and 89 years seen personally by the author have been reviewed to give an indication of the type of pathologies encountered in this particular setting. In 25 there was no specific associated diagnosis. In those who had a specific diagnosis associated with learning disability, the majority had cerebral palsy, perhaps a reflection of a particular interest in neuromuscular conditions. The associated conditions were as shown in Table 4.1.

CEREBRAL PALSY: WALKING PATIENTS

In the 36 patients who were able to walk (age range 20 to 87, mean 38 years) the presenting problems were as shown in Table 4.2.

For those presenting with foot problems, seven were provided with adapted shoe wear, four with ankle foot orthoses, three with gastrocnemius lengthenings

Table 4.1. Associated conditions seen at Gogarburn Hospital

Condition	Number
Cerebral palsy	69
Autism	1
Multiple congenital anomalies	1
Cortical dysplasia	1
Hydrocephalus	2
Hypocellular dwarfism	1
Microcephaly	5
Primary osteoporosis	1
Myelodysplasia	4
Muccopolysaccharidosis	1
Traumatic brain injury	1
Idiopathic scoliosis	2
Schizophrenia	2
Rett syndrome	3
No specific associated diagnosis	25

Table 4.2. Problems of walking in patients
with cerebral palsy

Problem	Number
Foot problems	19
Deteriorating mobility	5
Crouch gait	5
Hip pain	3
Gait assessment	2
Wrist pain	1
Backache	1

for equinus, two received fusions – one of the first metatarso-phalangeal joint for a severe bunion and the other a subtalar joint for a fixed hindfoot valgus – and two no specific treatment. Foot pain, particularly in spastic diplegia is a well recognised cause for patients to go off their feet, and foot problems were the commonest cause for consultation.

Crouch gait in diplegics presents either as a flexed hip, knee and ankle pattern or as a flexed hip, knee and excessively dorsiflexed ankle pattern. The first pattern was seen in these five patients. One did not require any treatment as the problem was mild but the remainder all received surgical treatment. This consisted of intramuscular lengthening of psoas and gastrocnemius in the first, hamstring and gastrocnemius in the second, psoas adductor and hamstring in the third and a femoral extension osteotomy in the fourth. Surgical management was appropriate in this group as all had severe functional problems. There were no postoperative complications.

The hemiplegic patient presenting with wrist pain was treated with a wrist fusion as the pain was associated with a severe flexion deformity and skin hygiene problems. The 45-year-old patient complaining of mechanical backache had a diplegia and an associated hyperlordosis. He did not require surgical treatment.

In this group, 35 out of 36 patients had a mobility problem necessitating a consultation. Those seven patients presenting specifically with a deteriorating gait and for a gait assessment (age range 26 to 38) represented a group who had been mobile without undue difficulty in their late adolescent years but who were now facing increasing difficulty. Although there is little information on the longer term outcome of gait efficiency in the older cerebral palsy patient there is a clinical impression that walking efficiency seems to deteriorate with time. There is a range of potential causes for deteriorating walking efficiency, which may include hip or foot instability, contractures, prolonged sitting, muscular weakness, increasing weight and pain arising from the lower back, patello-femoral joint or feet. Foot problems – both postural and involving pain – were the commonest reason for presentation in this group. These can be complex problems as often the underlying cause may not actually lie in the foot but in a more proximal area and the presenting foot problem is a compensation for this. For example, pes valgus may be secondary to an external tibial torsion, which might in turn be associated with excessive internal femoral torsion. Under these circumstances one may have to accept that correction of these multiple-level problems is not a practical proposition for the foot problem. There is an increasing interest in correcting torsional problems in the younger hemiplegic and diplegic patient, but it is not known whether or not this will have a protective effect on foot function in adult life.

CEREBRAL PALSY: NONWALKING PATIENTS

The presenting problems in the 33 patients who were unable to walk (age range 17 to 76, mean 32 years) were as shown in Table 4.3.

Clearly in this group there was some overlap of presenting features as some patients with spinal deformity also had a hip dislocation. The main problem has been recorded above.

The patients with spinal problems all had a severe fixed neuromuscular scoliosis, which was beyond surgical correction. All were provided with a detachable lightweight thermoplastic underarm orthosis whose aim was to improve trunk stability and head control.

The seven patients who had seating problems all went on to have a formal seating assessment from the local bioengineering centre. They all received adaptations to their existing seating system and none required a moulded seat. Usually it has been possible to adapt a commercially available chassis for the individual's needs.

Seven patients had a hip dislocation and in four the dislocation was painless. Three had modifications of their seating to accommodate hip posture. The fourth had adductor and psoas tenotomies whose aim was to improve hip abduction sufficiently for seating purposes, but not reduce the hip which would have entailed a much greater procedure. Three patients had a painful disloca-

Table 4.3. Problems of nonwalking in patients with cerebral palsy

Problem	Number
Spinal deformity	8
Seating problems	7
Hip dislocation	7
Foot problems	6
Wrist pain	4
Perineal access difficulties	2
Hip pain	2

tion. In the first, hip reduction was achieved by pelvic and femoral osteotomy. The remaining two patients both had a proximal femoral excision for high riding, painful, irreducible hips.

Successful outcomes in terms of seating and hip pain were seen in all those undergoing surgery. No attempt was made to treat fixed pelvic obliquity and associated severe scoliosis. It is easier technically to reduce a hip surgically if there is reasonable acetabular and femoral morphology and there is a good case for intervening early where the hip is clearly symptomatic and dislocating. The difficulty lies in the case of patients who have a painless dislocating hip and no functional deficit to decide whether or not prophylactic intervention is justifiable before the hip becomes unreconstructable. It has been reported that approximately 50 % of institutionalised patients with severe cerebral palsy go on to develop a painful hip dislocation (Cooperman et al., 1987). For this reason it is important to be able to distinguish between a painful and nonpainful dislocated hip and whether or not the hip is reconstructable. The views of the patient's carer help greatly in deciding management. The painless dislocated hip can be treated by an abduction osteotomy to improve perineal access and seating posture, if this is a problem. However if the joint is painful, a different approach is necessary – either hip reduction or excision. In the dislocated hip there is usually a combination of femoral and acetabular deformity. On the femoral side the deformity may consist of lateral flattening of the head due to pressure of the glutei or of flattening on the medial side due to pressure from the dislocated hip abutting against the side wall of the pelvis. In addition, the head can be notched by the psoas tendon. On the acetabular side there is usually a saucer-shaped elongation of the acetabulum in the direction of the dislocating femoral head. The aim of reduction is to produce a pain-free mobile joint.

Perineal access problems were seen in two patients who had congruent hip joints. These were both treated by anterior obturator neurectomy and division of the adductor longus and gracilis. Two patients had hip pain caused by hip subluxation and these were treated successfully with femoral varus derotation osteotomy. It is essential before undertaking these major procedures to ensure that the source of pain is correctly identified and that the likely functional gains for the patient are considered from the point of view of the patient and carers.

Six patients had severe foot deformities. Five underwent surgical treatment to give a foot that could be accommodated in a shoe and the sixth received adapted footwear. Even though these patients were nonwalkers, they required footwear that could be fitted and also a foot posture that would allow the foot to rest comfortably on the foot plate of their wheelchair.

Wrist pain was seen in four patients and all four had, in addition, hygiene problems with their flexor wrist creases. In all there was no useful hand function and all underwent a flexor release and wrist fusion.

A recent report has studied the expectation of cerebral palsy patients attaining the age of 40 years. It was shown that 85 % of total body involved patients could expect to achieve this in the absence of severe epilepsy, which worsened the outlook (Crichton et al. 1995). This suggests that there is a cerebral palsy population, who will require long-term care, for whom survival to midlife is a very real possibility. This has resource implications and is also a justification for treatment to improve function to assist the patient and their carers.

LEARNING DISABILITY AND NONSPECIFIC ORTHOPAEDIC PROBLEMS

Twenty-five patients had no recognised orthopaedic problem associated with their condition. Unlike the cerebral palsy groups, these patients were very likely to reflect the type of orthopaedic problems that might occur in the population at large. Their orthopaedic conditions were much more in keeping with those seen in routine adult practice. Three had Dupuytren's contracture and all were on medication for epilepsy; there is a well recognised association between the two conditions. One presented with a flexed knee walking pattern (although in the absence of any upper motor neurone lesion suggestive of cerebral palsy) and another presented with knee hyperextension associated with generalised joint laxity.

Five older patients aged 55 to 84 presented with osteoarthritis of the hips. In three the pain was severe enough to justify a hip replacement. From a technical standpoint, it was important to recognise that none of these three patients would be able to cooperate with a standard hip replacement rehabilitation regimen and so allowances had to be made for this. A lateral surgical approach to the hip was used and a prosthesis with a large diameter head selected to minimise the risk of dislocation. All three rehabilitated well and none suffered a dislocation. Good pain relief was obtained in all. However, one man developed profuse heterotopic bone formation around the hip, which limited the range of movement of the joint – but this remained painless.

One elderly man presented with osteoarthritis of the shoulder, another with spinal stenosis and a third with scoliosis. None required surgery.

One patient presented with an intracapsular fracture neck of femur that had occurred some time earlier and another with a loose hip replacement that had been inserted for a femoral neck fracture several years before. Both required surgery.

Ten patients had foot problems as shown in Table 4.4. All received functional foot orthoses and modified footwear where necessary.

One schizophrenic patient presented with bunions that were managed with footwear adaptations. One patient who had primary osteoporosis and another a muccopolysaccharidosis had gait assessments.

Table 4.4. Foot problems among patients

Problem	Number
Bunions	1
Metatarsalgia	1
Mild equinus	2
Idiopathic club feet	1
Pes cavus	1
Valgus hypermobile feet	4

LEARNING DISABILITY AND ASSOCIATED ORTHOPAEDIC CONDITIONS

Two patients had hydrocephalus. One presented with a hyperlordotic lumbar spine that did not require any specific treatment and the other with severe bunions, which were treated by first metatarsophalangeal fusions. One patient with hypocellular dwarfism and epilepsy developed mild equinus, which was treated with serial plaster casts.

Five patients had microcephaly and severe learning difficulties. Two were nonwalkers and of these one required an underarm jacket for a neuropathic scoliosis and the other footwear adaptations for a mobile valgus foot. One, who was a therapeutic walker, required a seating assessment, another, who was fully ambulant, needed advice for hip pain and one required footwear adaptations for a mild equinus.

Four patients had myelomeningocoele. Three were nonwalkers and had mid-thoracic paraplegias. All had a significant spinal deformity that was not amenable to surgical correction and received an underarm spinal jacket. The fourth, who was a walker, had a crouch gait associated with a low lumbar lesion and benefited from the provision of floor reaction ankle foot orthoses.

Three patients had Rett syndrome. Two had a spinal deformity, one of which was managed with an underarm orthosis and the other by spinal fusion. The third had developed a mild equinus that was treated with a heel raise.

The last patient had a traumatic brain injury and had developed severe hip, knee and ankle contractures that precluded stable sitting. He underwent multiple level surgery to produce a sitting posture.

ILLUSTRATIVE CASE REPORTS

OSTEOARTHRITIS OF THE HIP

The patient, a 64-year-old woman, was a long-term resident at Gogarburn Hospital. She had severe learning difficulties and behaviour problems consisting of screaming, pinching and poking other individuals, was unable to communicate her needs and required supervision of all of her day-to-day activities. She was normally able to walk out of doors under supervision. In the preceding two years she had been noted to develop a painful left-sided limp and limitation of her walking so that latterly she would no longer go outside. In addition it was noted that she appeared to have pain when her left leg was moved by her carers.

Examination and subsequent X-rays confirmed advanced osteoarthritis of her left hip. After discussion with her carers and her brother and sister it was decided to offer a hip replacement. This posed several potential problems. First, the patient was unlikely to have any understanding of the proposed procedure and would not be able to cooperate with a standard postoperative rehabilitation programme after hip replacement. Second, she was likely to be at a greater risk of dislocation of the hip. Third she would be noisy in an open ward and probably upset other patients also undergoing elective orthopaedic surgery.

It was decided to use a prosthesis with a larger diameter head than usual to minimise the risk of dislocation. She was looked after in a side room so as to minimise any disturbances on the ward and an early return to her normal environment at Gogarburn Hospital was planned for her own wellbeing. In addition, there was excellent coordination between the nursing staff of both hospitals and nursing staff from Gogarburn came to the orthopaedic ward to assist with her care. No attempt was made to follow a conventional rehabilitation programme and the patient mobilised at 48 hours without difficulty. She made surprisingly good progress and was well enough to return to her usual environment five days after surgery. Her subsequent progress was uneventful: her walking pattern improved; her limp resolved and her carers noted that she did not appear to have hip pain. Her progress has been maintained two years after surgery.

WRIST PAIN IN A HEMIPLEGIC

The patient, a 37-year-old man, had a congenital hemiplegia and learning disability. He was unable to communicate verbally but appeared to have reasonable comprehension and lived with his elderly mother. There had been, over the years, a progressive flexion deformity of his right wrist and increasing wrist pain. He did not have any useful hand function but used the arm as a prop. In addition, he had increasing problems with hygiene of the flexor creases of the wrist.

After discussion, he was offered surgery to lengthen the forearm flexors and to fuse the wrist. This was carried out successfully two years ago and relieved him of his wrist pain and hygiene problem. There was no functional gain or loss. The preoperative and postoperative appearances are shown in Figures 4.1 to 4.3.

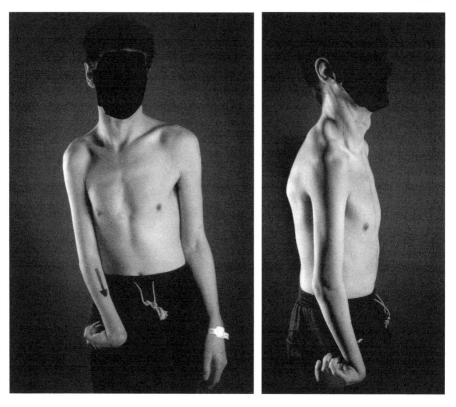

Figure 4.1. Preoperative appearances of the wrist.

EQUINUS IN A PATIENT WITH A CHROMOSOME DISORDER

The patient, a 35-year-old woman, had a severe learning disability and was unable to communicate verbally. She was able to walk using a rollator with assistance from daycare staff but her ability to do so was hampered by a high-riding, longstanding painless dislocation of the left hip and a progressive equinus of the left ankle. Her functional difficulty was an inability to contain her left foot comfortably in a shoe. This resulted in bottom shuffling in a wind-swept posture as her chosen method of mobility. She was no longer able to walk and use a standing frame. After her mother's death she lived in a house run by the Cheshire Foundation.

After discussion it was decided to offer calf muscle surgery to improve the foot posture and to produce a plantargrade foot. The hip dislocation was painless and so did not require treatment and it was anticipated that she would require an ankle-foot orthosis and a compensatory shoe raise postoperatively.

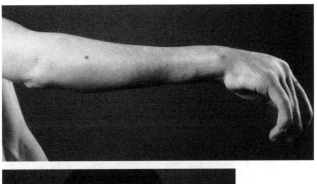

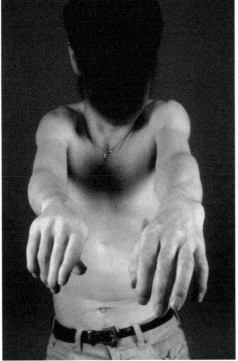

Figure 4.2. Postoperative appearances of the wrist.

She underwent an elongation of gastrocnemius, tibialis posterior and flexor hallucis longus of the left calf, which produced a plantargrade foot. Her post-operative recovery was uneventful and her foot posture and mobility have been maintained two years after surgery. She does not object to wearing her orthosis and is able to walk independently at her day centre using a rollator.

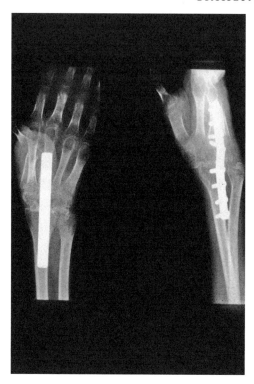

Figure 4.3. Postoperative radiological appearances; the wrist has fused and the plate has been used to align the third metacarpal to the radius and has been contoured to give some dorsiflexion.

SEATING DIFFICULTIES IN SEVERE CEREBRAL PALSY

The patient, a 28-year-old man, was a long-term resident at Gogarburn Hospital. He had total body involvement cerebral palsy and difficulties with seating. This was due to a combination of a severe scoliosis, a flexed and adducted right hip and a fixed extension deformity of the left knee. He had severe equino-varus of the left foot and calcaneus of the right foot and was only able to wear slipper socks. There were also severe flexion contractures of both elbows and wrists. He was unable to sit in any conventional form of seating and had a moulded seating device to accommodate his extended left knee. He had several other functional problems: difficulties of perineal access due to the fixed flexion deformity of the left hip of 80° and fixed adduction of 60°, hygiene problems with the elbows and wrists and an inability to wear normal footwear.

The difficulties with perineal access and seating were identified as the dominant problems by his carers and after discussion with them and the patient's father, it was decided to offer surgical treatment. This consisted of an abduction osteotomy of the right femur (Figures 4.4 and 4.5) and division of adductor longus, gracilis and the anterior obturator nerve and a left quadricepsplasty to gain knee flexion. This produced abduction of 5° on the right side and 90°

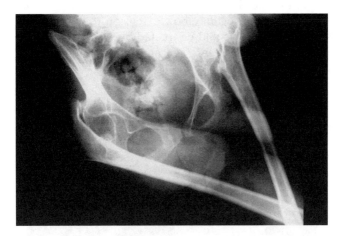

Figure 4.4. Preoperative radiograph of the pelvis. The right hip is in severe adduction and the hips are dislocated.

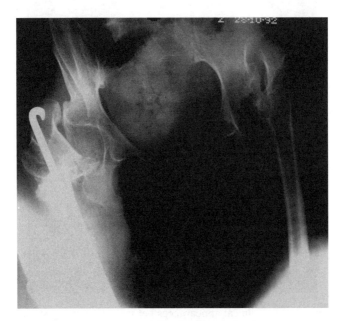

Figure 4.5. Appearances following the abduction osteotomy.

of knee flexion on the left side. Both were sufficient to permit perineal access and the use of conventional seating rather than a moulded device. His severe scoliosis was inoperable. This surgery was undertaken seven years ago and the postoperative position has been maintained (Figures 4.6a and 4.6b).

One year later, it was felt by his carers that the hygiene problems of his elbows and wrists were causing a persistent disagreeable odour and surgical treatment was requested. These were longstanding deformities and it was felt that it would be possible to gain elbow extension to about 90° but no more and that the wrist problems could be treated by wrist fusion. Both these procedures were carried out six years ago and have been successful in dealing with the hygiene problems.

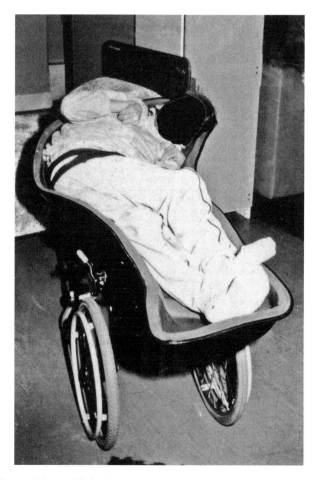

Figure 4.6(a). Clinical appearances before and after hip surgery.

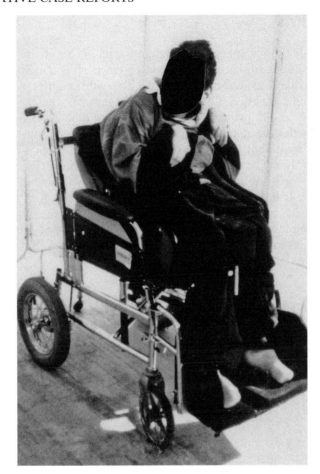

Figure 4.6(b). *Continued*

Two years later there were increasing concerns about the posture of his left foot and because of severe equino-varus the skin on the outer border of the foot had begun to ulcerate. This was treated by a wedge tarsectomy, which produced a plantargrade foot. This, and the provision of an ankle-foot orthosis on the right side, enabled him to be provided with conventional footwear and to be able to rest both feet on the footplate of his seating system.

This patient received the most surgery of all those seen in the clinic. Such procedures are justifiable if clearly defined problems and goals of treatment are identified.

CONCLUSION

There was inevitably a spectrum of patients seen in this environment. Some had orthopaedic conditions as a direct consequence of the condition producing their learning disability. Others were seen with conditions that were additional to their learning disability. Orthopaedic management, whether operative or not, can be of benefit, providing realistic aims and functional goals are set in conjunction with the patient's carers and therapists. Disability and age should not preclude treatment. Even the most severely handicapped patients were able to cope with major surgery. Having a long established clinic with a tradition of open discussion and cooperation has been invaluable in assisting this patient group. It has already been shown that expectation of life in severe cerebral palsy has improved and this has implications for the longer term care of more profoundly handicapped adults. More are now living in the community and it is not known what effect this may have on future referral patterns and morbidity.

REFERENCES

Cooperman, D.R., Bartucci, E., Dietrick, E. and Millar, E.A. (1987) Hip dislocation in spastic cerebral palsy: long term consequences. *Journal of Paediatric Orthopaedics*, **7**, 268–76.
Crichton, J.U., Mackinnon, M. and White, C.P. (1995) The life expectancy of persons with cerebral palsy. *Developmental Medicine and Child Neurology*, **37**, 567–76.

II Assessing Physical Ability and Planning Intervention

5 The Multiprofessional Learning Disability Team

PATRICIA ODUNMBAKU AUTY AND JEANETTE RENNIE

INTRODUCTION

Chapter 1 described the historical development towards multiprofessional teamwork with people who have learning disabilities. This chapter aims to describe benefits that can result from this working practice and problems that can impede its practical development.

For many years different professionals have used their skills for the benefit of people who have learning disabilities and associated disabilities. In a minority of hospitals teamwork was routine practice. In many, however, departments or individuals tended to work in isolation with little consultation or cooperation. Therefore, clients were unable to benefit from a coordinated programme, which is necessary before the various skills can be focused in one smooth operation.

Working in isolation prevented treatment and management from reaching their optimum level and achieving the desired outcomes. For example if a physiotherapist established a programme of activity without knowing the linguistic skills, comprehension or sign language of the client, then that programme was bereft of an essential component. This interfered with the client achieving his or her potential. Similarly, if an occupational therapist was not conversant with the programme for the client's challenging behaviour, that programme could not be completely effective.

This has now changed and multiprofessional working is the desired goal even if it is interpreted in a variety of ways. The results range from excellent to indifferent.

Originally the healthcare element of Community Mental Handicap Teams (Chapter 1) was drawn from nursing and therapy departments of the large hospitals as the clients moved into the community. Allen, Pahl and Quine (1990) described the fears and misgivings felt by staff on being redeployed in the community. They noted that morale and confidence was affected by;

Learning Disability: Physical Therapy Treatment and Management. Edited by Jeanette Rennie
© 2007 John Wiley & Sons Ltd

- change of work setting
- job redefinition
- multiagency work
- training for a new service
- worries about staff recruitment

These were very real concerns especially where clinical line management was no longer on site and where special equipment, large spaces and a hydrotherapy pool were required for treatment, particularly for physiotherapy.

EXAMPLES OF TEAM CONFIGURATION

Teams combined a number of different professions with different configurations. In 1991 Cheseldine wrote that:

> the core membership of a Community Mental Handicap Team typically consists of a social worker, community mental handicap nurse and clinical psychologist.
> Clients' needs may require involvement from other people including a consultant psychiatrist, occupational therapists, rehabilitation officers, home support workers, social work assistants, pre-school teachers, liaison health visitors and volunteer co-ordinators.

In other areas of the country teams were developing along different lines, obviously with a slant towards people with more severe physical disabilities (Hollins 1985). They included:

- many nurses and a single physiotherapist or occupational therapist
- a psychology manager, a predominance of psychologists and challenging needs specialist and a single representative from different therapies
- equal number of specialists

Teams ranged from a single professional representative of each healthcare profession to three or more members of each. Many have always included a consultant psychiatrist. Social work representation varied according to the division between specialist and generic teams within the area.

Gradually new government directives were enacted. Some have since been superseded but all have influenced the development of multiprofessional work. They have included:

- the role of Social Services, health authorities or boards as purchasers and not direct providers
- GP fund holding
- the introduction of care managers (Macadam and Rodgers 1997), primary care groups in England and Wales and local healthcare cooperatives in Scotland, and the Partnership in Action programme following the Health Act 1999

- devolution of health affairs to Scotland and Wales
- increased use of person-centred planning
- community health partnerships introduced in the National Health Service Reform (Scotland) Act 2004
- collaboration of services outlined in Working Differently (Department of Health 2005) (see Chapter 1)

Team configuration has changed because the structure is led by the needs of the people with learning disabilities and resources are distributed proportionally to suit the local requirements. They may now include

- a dietician
- art therapist
- music therapist

depending on need and availability of staff.

In some teams community nurses operate an emergency on-call service.

RESOURCES

Resources continue to be scarce both in finance and staff skills, and experience. This can lead to professions that are small in staff numbers having to participate in more than one team and attempting to attend a number of team meetings. If care is not taken then members of staff can begin to feel that they do not belong fully to any team. Conversely a feeling of guilt may be generated if meetings seem to be attended at the expense of direct client contacts. It can also lead to the rest of the team neglecting that member's potential contribution. In most areas the problem of staff shortage is resolved by regarding the team as a coordinated group of professionals and accepting that not all members are likely to be available to attend every meeting, so clients are deferred for discussion until such time as key staff are present. Everyone receives all minutes and correspondence.

Despite lack of resources, continuing development of community learning disability teams was clearly anticipated in a report from the NHS executive immediately prior to devolution. It referred to the usual model of service delivery as 'that of multidisciplinary community teams for people with learning disabilities. These provide a single point of access and assessment leading to a range of specialist provision on a peripatetic or outpatient basis.'

It recognised that, in a few areas, specialist services had been integrated into unidisciplinary teams or 'ordinary community services' (Lindsey 1998). The concept of placing learning disability services in the primary and community care trusts was welcomed by MENCAP on condition that their specialist identity was preserved (Band 1998). In some areas community learning disability teams are now accommodated in large community health centres together with a number of other specialist or independently managed services, for example general practitioners' practices, health visitors and generic community physiotherapists.

> Team = a set of people working in combination = a coordinated group of professionals. (*Chambers Dictionary*, 1993 edition)

ESTABLISHING A TEAM

The gathering together of a multiprofessional group of individuals does not constitute team working. Many steps are required before a truly coordinated group is established that can provide a holistic programme for the benefit of clients without diminishing the unique contribution of each professional group. Underpinning any multidisciplinary learning disability team is a shared philosophy, frequently expressed by O'Brien's five essential accomplishments for quality of life (see Table 1.5).

COMMUNICATION AND DYNAMICS

Ignorance of each other's professional roles can present difficulties and sensitivities where professional boundaries overlap. To help to overcome this many teams hold in-service training on roles and responsibilities. Some have resulted in the production of leaflets for the public, which have enabled referrals to be directed to the appropriate services.

Establishing a base office is critical for success, as a good working environment and administrative support is an important factor in effective work. Close proximity assists communication in the base. Distribution of room space for different professionals allows for further integration. Multiprofessional working begins slowly, developing as friendship and respect grow.

POLICY

A clear team operational policy, prepared and shared by all while respecting each set of professional standards, assists development of a successful service. It includes the general purpose of the team, its aims and priorities, membership, meetings, team leader role and professional management roles. It also includes case allocation and priorities. Each profession within the team will have their own professional clinical guidelines and will accept referrals and pritorise these according to the local protocol within the providing service. Since the modernisation of services and the reorganisation within the NHS and the establishment of PCTs, Learning Disability teams have become more autonomous and the professionals make referral decisions based on agreed professional, legal and team protocols. A strong operational policy also clarifies the issues surrounding shared or separate professional case files. Some trusts operate the system of integrated care pathways as a flow chart to clarify a client's progress through the system and to specify who is responsible for decision making at each stage of progression (Baldry and Rossiter 1995).

REFERRAL SYSTEM

Referrals may be made by:

- the paediatric department
- transition team
- local general practitioners
- social services via social workers and day carers
- residential care staff
- individuals and their families
- individuals from their person-centred planning meeting
- general hospitals and outpatient clinics
- the remaining long-stay residential learning disability hospitals in anticipation of closure

It is possible that only 30 % of the team's caseload requires input from more than one professional. However, it may be that following the initial assessment other needs become apparent and other professionals are required. To share this information a multidisciplinary meeting at frequent and regular intervals is established. It is at this forum where difficulties can be discussed, support given and quality issues can be voiced. New referrals can be discussed and appropriate information on clients shared.

Once all this information is received and the client allocated to the appropriate profession, a screening takes place to make priorities of his or her needs.

METHODS OF MAKING PRIORITIES

One method of prioritising is through the use of waiting lists, either explicitly via a system of chronological referral or implicitly following discussion on the basis of clinical need.

An alternative is the structured points system. The following example of a points system used in case weighting was designed for physiotherapists. It could be transferred to other professionals or adapted for the team as a whole. Papathanasiou and Lyon-Maris (1997) based their system on the principles devised by Williams (1991) as shown in Table 5.1.

In any system of determining priorities where there is also paediatric involvement the team will be influenced by the statement of needs assessment,

Table 5.1. System of Papathanasiou and Lyon-Maris

- Clients are weighted by five factors:
  1. Type of input required
  2. Other support services involved
  3. Management of physical status
  4. Client/therapist interface
  5. Client/carer compliance
- Scores for each factor range from 1 to 5
- Minimum intervention would be required for a score of one point or less in each factor. Total case intervention score (CIS) of between 21 and 25.
- The CIS is classified by a case band A – E (minimum to maximum)
- Estimated physiotherapy intervention hours for case band A is 3 hours in 6 months and case band E is 48 hours in 6 months

---

Before the age of 16 years while still at school
Start of transfer from paediatric nurse to adult learning disabilities nurse
Start of transfer from children and families social worker to adult learning disabilities social worker

Before leaving school
Statement of needs assessment, future needs assessment
Person-centred planning meeting
Transition clinic: consultant paediatrician, paediatric physiotherapist, school nurse, lead physiotherapist for learning disabilities, other allied health professionals as required.
Refer to citywide transition team led by a coordinator and including transition facilitators (nurses) and lead physiotherapist.

↓

Relevant community learning disability team

Figure 5.1. Example of transfer from paediatric to adult services.

future needs assessment and the newly developing transition team's recommendations.

Discussion at a multiprofessional meeting does not replace a case conference or planning meeting in which progress and problems are discussed in depth.

CASE LOAD MANAGEMENT

The number of people that the team can be expected to reach is estimated in a variety of ways in different areas of the country – for example via a learning disability or community care register. With pressure of clients, caseload management is essential to ensure that the clients who are treated receive quality interventions, that notes comply with clients' needs and with legal responsibilities, and that discharge letters are written and statistical information is recorded before other clients are accepted.

Many professions have one or more recognised methods of estimating staff/client ratios. The most recent estimates for speech and language therapists indicate that most newly qualified staff spend 60 % of their working hours in client contact time. This will gradually shift from 60 % to 40 % for more senior staff as training and lecturing responsibilities increase.

Table 5.2 is one model, which was produced by Joyce Wise and may be used as a basis for estimating physiotherapy staffing levels. It does not differentiate between levels of physiotherapy experience or conditions under which people are treated (centre based or domiciliary). As with speech and language therapy, client contact time will decrease with seniority. Table 5.3 is Wise's model for physiotherapy case management. Both models in Table 5.3 may be multiprofessional although this is less likely in the case of the therapeutic model.

Joint working can be advantageous for clients

For example:

- eating and drinking referrals
- speech and language therapists, dietician, physiotherapist, community nurse may have input from psychologist and psychiatrist
- challenging behaviour
- psychiatrist, psychologist, community nurse, speech and language therapist, may have input from occupational therapist and on occasion physiotherapist.
- housing needs and adaptations
- occupational therapists, physiotherapist, community nurse

Community nurses will be involved with health needs and liaison with local hospitals but will gather information that is appropriate to the specific episode or treatment from all who provide services to the client. Occupational therapists are involved with skills teaching and are closely linked to the social services and non-profit agencies.

EDUCATION AND TRAINING

Training takes a large proportion of time. Skills are passed from individual members of the immediate team to carers at home and in day centres and

Table 5.2. An example of staffing level requirements for
physiotherapists for one year

Physiotherapist	Patient contact hours
1 Whole time equivalent	36 hours × 45 weeks = 1 620 hours/year
70 % contact	1 134 hours (in learning disability this can reduce to 50 % as a result of clinics, meetings, telephoning and modifying seating and equipment)
Individual patient treatment hours/year	**Number of patients who can be treated**
Patient receiving recognised General Practitioner referral requirement of treatment.	5 sessions at 0.5 h/session = 2.5 h in the year = 453 patients/year
Patient × 1 h in the year.	1 134 patients in the year
Patient × 5 h in the year.	226 patients/year
Patient × 45 h in the year (Many of the learning disability clients).	25 patients in the year

Joyce Wise ACPPLD Conference 1998.

Table 5.3. Models of physiotherapy case management

Therapeutic model – largely gate kept by doctors
This is treatment that is in direct response to medical problems.
  Assessment
  Intervention
  Episodic
  Discharge
    complete
    onward to wellness model

Wellness model – open referrals
Maintenance of optimum health/fitness
Preparation for therapeutic intervention
Maximising and maintaining health gains obtained from therapeutic model
Interface between childhood/adolescence and adulthood
Multidisciplinary
Multiagency
Long term, seldom complete discharge.

Joyce Wise ACPPLD Conference 1998.

inclusion projects. Clients and staff are assisted to understand and carry out programmes as described in various chapters in this book.

It is also inevitable that the professionals learn from each other and develop a mutual respect for each other and for their various professional skills. As teams develop into more cohesive units they may invite informal speakers to their meetings or form their own journal club.

Members of the immediate multiprofessional team also learn from other professionals as they liaise with them over specific clients. For example, an audiologist's report influences the method by which speech and language therapists enable clients to achieve appropriate communication. More detailed examples are given in the case studies.

REPORTS

Joint reports are written when it is appropriate. These may be produced from case conferences and individual meetings around the clients in which all who provide a service participate. Any professional who is unable to attend will submit a report, which will be presented by a well briefed colleague.

Each profession uses uniprofessional clinical audit and progress reports and has a tool for outcome measurement (see Chapters 7 and 8). A client and staff satisfaction scale can be used to evaluate training of carers.

Trying to find a measurement of outcomes to reflect an efficient, effective and beneficial team service to clients takes much thought and effort. Current methods include:

- individual professions' outcome measures placed in the medical records
- simple rating based on the initial team assessment of needs using a scale of 0 to 2
- base line assessment unique to the team followed by a written report after a specified time span
- recognised multiprofessional outcome measure (see Chapters 7 and 8)

STAFF SUPPORT

Increased stress levels can arise within a multiprofessional team. However, mutual staff support from a group of people working together with the same client compensates for this.

Teams tend to be coordinated by one of their members and managed by a , therapist or psychologist who reports to a general manager.

Professionally, members of staff need to retain their identity, have the opportunity for personal development and feel valued. This can only happen if opportunity is afforded for continuing education.

Higgs and Titchen (1995) suggested that three types of knowledge were required as a basis for clinical reasoning. These were

- *continuing propositional knowledge*, gained through research, conferences, meetings and courses within the individual profession

- *professional craft knowledge* – practical expertise and skills that develop over the years; the type of knowledge that passes from experienced to less experienced staff, and
- *personal knowledge*, which is a deepening understanding of oneself and through others

All of these elements are required for what has become mandatory continuing professional development.

It is essential, therefore, that all professionals are encouraged and assisted to participate in relevant courses and conferences organised by their own professions. Opportunities should have been strengthened by the introduction of 'clinical governance' in 1999, which made trust chief executives accountable for the quality of patient care in their trusts. This is reinforced in *Valuing People*, and the health needs assessment report for people with learning disabilities in Scotland (see Chapter 1), and through the development of clinical effectiveness networks (e.g. NHS QIS Web site see Appendix B). The service as a whole benefits if such encouragement and assistance is made known publicly whenever staff are being recruited.

It is also essential that all professions have access to appropriate clinical supervision and appraisal. In trusts or health service divisions that have maintained line management within professions in learning disability there should be no problems. Where professions have no clinical manager within learning disability, support is reduced and there may be no obvious professional development structure. This can exacerbate recruitment difficulties. In such cases structures may be established to allow supervision and appraisal by a therapist of the same profession in another speciality while concurrently developing peer assessment within learning disability in the local area. Some professions are discussing the possibility of mentoring through the national clinical interest group of the professional body.

The strength and quality of the team is only achieved by the updated expertise of the members of each individual profession. However, growing knowledge within individual professions cannot replace multiprofessional training. They must be seen as complementary to one another and it is through training and working together that personal knowledge is most likely to become fully developed. This may be achieved through the concept of peer coaching (Ladyshewsky 2006) and practice development (Manley 2000), which could apply equally well to individual professions and the multiprofessional team.

CONCLUSION

Professionals work together as coordinated groups to reinforce each other's aims and objectives. They provide sound practical assistance for people with learning disabilities in their aim to lead an active life in the community. In stressful home and family situations, strong co-ordinated support instead of indiscriminate attention from individuals is invaluable. In such situations joint voices are a powerful and influential tool.

CASE STUDIES

CASE STUDY 1: JA

Community support for Miss JA is illustrated in Figure 5.2.

Miss JA transferred to a home for elderly people from a long-stay hospital where she had lived for 35 years. She has severe learning disability.

History

- She was a 69-year-old woman.
- She had a history of depressive illness, which can result in withdrawal and unwillingness to speak, eat or take medication.
- She had a history of tardive dyskinesia resulting in a slight parkinsonian tremor of the hands.
- She was prone to urinary tract infection and constipation.

A comprehensive community care assessment was compiled by her social worker/care manager at the hospital in conjunction with the ward and all departments with whom she had contact. This was used as the basis of her care plan.

During the transition from hospital to residential home her care manager referred her to the local learning disability team psychiatrist and community nurse. Her residential home referred her to the district nurses and a voluntary befriender.

Three weeks after moving she was referred to a physiotherapist in the team because of swollen and apparently painful hands. Before treatment an x-ray was requested. She resisted all attempts to take her to a radiography department until six weeks later. For three months she resisted any contact other than gentle passive exercises undertaken in her chosen position, which was frequently walking round the building. It was established that she had psycho-flexed hands. At one time a fungal condition developed in the palm of her hands, which required daily treatment from the district nurse with assistance from the physiotherapist. The physiotherapist continues regular passive stretching and, as Miss A has become more amenable to having her hands touched, the home staff incorporate gentle finger movements during hand washing.

She has sharply fluctuating mood swings necessitating adjustment in her level of medication and she has suffered severe weight loss. The dietician and

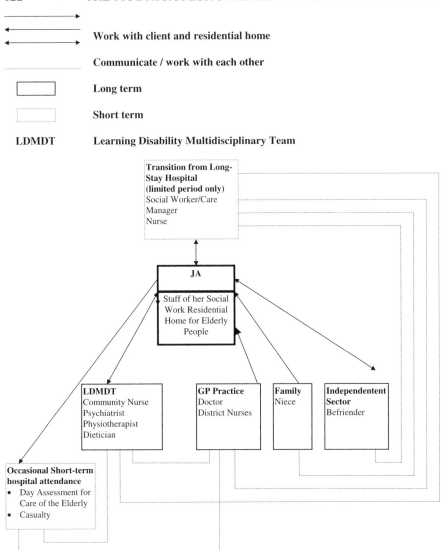

Work with client and residential home

Communicate / work with each other

Long term

Short term

LDMDT   **Learning Disability Multidisciplinary Team**

Transition from Long-Stay Hospital (limited period only)
Social Worker/Care Manager
Nurse

JA

Staff of her Social Work Residential Home for Elderly People

LDMDT
Community Nurse
Psychiatrist
Physiotherapist
Dietician

GP Practice
Doctor
District Nurses

Family
Niece

Independentent Sector
Befriender

Occasional Short-term hospital attendance
• Day Assessment for Care of the Elderly
• Casualty

Figure 5.2. Case study 1: J.A.

community nurse have established food intake charts with the home staff and monitored her weight and body mass index (BMI) weekly.

Miss JA is routinely placed on a list for three-monthly discussion at the team meeting. However, the variety of conditions that she has and their impact upon each other frequently necessitate an update discussion. This enables all staff to work in a concerted manner.

CASE STUDY 2: BH

Community support for BH is illustrated in Figure 5.3.

Mr BH married and moved into a voluntary agency 'good neighbour scheme' flat from a long-stay hospital in 1983 when multidisciplinary community care

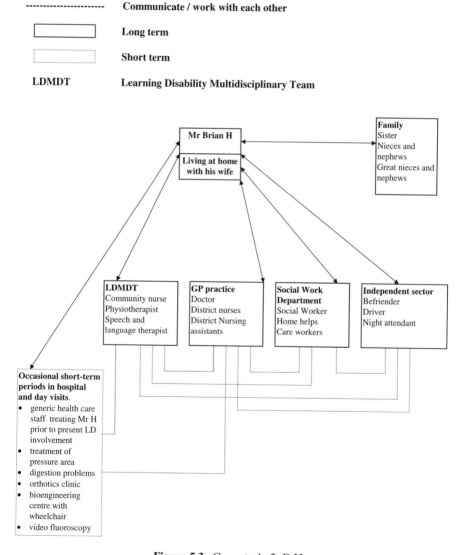

Figure 5.3. Case study 2: B.H.

was becoming established. He was described as being in the dull normal range of intellectual ability and perhaps should not have been admitted to a long-stay learning disability hospital; his wife has moderate learning disability.

History

- A 73-year-old man.
- He had an uncertain early history, which suggested postencephalitic syndrome.
- The eventual diagnosis was ataxic diplegia with some extrapyramidal features presenting as pyramidal involvement of all four limbs, cerebellar inco-ordination of upper limbs, marked spasticity of lower limbs, facial grimacing and dysarthria, which was possibly cerebellar.
- He reportedly walked at five-and-a-half years of age.
- He attended a special school.
- He could become extremely frustrated and angry.
- At age 25 years and after the death of his father he was admitted to a long-stay hospital.
- On admission he was still able to walk, with a scissors-gait pattern.
- Five years after admission became confined to a wheelchair.
- In 1968 he was referred for physiotherapy and speech therapy.
- Treatment continued until he left the hospital.
- He attended further education classes in and outside the hospital.

The couple attended separate day centres three times a week. Mr BH ceased attending because it lacked stimulation. He was an active member of the Regional Rights Group and Division Planning Group for people with mental handicap and was invited to discuss proposals on the Disability Bill. He continued to expand his interests and activities in the community.

Daily contact was maintained with district nurses, home help, his volunteer driver, his befriender and neighbours, so formal contact with the learning disability team community nurse was regular but infrequent.

At his request all therapy ceased until 1987. On discharge from a general hospital he was referred to the generic community physiotherapy department, which referred him to learning disability physiotherapists again. He participated in hydrotherapy sessions at his former long-stay hospital and subsequently self-referred whenever he felt that it was necessary.

In 1995 his learning disability team social worker referred him to the team physiotherapist. He was more frail and dependent and required professional intervention to accelerate work on his wheelchair. Sadly, before this referral had been made, several months' retention of his wheelchair for major modifications had confined him to bed and resulted in an open pressure area.

It transpired that between 1983 and 1995 he had periodically been admitted to a hospital for care of the elderly for treatment of a pressure area and had been treated for a right cervical neuropathy. Both upper limbs had become severely affected. Limb function was limited to pointing with his left arm.

From 1995 he participated in weekly physiotherapy at home. This included a short period of laser treatment in conjunction with a specific nursing regime for his pressure area – which remained healed for over three years – modifications to his wheelchair, regular positioning, active and passive exercise and chest physiotherapy. His wife and carers were taught how to position him correctly and undertake simple passive movements. The speech-and-language therapist, nurse and physiotherapist worked together regarding mealtime positioning. His wife and home help were shown how to position him at mealtimes. During that period he sustained several transient ischaemic attacks, which needed attention.

Despite his increasing level of dependence he continued to be the pivotal figure within his household and took responsibility for his own decisions. Good community care and frequent discussion at and between meetings continued until his death. His widow continued to be supported and treated for her physical disability by members of the team and was made welcome by her late husband's family.

CASE STUDY 3: KT

Community support for KT is illustrated in Figure 5.4.

Miss KT lives at home with her parents. She has a lively, very strong-willed personality. When first known to the team she was emotionally labile. She has matured greatly.

History

- Miss KT is a 25-year-old woman.
- She has moderate to mild learning disability.
- She has moderate cerebral palsy, which was presenting with increasing balance problems and diminishing walking distance.
- Standard ankle foot orthosis (AFO) is supplied by the generic physiotherapy service.

On leaving school she was referred to the community nurse in the team and later to a citywide clinic for people who have physical disabilities in addition to learning disability. This was originally conceived to aid transition from the paediatric sector to adult sector. It is primarily for people with severe learning disability but can accommodate those who have multiple though less severe needs. It is run by a consultant psychiatrist in learning disability and attended by a community learning disability nurse and physiotherapist. It provides time and opportunity for full examination by the three professionals.

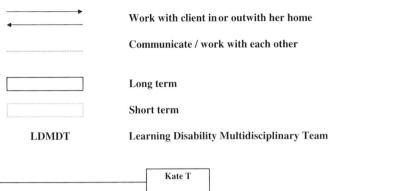

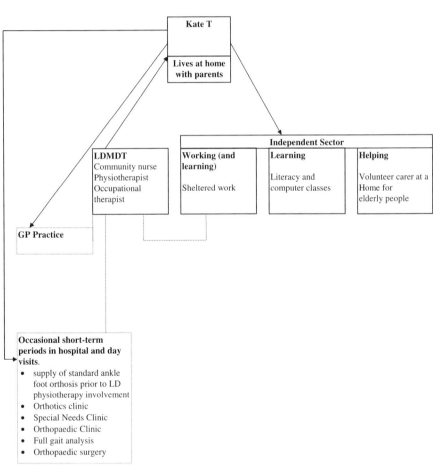

Figure 5.4. Case study 3: K.T.

It was decided to continue to monitor her progress through the clinic and her learning disability team, encourage use of the standard AFO, undertake individual physiotherapy if the need arose and refer her to her team occupational therapist.

Recommendations from the occupational therapist included:

- increase domestic activities in the house
- attend local groups and courses with her own age group
- continue classes to extend literacy and computing skills
- work as a volunteer at a nursing home
- continue search for respite care

Six months later the team community nurse re-referred her for physiotherapy because of problems with the AFO and concerns about deterioration in walking, which seriously affected her independent lifestyle.

She was referred to the orthopaedic clinic. Her walking pattern was considered to be secondary to calf muscle contractures. Full gait analysis confirmed that she would benefit from gastrocnemius lengthening. She had a lengthening of bilateral gastrocnemius and the right tibial posterior tendon.

Following her hospital discharge physiotherapy continued with the learning disability team physiotherapist at home once weekly for four months. The main advantage of home treatment was the involvement of the whole family, which promoted discussion that led to integration of daily exercises into a step routine and swimming with her mother. Physiotherapy reduced to two monthly visits for a further one year with one visit four months later when she was discharged from physiotherapy. She still had an abnormal gait pattern but no longer required an AFO, rarely fell, negotiated stairs well at home and at work, travelled independently on the buses and went to the cinema with friends.

She continues to be seen by the team community nurse in relation to her new sheltered work and relationships with boyfriends. She can be referred to other members of the team again when required.

REFERENCES

Allen, P., Pahl, J. and Quine, L. (1990) *Care Staff in Transition – The Impact on Staff of Changing Services for People with Mental Handicaps*, Stationery Office, London.

Baldry, J.A. and Rossiter, D. (1995) Introduction of integrated care pathways to a neuro-rehabilitation unit. *Physiotherapy*, **81** (8), 432–4.

Band, R. (1998) *The NHS – Health for All*, Royal Society for Mentally Handicapped Children and Adults, London.

Cheseldine, S. (1991) Community mental handicap teams, in *Hallas' Caring for People with Mental Handicaps* (eds W.I. Fraser, R.C. MacGillivray and A. Green), Butterworth Heinemann, Oxford, pp. 215–24.

Department of Health (2005) *Working Differently: The Role of Allied Health Professions*, Allied Health Professions Federation, London.

Higgs, J. and Titchen, A. (1995) Propositional, professional and personal knowledge in clinical reasoning, in *Reasoning in the Health Professions* (eds J. Higgs and M. Jones), Clinical Butterworth Heinemann, Oxford, pp. 129–46.

Hollins, S. (1985) The dynamics of teamwork, in *Mental Handicap* (eds M. Craft, J. Bicknell and S. Hollins), Bailliere Tindall, Eastbourne, pp. 281–7.

Ladyshewsky, R.K. (2006) Building cooperation in peer coaching relationships: understanding the relationship between reward structure, learner preparedness, coaching skill and learner engagement. *Physiotherapy*, **92**, 4–10.

Lindsey, M. (1998) *Signposts for Success in Commissioning and Providing Health Services for People with Learning Disabilities*, Stationery Office, London.

Macadam, M. and Rodgers, J. (1997) A multi-disciplinary, multi-agency approach, in *Adults with Learning Disabilities* (eds J. O'Hara and A. Sperlinger (eds), John Wiley & Sons, Ltd, Chichester, pp. 187–204.

Manley, K. (2000) Practice development revisited: clarifying the concept. *Nursing in Critical Care*, **5** (4), 161–2.

Papathanasiou, I. and Lyon-Maris, S.J. (1997) Outcome measurements and case weightings in physiotherapy services for people with learning disabilities. *Physiotherapy*, **84** (12), 633–8.

Williams, J. (1991) *Calculating Staffing Levels in Physiotherapy Services*, Pampas Publications, Rotherham.

6 First Steps in Communicating with People Who Have Learning Disabilities

SUE STANDING AND SUE SMITH

INTRODUCTION

Therapists meeting a person with learning disabilities for the first time are faced with many challenges. First, their own perception of learning disability: what does it mean to them? Their own beliefs, values and experience will dictate the way in which they react. Second, fear of communication difficulties may lead to the embarrassment of misunderstanding. Third, the inability to identify the client's need accurately could lead to inappropriate goals and plans being developed which will promote failure rather than achievement.

EXAMINATION OF THE THERAPIST'S PERCEPTION OF LEARNING DISABILITY

Professionals often state that they hold positive beliefs about people with learning disabilities because they have had appropriate training and clinical experience. This can be challenged. First, their response may reflect Oppenheim's (1992) opinion that people answering questions conform to the most socially desirable views. Second, if offered the chance, would you change places with a person with learning disabilities?

Despite these two reservations, Gething (1993) found that the accepted view was largely true with regard to physiotherapists. She discovered that their attitudes towards people with disabilities were more positive than those of the general population, a fact that she attributed to preregistration disability awareness training and in-service education. Both stimulated positive and realistic attitudes and beliefs, which enhanced effectiveness and appropriateness of practice. In writing about the shaping of social oppression, French (1993) suggested that examination of disability issues develops and deepens knowledge, which enables attitudes to change – a view supported by a small

Learning Disability: Physical Therapy Treatment and Management. Edited by Jeanette Rennie
© 2007 John Wiley & Sons Ltd

study on attitudes of physiotherapy students and qualified physiotherapists towards people with disabilities (Atkinson 1994). Since these studies were completed, disability awareness training has been increased in preregistration courses for all healthcare professionals. *The Same as You?* (Scottish Executive 2000), *Valuing People* (Department of Health 2001) and The Surgeon General's Conference on Health Disparities and Mental Retardation in the USA in 2002 all reinforced this by placing great stress on improving communication between people with learning disabilities and health professionals (see Chapter 1).

The social construction of disability theory (Berger and Luckman 1987) assumes that people discover their identity through interactions with others. It highlights influences in society that affect the experience of disability. These influences have generally led to negative attitudes towards people with learning disabilities and to their social alienation. It is, therefore, important to define disability correctly, acknowledging that it has a social dimension (Oliver 1993). Gates (1997) suggested that professionals working with people who have learning disabilities should stop and reflect on the meaning of such definitions as learning disability, profound handicap and complex needs. This social approach (French 1994) sees the problem located in the minds of the nondisabled. It implies that if the attitude of nondisabled people changed some of the problems of disability would be resolved. On the other hand, Morris (1991) stated: 'we can insist that society disables us by its prejudice and by its failure to meet the needs created by disability, but to deny the personal experience is in the end to collude to our oppression.'

There is much debate about the social model and the personal tragedy model. The experience of institutional practices has led to prejudices by society that are perpetuated in many aspects of life (see Chapter 1). The experience of disability, therefore, is affected profoundly by social practice. Why do people with learning disabilities continue to travel on vehicles marked 'ambulance'? Why are they still segregated despite the consultations listed in Chapter 1? Who segregates them? Why, despite improvements following implementation of the Disability Discrimination Act 1995 in 2004, are any buildings difficult to access?

BARRIERS TO GETTING TO KNOW A PERSON WITH LEARNING DISABILITIES

Getting to know another person is a two-way process. A more developed and deeper understanding of the perspective of the experience and history of people who have a learning disability will produce a more positive attitude towards them.

People with learning disabilities face many barriers in getting to know other people. The experience of being disabled is one of social restriction, prejudice and oppression (Swain et al. 1993). They may be out of reach of relationships with people without disabilities because they live or work in segregated environments. They may lack the opportunity to frequent places where others meet and interact because they cannot afford the entrance fee or price of food and drink, are physically impaired, access to buildings is poor or transport costs are prohibitive (Emerson et al. 2005). They may have additional communication difficulties and sensory impairments. They may lack confidence due to past experiences of rejection by others.

Without both aspects of this two-way process, relationships cannot be established. Relationships help to define who we are. By helping us to build and reinforce our self-esteem they can in turn allow us to choose to be either the same as or different from other people. Without them we cannot know what we are like, or what kind of people we would like to be. Relationships allow us to learn about others, from others, through others and about ourselves (Firth and Rapley 1990).

One of the key factors in getting to know people with a learning disability is to give time to them. Research their background, abilities, style of communication and behaviours. Do not take their reactions at face value. Remember that each person is unique and responds differently in different situations. Investigate their problem thoroughly.

Case history 1

Mr A has cerebral palsy with no verbal communication. He recently moved to a new home. The carers note that he grimaces and develops spasms, especially around his hips. On movement he seems to show signs of discomfort. On examination and gentle moving of his hip joints he is able to relax. It is noted that during the move some of the supports and the footrests of his armchair were mislaid. Having located these he sits more happily in his chair. But the grimacing and spasms continue. Further examination of his hips and back are made and a referral to the orthopaedic consultant is made. On X-ray a dislocation of the hip is found. Conservative management with daily posture control is established. It appears that the grimacing and spasms increase after eating. He undergoes an investigation into his bowel and abdomen. A friend of his visits and in discussion discloses that he has often displayed these actions especially when frustrated and unable to make himself understood.

COMMUNICATION SKILLS OF ADULTS WITH LEARNING DISABILITIES

Communication is one the most basic needs and functions of human life. The range of methods used to communicate is vast as are the reasons for using them. Everybody, regardless of their cognitive ability has methods of communication that are both verbal and nonverbal. These are used as part of their normal communicative repertoire.

Most adults use spoken language as their primary verbal mode of communication and a range of nonverbal communication methods to complement speech. For example, someone telling a story will convey the basic content of the story using spoken words but will convey a range of other aspects using nonverbal communication skills. The emotion of the story may come across through the speakers' intonation, their facial expression, and body language. Descriptive information may be expressed through gesture and mime. Emotions of the characters may be portrayed through the volume of speech used by the storyteller. For many adults with a learning disability, speech may not be their strongest modality and the range and importance of nonverbal skills in conveying the basic contents of their message can become far more significant. It is important to note that any behaviour is potentially communicative (Coupe and Goldbart 1988) and adults with learning disability will have a very wide range of behaviours that could be potential communicative messages to those around them.

Adults with a learning disability may also use some nonverbal methods of communication at a more sophisticated level than their counterparts who are not learning disabled. Many will have been taught to use some kind of signing system such as Makaton (Walker 1971, 1977, Walker and Armfield 1981). However, not all people with learning disabilities will be able to use such a system. Some may more recently have been taught to use a basic object based system known as 'objects of reference' (Ockelford 1994). Other people will use pictorial systems of communication of varying levels of sophistication depending on their cognitive skills.

> 'An adult with learning disabilities is only going to learn to communicate if they have a reason, a purpose for that communication' (Coupe and Goldbart 1988).

East (1991) identified a range of what she terms 'functions' of communication. The most fundamental were:

NEEDS SATISFACTION

A person has some kind of need that requires another person to satisfy it. Examples could be a hungry person requiring food, an unhappy person requiring a hug, a bored person requiring stimulation. This need provides the reason and motivation to communicate with another person.

ATTENTION TO SELF/OTHER OR AN ACTION

This is a complex and absolutely fundamental function of communication. Before beginning any communication, if it is to be successful, the attention of the listener must be gained. Frequently, attention is discussed in a negative sense, for example: 'he is only doing it to gain attention.' There are, however, a number of very positive scenarios in which gaining attention is a very valid reason to communicate.

A person may want to gain attention in order to communicate 'look at me I want to tell you something' or so that he can focus his communication partner on something of joint interest ('look at that thing with me') or to focus his communication partner on himself ('look what I'm doing').

If that initial attention cannot be successfully gained then any further attempts at communication become redundant. To give a practical example, a client may be able to sign 'drink' perfectly but if he cannot gain attention he won't get his drink.

PROTEST

A person has the desire to express unhappiness with a situation to stop or change it. Some clients with learning disabilities use such a dramatic method of protesting – for example kicking, throwing, smearing – that it distracts their communication partner from their original message. This may particularly be the case if the client is poor at gaining attention and as a result is forced to protest. At the opposite end of the scale, some clients present with such a high level of passivity that it is difficult to establish when they are unhappy about anything.

ANSWERING

Answering a question is a reason to communicate. This may be a simple 'yes' or 'no' response. It is common, particularly for people with primarily nonverbal communication to find that they are rarely given encouragement to answer and that communication partners may answer for them.

GAIN PERMISSION/CLARIFY

Another reason to communicate is to check that it is going to be all right to do something, or to make sure that something is understood correctly. This is a function that, for people with mainly nonverbal skills, could easily be mistaken for requesting or protesting

GIVE INFORMATION

This is a means of giving information to others, for example 'I am tired' or 'you have forgotten something'.

GREETING

Although this may in some cases be a way of gaining attention to communicate, there are other times when communication is used simply as a way of being polite and sociable with those in the environment, most commonly 'hello' and 'goodbye'.

There can be a wide range within these basic categories. More often than not more than one of these communication functions will be used at one time. For example, in order to communicate it may be necessary to gain a person's attention before a request can be made for a need to be satisfied. In another scenario, a client may be answering a question by protesting and trying to divert communication partner's attention onto the cause of their protest.

For people with learning disabilities both the methods of communication and the functions of communication may be impaired.

FORMALISED COMMUNICATION

Formalised communication refers to any organised system of communication. This can include both spoken systems and signed systems.

SPOKEN LANGUAGE

People with learning disabilities may present with disorders in either understanding or expressing themselves using spoken language, or with both. This could be a profound problem resulting in no spoken expression or comprehension. It may present as a subtler problem – for instance a difficulty understanding and/or expressing language related to a specific concept. This could be time ('we *will be* going out'), negatives ('the bus *isn't* coming') or position ('the pen is *under* the table').

These difficulties may be part of an overall syndrome/condition from which the person suffers or may be linked to brain damage that has resulted in their learning disability. In some instances these difficulties may be related to traumas such as head injury or stroke, which have no link to their learning disability. It is also possible that a lack of experience may relate to subtler problems – for example, very limited mobility may cause difficulty in understanding positional language such as 'in', 'on', 'behind'.

People with learning disabilities are frequently taught signed systems of communication because of their more concrete nature. These, however, will be very specialised systems and approaches like Makaton (Walker 1971). A system such as British Sign Language is a language in its own right and therefore just as complex cognitively as spoken language.

NONFORMALISED COMMUNICATION

People may be impaired in their ability to express themselves nonverbally. For example they may lack eye contact, or have very unusual patterns of eye contact; they may have an abnormally flat or extreme intonation pattern; they may lack the ability to use facial expression. These difficulties are frequently those that have the biggest social implications for people as they will frequently be judged by communication partners as 'odd' or possibly even dangerous because they give the wrong nonverbal messages.

People may present with difficulties of formalised communication or informal communication, or very commonly, with difficulties of both.

WHY DOES COMMUNICATION PRESENT A PROBLEM FOR PEOPLE WITH LEARNING DISABILITIES?

Primary difficulties for people with learning disabilities involve generalising learned skills and dealing with more abstract concepts and information. Language in itself is symbolic. This means that it involves something, in this case a spoken word or formalised sign, being used to represent something else, in this case an object, action or concept. Take for example the word 'tree' or formalised sign for tree. This is used to represent a living object and when the word or sign is used it instantly brings to mind a picture of an actual tree. This is an example of the way in which spoken or signed language is symbolic of real objects.

For people with learning disabilities, speech is frequently the most difficult level of communication for them to acquire and they often need other systems in place to support it. This is because spoken language is the most abstract way in which we can represent a concept in communication.

As Figure 6.1 demonstrates, the spoken word represents the most abstract way in which the concept of 'tree' can be represented communicatively. The most concrete is using the actual tree itself. It should be assumed that those communication methods that are at the most abstract end of the scale, signing and speech, are so lacking in sensory clues that their relationship to a particular object, action or concept will have to be taught. It is a common misapprehension that a system such as signing will automatically be easy for people with learning disabilities. The diagram shows it is less abstract than speech but is not necessarily obviously linked to the object or concept that it represents.

MOST CONCRETE

Real Tree

(Sensory support: colour of tree, shape of tree, size of tree, sound and smell of tree,

and 3D, is situated in context)

Miniature of tree

(Sensory support: colour of tree, shape of tree, 3D)

Photograph of tree (actual tree)

(Sensory support: colour of tree, shape of tree)

Photograph of tree (any tree)

(Sensory support: some aspects of colour and shape)

Line drawing of tree

(Sensory support: generalised shape)

Sign for tree (MAKATON)

(Sensory support: gross link to generalised shape of a tree)

Word tree

(Sensory support: NONE)

MOST ABSTRACT

Figure 6.1. Communicating the concept of 'tree'.

It is vital, when considering communicating needs of people with learning disabilities, to consider the level of abstraction with which they will be able to cope. This is not to say that someone cannot progress to using a more abstract system. For example it is possible that clients who related to photographs may progress to understanding line drawings/symbols. However, it is necessary to start at the level that matches their cognitive skills and gradually introduce the more abstract system, the line drawing, alongside the one that they understand, the photograph.

To give a practical example, take a client who is currently able to make a choice by eye pointing at one of two objects. That system, although effective, lacks portability and relies on other people to produce the required objects to choose between. A way to move on would be to present the objects as before but with a photograph of the actual object alongside each object to help the client learn that they are linked and are symbolic of the same thing. After a while, the objects could be gradually faded into the background to see if the client could make a choice between the two photographs by eye pointing instead. This would represent a more portable and adaptable communication system. It should be noted that the transition between these two types of symbols for some people might take a considerable period of time.

For some clients either because of cognitive difficulties or visual disabilities the most appropriate level of communication may remain at the level of objects. This could involve using the system known as 'objects of reference' (Ockelford 1994). This involves teaching a client to relate to objects as symbols for communication. For example, learning that a spoon represents food, or a piece of flannel represents 'toilet'. This system has the advantage of being both concrete and tactile and can be very simple or quite sophisticated. It is a system that relies heavily on consistent teaching and use by carers.

HOW DOES COMMUNICATION DEVELOP FOR A PERSON WITH LEARNING DISABILITIES?

There are a number of models of communication development; probably the most useful in terms of practical intervention with people with learning disabilities is to look at the development of intentional communication. This is particularly helpful in terms of the communication skills of people with profound learning disabilities.

Table 6.1 is a representation of the way in which intentional communication occurs in normal development. 'The focal person' can potentially represent a person of any age or level of cognitive ability. It is however easiest to look at the examples in terms of the early development of a baby.

When individuals grasp the concept that they can use their communication to control their environment then they are truly intentional communicators. As this diagram shows there are steps along the way that rely heavily on appropriate 'interpretations' and responses to ensure that those skills develop.

This behaviour comes naturally when adults are with very small babies and the results of this in terms of the speed of children's development of communication speak for themselves. Current thinking is that this sort of philosophy should be applied when working with adults with learning disability who present as 'pre-intentional' in their communication skills (Hewett 1996; Nind and Hewett 2001).

Table 6.1. Development of normal intentional communication

Focal person's behaviour	Communicative partner's interpretation of behaviour	Communicative partner's response	Focal person's learning
Earliest Stage			
Reflexive crying in response to hunger	Person has a need, may be hungry	To give food whilst telling the person what their interpretation of the behaviour was 'Are you hungry?' with a soothing inflection	With repetitions of this pattern the person begins to learn that their behaviour has a rewarding effect on those around them
Smiling in response to a friendly voice and face	Person likes individual doing the talking and wants to hear more	Says something else and smiles each time the person smiles at them	With repetition person begins to learn about turntaking and that their actions get reaction from others
Later stages			
Makes 'word-like' noise e.g. 'di' and points at a drink	Wants a drink and is trying to say it	Gives drink and reinforces the vocalisation saying 'you want a **drink**', with heavy emphasis on the key word	With repetition person begins to learn that speech is a powerful tool and that particular sound combinations link to particular objects/actions
Points at ball, and looks at carer (Anne)	Wants ball and wants carer to help	Gives ball saying 'you want Anne's Ball?'	Person learns to control people using communication

HOW CAN CARERS IMPROVE COMMUNICATION SKILLS FOR ADULTS WITH A LEARNING DISABILITY?

There is no doubt that, looking at all the theory, a great deal of responsibility for the effectiveness of the communication of people with learning disabilities lies with the individual who is communicating with them on a day-to-day basis.

The following is a checklist of basic questions to ask and actions that could relate to the answers to these questions:

- *How is the person with a learning disability communicating?* It is important to observe the ways in which clients are communicating and to decide whether the methods they are using are effective. This may lead the carer either to try to introduce a new method or to work at reinforcing the existing ones to improve their usefulness.
- *Why are people with learning disabilities communicating?* Do they have reasons to communicate? The carer would need to create situations in which clients were motivated to communicate. For example, this may involve setting up more choice-making situations. It may involve re-evaluating their environment so that they need to use their communication methods to ensure that their needs are met.
- *Are carers 'speaking the same language' as the client?* If a client is nonverbal it is important that carers also use clear nonverbal communication. This may be a system such as Makaton signing (Walker 1971) or may involve using facial expression, touch, and other nonverbal signals to communicate. It makes good sense to consider the way in which people mirror and extend the communication skills of normally developing children and consider how this could be done for the adult learning disabled person.
- *How much language does the person with a learning disability understand?* This can be established with the assessment from the speech and language therapist and is essential in order to decide at which level to pitch an interaction. Careful observation can begin to establish this, looking particularly at the way clients respond to instructions when they are out of the normal routine and context and when clues such a facial expression and gesture are kept to a minimum.

Developing the communication skills of a client with learning disabilities is a big task and one that should be embarked on in a structured way. A key factor to bear in mind is that a very small improvement in an individual's communication skills has the potential to make a massive impact on his or her quality of life.

WORKING WITH PEOPLE WHO HAVE A VISUAL PROBLEM

The Royal National Institute for the Blind (RNIB) produces informative literature and references about the experience of visual impairments. With this knowledge an understanding can develop on how to aid communication and get to know and develop relationships with visually impaired people. The RNIB state that the term 'blind' is not really accurate. Only a minority of blind people are totally blind or just see light and dark. The majority have some sight, which they can use in their daily lives. Unfortunately, many adults with visual and learning disabilities have not been helped to use their sight and so tend to give the impression of being more disabled than they really are.

The RNIB describes five main factors that aid a visually impaired person's environment: lighting and the use of colour contrast, sound, walls, surfaces (floors) and furniture and equipment. It is important that these are taken into consideration when assessing clients. A referral to a physiotherapist for a client who 'shuffles' and has mobility problems on the stairs might not mean that client has a physical difficulty but perhaps has tunnel vision and therefore can only see a very small area in front of her. Her vision is limiting her physical progress; she lacks confidence as she is unsure where to place her feet and is reluctant to stride out into the unknown. In this instance it would be helpful to have white edging to the stairs and tactile indicators on the wall and banister.

It is necessary for people with a visual impairment to make use of other senses, usually hearing and touch. A visually impaired person may need help to learn by discovery whereas a sighted person quickly assimilates surrounding information. For example, a blind child may not know that it is worth crawling across a room to get a sweet because their hearing cannot tell them that it is there.

Communication skills are impaired because it is difficult to observe non-verbal communication or body language. A smile to show encouragement is not noticed and signs of sadness or crying may pass without recognition, so a visually impaired person may often seem passive, withdrawn and unsociable. Such people are often dependent on others to interpret their surroundings.

People with a learning disability and visual impairment need to be offered structured activities in environments that enhance their opportunities. Good lighting and reduced background noise enable them to focus on important sounds. Tactile clues are essential. For each person with a visual impairment the experience is unique. The therapist must take time getting to know that person and understanding their responses and behaviours.

In many small group homes and day facilities used by adults with learning disability and visual impairment this understanding is developed to high levels by using an adapted form of 'intensive interaction' (see Table 6.1). One independently funded organisation gives the guidelines in Figure 6.2 to its care staff.

WORKING WITH PEOPLE WHO HAVE A HEARING IMPAIRMENT

People with learning disabilities are prone not only to visual impairments but hearing impairments. Studies consistently reveal that around 40% of people with severe learning disabilities also have hearing problems. Unfortunately many of these people go through their lives without staff and carers

How do I 'do' Intensive Interaction?

There are no hard and fast rules – GO WITH THE FLOW

The most important things you need to do are to *watch* and to *follow.*

Watch

Observe your partner for little movements, gestures, facial expressions, indications of pleasure.

Take time to notice things - little things grow into big things but if you're too busy to notice them they don't get the chance. For example:

Gestures --------------------------→ signs

Sense of control over noise--------→ sense of control over more important things

Fun from one small interaction----→ potential fun in lots of other interactions

Wait

Be patient, give partner time.

Don't try to push things along - sometimes nothing will happen for a while.

If there is a 'lull' don't assume that this is the end - share the quiet, your partner will know you are still 'available'.

Follow

Follow the lead of your partner. Keep your focus on them and what they do, and respond to what they initiate.

Make an effort to *control* less and to *receive* more from the individual.

Figure 6.2. How do I 'do' intensive interaction?

How do I build on what happens?

You can begin to build on things that you observe by:

• responding to actions / things observed

• interpreting them i.e. giving them some kind of 'meaning'

• exaggerating them

• adding a variation . . .

Why have specific sessions for intensive interaction?

By setting aside specific time for intensive interaction sessions, you create a regular time when the individual knows that you are there. They won't necessarily take you up on the offer but what is important is that you make yourself available to them. This is unconditional – there should be no sense of you imposing your ideas about what's acceptable/ appropriate – anything goes!

Also, a session is more focused than the spontaneous interactions that occur during the course of the day. This means fewer distractions, less chance of the 'flow' being interrupted, more chance to build on things.

From training notes for care staff at 'Visualise', Fountain Hall Road, Edinburgh.

Figure 6.2. *Continued*

recognising this loss. People who have poor hearing may not be aware that other people hear better than they do. It is important to recognise that improvements can be made if a person with learning disabilities has hearing impairments. Often a relatively simple problem such as wax in the ears can be the cause and can be treated. Others may have longstanding ear infections, which should be treated as soon as possible. Some people may need to wear a hearing aid or even have surgery. A hearing aid may not solve all the problems and in some cases is not tolerated by the client, but it may assist in communication.

Case study 2

Client B was admitted to a long-stay hospital aged 8, and described as profoundly handicapped. Her deafness was not identified until she left the long-stay hospital 25 years later. Staff felt that her inability to hear and communicate contributed to her challenging behaviour. Her deafness isolated and frustrated her but she has gained considerable self-confidence and new skills since she learnt sign language.

WORKING WITH PEOPLE WHO HAVE VISUAL AND HEARING IMPAIRMENTS

People with learning disabilities can have both visual and hearing impairments along with or without other physical or behavioural problems. The organisation SENSE provides useful literature and courses to train therapists, teachers and carers. If a therapist is working with these people it is important that all the relevant information is found about them so that their needs can be adequately met if possible. This process will involve time spent watching and listening, identifying clues that will produce regular and reliable responses and working through the barriers to enable progress to develop.

Case history 3

Client C is a 45-year-old woman with Down syndrome. She has a hearing impairment and has very deformed eye sockets, causing visual impairment. She lived in a long-stay hospital for 27 years. It is understood that at one time she walked. She has now moved into a small community home where she will stand to be washed and changed. The staff have requested advice on how to encourage her to walk again.

It seems that she will bear weight in certain situational activities but she very quickly just sinks to the ground without warning. She is a heavy woman and there is risk of damage to herself and her carers. To achieve the goal required the client has to want or enjoy the experience and has to have the opportunity to practise safely. In this case a regular routine of standing in a standing frame with knee gaiters to prevent sudden 'sinking' to the ground was established. Client C would initially stand for 10 minutes twice a day. To achieve this staff put her into the frame, giving her a vibrating pad to hold, which she was known to enjoy.

The client was also known to enjoy water activities. A weekly visit to the pool was established where she was encouraged to walk several widths in waist high water before venturing to the deep end where she loved to float.

This regime has continued for the last 6 months increasing the period in the standing frame, and the number of widths of the pool walked. The staff continue to encourage standing for functional activities. It has been noted that the client's standing time has increased and is much more reliable during functional activities. On occasions she has taken steps between two people. The staff are willing to continue with this regime with regular monitoring and advice from the therapist.

CONCLUSION

A high standard of treatment and management of the physical disabilities of an individual with learning disabilities can only be achieved if he or she and his healthcare professional can communication with each other. This requires healthcare professionals to examine their own attitudes towards people with learning and physical disabilities. It is then essential that healthcare professionals liaise with each other and with the carers to discover the client's method of communication. Finally, it is essential that all the carers and professionals take time to communicate with clients by using their particular methods of communication.

REFERENCES

Atkinson, J. (1994) *Physiotherapy in the Field of Learning Disabilities, A Study of Attitudes*, Unpublished BSc project, University of Central England, Birmingham.

Berger, P. and Luckman, T. (1987) *The Social Construction of Reality*, revised edition, Pelican Books, London.

Coupe, J. and Goldbart, J. (1988) *Communication Before Speech: Normal Development and Impaired Communication*, Croom Helm, London.

Department of Health (2001) *Valuing People – A New Strategy for Learning Disability for the Twenty-first Century*, Stationery Office, London.

East, C. (1991) *Intent to Communicate*, Unpublished MSc thesis, Southampton University.

Emerson, E., Malam, S., Davies, I. and Spencer, K. for The Department of Health (2005) *Survey of Adults with Learning Difficulties in England*, Department of Health Publications, London.

Firth, H. and Rapley, M. (1990) *From Acquaintance to Friendship – Issues for People with Learning Disabilities*, BIMH Publications, Kidderminster.

French, S. (1993) Disability, impairment or something in between, in *Disabling Barriers – Enabling Environments*, 1st edn (eds J. Swain, V. Finklestein, S. French and M. Oliver), Sage, London, pp. 17–25.

French, S. (1994) Attitudes of health professionals towards disabled people. *Physiotherapy*, **80** (10), pp. 687–93.

Gates, B. (1997) *Learning Disabilities*, Churchill Livingstone, Edinburgh.

Gething, L. (1993) Attitudes towards people with learning disabilities of physiotherapists and members of the general population. *Australian Journal of Physiotherapy*, **39** (4), 291–6.

Hewett, D. (1996) How to do intensive interaction, in *Interactive Approaches to Teaching 0- A Framework for INSET* (eds M. Collis and P. Lacy), David Fulton, London.

Nind, M. and Hewett, D. (2001) *A Practical Guide to Intensive Interaction*, BILD Publications, London.

Ockelford, A. (1994) *Objects of Reference. Promoting Communication Skills with Visually Impaired Children who have Other Disabilities*, Royal National Institute for the Blind, London.

Oliver, M. (1993) Redefining disability: a challenge to research, in *Disabling Barriers – Enabling Environments*, 1st edn (eds J. Swain, V. Finklestein, S. French, M. Oliver), Sage, London, pp. 61–7.

Oppenheim, A.N. (1992) *Questionnaire Design, Interviewing and Attitude Measurements*, Pinter Publisher, London.

Scottish Executive (2000) *The Same as You? A Review of Services for People with Learning Disabilities*, Scottish Executive Health Department, Edinburgh.

Swain, J., Finklestein, V., French S. and Oliver, M. (1993) Taught helplessness? Or a say for disabled students in schools, in *Disabling Barriers – Enabling Environments*, 1st edn (eds J. Swain, V. Finklestein, S. French and M. Oliver), Sage, London, pp. 155–62.

US Department of Health and Human Services (2002) *Report of the Surgeon General's Conference on Health Disparities and Mental Retardation. Closing the Gap: A National Blueprint to Improve the Health of Persons with Mental Retardation*, Office of the Surgeon General, Rockville MD.

Walker, M. (1971) *The Makaton Vocabulary Development Project*, Makaton, Camberly, Surrey

Walker, J. (1977) Teaching sign language to deaf mentally handicapped adults, in *Institute of Mental Subnormality Conference Proceedings* 3, *Language and the Mentally Handicapped*. British Institute of Mental Handicap, Kidderminster, 3–25.

Walker, M. and Armfield, A. (1981) What is the Makaton Vocabulary? *Special Education: Forward Trends*, **8** (3), 19–20.

7 Assessment

ANNELIESE BARRELL

INTRODUCTION

This chapter relates primarily to physiotherapy assessment but much of it could be used by anyone undertaking an assessment with people who have learning disabilities.

In general, assessments can take anything from one hour to one week. When working with people with learning disabilities, however, a month or longer may be required to establish a realistic pattern of ability and need. It is common to gain the wrong impression of their ability even after several attempts at an initial assessment. Therapists must not give up at the first hurdle.

All assessments should be recorded, signed and dated according to the standards of professional practice, for example: *Standards of Physiotherapy Practice* (Chartered Society of Physiotherapy 2005), *Communicating Quality 3* (Royal College of Speech and Language Therapists 2006), *Professional Standards for Occupational Therapy Practice* (British College of Occupational Therapists 2003).

ASSESSMENT

An assessment is a systematic method of establishing a baseline for intervention – for treatment and management. It involves an audit of the client's skills, abilities and pathology and the resources available to undertake any intervention. Outcome of intervention cannot be measured without an effective assessment. It should be holistic and needs to be valid, responsive, appropriate and sensitive to the needs of the client. It comprises markers to judge change as a result of:

- Developmental status. Is the client maturing neurologically after the chronological time span?
- Pathological deterioration.

- The impact of intervention: this is difficult to measure as so many influences and factors impinge upon the client's life.
- Habituation: the repetitious bombarding of pathways in the brain.
- Compliance (carer and client).
- Mood.

It can be:

- Multiprofessional: for example community team assessments (see Chapter 5) or dysphagia team assessments.
- Uniprofessional
- Condition specific, for example: musculoskeletal, including Cyriax (1982); McKenzie (2003), Maitland et al. (2005); neurological, including Parkinson's (Wade 1992), gross motor function measure (GMFM) (Russell et al. 1989, Russell et al. 2002); general health profile, including Rivermead (Collen et al. 1991)

It should also encompass the needs of the carers.

EVALUATION

An evaluation is the analysis of the outcomes of the goals set, based on the findings of the assessment. This is described in Chapter 8.

REASONS FOR ASSESSMENT

Physiotherapy assessments for people with learning disabilities are carried out for a variety of reasons, which include the following:

- To establish health status, diagnosis and prognosis and the effect of disease.
- To determine position and posture for effective and functional seating and the provision of the most suitable wheelchair (in some multiprofessional teams this may be the role of the occupational therapist or it may be a combined role).
- To determine the suitability of a person with learning disability for and to aid the physiotherapist's decision on the most effective use of treatment modalities such as those described in Chapters 9 to 17.
- To identify the requirements for orthotics, such as spinal jackets and specialised footwear, and for specialised equipment to aid mobility.
- To ensure that assumptions are not made that may lead to inappropriate goal setting, which could lead to a reduction in quality of life and/or deterioration of health status.
- To indicate an individual's problems/needs including level of support, improvement, maintenance, skills level and functional ability.
- To highlight resource and service deficit and indicate service effectiveness and efficiency for service developments and contracts.

They are used as a baseline of health, social and/or educational status. They are also used to determine disability and handicap and the level of function and ability, which assists the physiotherapist in selecting the form of intervention to use and in measuring the outcome of that intervention be it improvement, maintenance or deterioration. (Maintenance should be viewed as improvement if deterioration is slowed down or halted.) The assessment will highlight any necessity for further intervention by another profession or agency and will form the basis of a referral on to the most appropriate person according to the client's needs. It can provide a valuable contribution towards person-centred reviews by giving an accurate indication of the level of support and help required to stay 'healthy and safe' (Smull and Sanderson 2001).

MULTIPROFESSIONAL TEAM ASSESSMENT

As part of its initial screening process a multiprofessional team may complete an assessment that is not therapy specific prior to determining which professions will need to be involved with the client. One example is social service core assessment carried out by care managers such as the 'OK Health Check' (Mathews and Hegarty 1997) and the *Face* Profile Learning Disability Walnut Assessment (see Appendix B). These assessments should be considered as part of the holistic assessment thus enabling efficient and effective care programming (see Chapter 8).

Teams, or individual members from the team, may undertake assessments in conjunction with transition services, where they have been established to facilitate a smoother transfer from child to adult services (Morris 2002; Bent et al. 2002; Smith 2002).

FACTORS THAT CAN AFFECT THE ASSESSMENT PROCESS

Time of Day

It is important that physiotherapists familiarise themselves with clients' likes, dislikes and daily routine.

Time of day can severely disrupt and/or prevent the assessment process from taking place. Times to be avoided are immediately before or after a meal, after a long journey to a day centre, sports centre or swimming/hydrotherapy pool when the more disabled people have had much preparation handling, and at the end of the day. Conversely some clients react well to handling and travelling and have a very positive outcome to an assessment undertaken then.

Fear of the Unknown

Initial contact may provoke an out-of-character response such as unusual quietness, overconfidence, verbosity, aggressiveness, abusiveness or noncompliance. Time is required to get to know and establish a rapport with the client and their support workers before any attempt is made to start a formal assessment (see Chapter 6). It is good practice if time and geography allow for the therapist to make contact with the client, home, family and other carers in order to establish a rapport with all concerned prior to embarking on a formal assessment. It is possible at this point to gain valuable and often more accurate information on the following:

- clients' communication methods
- concentration span
- the relationship between the client and the carer
- reaction to new situations and people
- their mobilisation methods when unobserved
- their preferred posture and seating
- their use of leisure time
- do they prefer to be alone or with others and, if others, are these carers or peers?

All this information is important to the physiotherapist when deciding in which form and venue intervention should take place to achieve the best outcome and what advice and training are necessary for the family and carers.

This period of building a relationship becomes part of the informal assessment process, which is equally as important as the structured assessment.

- A rushed session giving insufficient time to establish a rapport between physiotherapist and the person with learning disabilities can produce nothing except a frustrated physiotherapist and a noncompliant client, not to mention the negative compliance of the carer or support worker who feels angry because the person with learning disabilities is not being valued.
- The presence of the parent or carer may help or hinder the assessment process and affect the outcome. Major problems can be caused by people with learning disabilities who react to their parents or carers being present and so prevent an accurate assessment of skills or function taking place. On the other hand the parents or carers know the client well and can offer assistance and information that can enhance the assessment outcome. The physiotherapist has to involve all those concerned in the care of clients and if possible the clients themselves.
- Consultation with all other members of the education, health and social care teams who are familiar with the client before the assessment is very valuable. Previous knowledge of difficulties, needs and successful or failed interventions can shorten or enhance an assessment process. In some teams all clients are discussed at team referral meetings before any intervention takes place, so the most appropriate people are involved at the outset of any assessment process. It is very easy for a physiotherapist to embark on a

first-time home visit, armed only with the referral information, to find later, from a chance remark by another member of the team, that there is some reason for not following that chosen route of assessment or that it has been tried before unsuccessfully.

WHEN SHOULD ASSESSMENT TAKE PLACE AND HOW OFTEN?

Following Referral

The assessment takes place before any treatment interventions begin. Referrals come in a variety of ways:

- Open referral. Where anyone – for example, client, carer, teacher or health professional – can refer to a team or to any one of the individual professions within the team. Teams operating an open referral system often have distinct referral and admission criteria stating the terms of reference of referral to the learning disabilities service. The teams can have a common referral source and allocation to physiotherapy will come following a multiprofessional referral discussion and screening for previous known contacts. Information given with open referrals may state only nonspecific problems or needs, such as problems with feeding.
- Specific referrals. The service admission criteria still apply. These referrals may come from general practitioners, hospital consultants and from other professionals in all agencies involved with the client usually for a defined problem or because they need help in determining the problem. Some generic therapists and other healthcare professionals routinely refer people with learning disabilities on to the specialist service. Referrals are becoming more appropriate, however, as suitably supported access to generic hospital facilities and healthcare services is being encouraged and fostered for people with learning disabilities (Lindsey 1998; Scottish Executive 2000; Department of Health 2001). A useful development has been for generic physiotherapists to refer people for necessary ongoing treatment on completion of an initial intensive block of treatment with them (Brown and Rennie 2003).

Informal Assessment

This takes place at every therapeutic intervention; change is recorded and adjustments are made to the client's therapy programme. This may be a 'one-off' change as client condition and compliance can change for a variety of reasons including: mood, time of day, who brings them for therapy, where therapy occurs. The therapist has to be prepared to be very flexible and to have infinite patience. Many physiotherapy departments use:

- S (subjective)
- O (objective)

- A (assessment)
- P (planning)

notes to record each physiotherapy intervention.

Before the Client's Individual Programme Planning Review

This is done as an indication of change in the client's condition and assists in setting team goals.

Placement Assessment

Social services or other providers may ask the therapist to assess the client for a specific need – for example the type of housing accommodation required or for the most suitable daycare provision. Such assessments are frequently carried out jointly with an occupational therapist or another member of the multidisciplinary team.

Regularly

This is done with clients whose therapeutic intervention is ongoing over a lengthy period; assessments should be undertaken at intervals decided on at the time of the initial assessment.

Before Change in the Client's Condition or Circumstances

This is done when there is, for example, a move to another area or change in residential or daycare accommodation.

On Request

This is on request by carers or the care manager.

On Discharge

This may accompany a discharge letter/plan to the client's medical practitioner.

Legal Assessments

Experienced specialist physiotherapists may be asked to carry out assessments in cases of compensation, for a disciplinary process, or complaint. Lawyers, health or service managers or the individual professional body would initiate these.

WHERE DO ASSESSMENTS TAKE PLACE?

Assessments can take place in a variety of settings:

- In a community daycare centre. It is usually possible to arrange for a quiet area in which to carry out the assessment but this is not always possible and the physiotherapist has then to be creative and flexible. Many daycare establishments have designated and equipped therapy areas.
- In the client's family home.
- In a private, voluntary or statutory residential home.
- In the physiotherapy department of one of the remaining hospitals or National Health Service long-stay accommodation for people with learning disabilities.

Assessments should be carried out in the place and at the time of day that is most appropriate for the person with learning disabilities as described in the Association of Chartered Physiotherapists for People with Learning Disabilities (ACPPLD) standards of good practice (Barnes et al. 1993), a revision of which has been proposed for 2007. Assessing for a feeding problem, for example, is usually best carried out during a mealtime, not in a simulated session. There are, of course, exceptions. If a client's behaviour at meal times with other clients around exacerbates the problem then a simulation would be desirable.

Wherever the setting the physiotherapist must ensure that:

- Enough time is allowed for the physiotherapist to carry out the assessment.
- The client is comfortable and feels at ease.
- There is a minimum of disruption and disturbance, for example by telephone calls, the presence of other clients, or interruptions by or conversations with other staff, the presence of unnecessary distractible equipment.
- The client and/or carer is aware of where the toilets are situated and where refreshments can be obtained, if they are available.
- The therapist has all equipment and assessment tools to hand, for example charts and measuring instruments.
- All involved in the assessment understand what is happening or about to happen.
- In cases of suspected disruptive clients an alarm/panic system/process is in place. This is usually part of a team policy for all staff working in hospital or community settings. Team policy could be: a panic button in a treatment area, having another staff member present in the building, leaving information in a team diary before embarking on a home visit, going accompanied on a home visit, having a code on known client files to alert all therapists of potential difficulties prior to arranging an assessment session, carrying a

mobile phone that is kept switched on at all times. In some general hospitals codes are also used on client files to denote that the client has a learning disability. These are to ensure that the client is valued and given time and understanding by all of the staff especially in a busy outpatient/accident and emergency department.

WHICH ASSESSMENT?

This will depend on the reason for referral, the desired outcome, the level of disability and whether there is a multiprofessional or uniprofessional approach to assessment.

Assessments vary in format and could be one of the following:

- McKenzie (2003)
- Bereweek (Jenkins et al 1983)
- gross motor function (GMF) (Russell et al., 1989, 2002)
- MOVE (Mobility Opportunities Via Education) (Kern County Superintendent of Schools 1990 – see Appendix B)
- The Caring Person's Guide to Handling the Severely Multiply Handicapped (Golding and Goldsmith 1986)
- Mary Marlborough Lodge Assessment (1997 – See Appendix B)
- The Functional Independence Measure (FIM) (Wright 2000) (see Appendix B)
- Barthel Index (Mahoney and Barthel 1965) and see Appendix B
- Goal Attainment Scaling (GAS) (Kiresuk et al. 1994; Reid and Chesson 1998; Young and Chesson 1998)

These highlight ability and deficiency, degrees of disability and handicap, problems and need. Results are easy to read and to evaluate. Intervention plans follow a logical pattern.

VIDEO ASSESSMENT

This gives a very useful record of movement.

- It can be used in situations where deterioration or maintenance is the expected outcome.
- Video assessment can highlight improvement that is so small and imperceptible that it cannot always be seen during day-to-day contact. The effect of this visual change often raises the morale of carers who find it difficult to believe that all is being done to assist the person they support.
- Behaviour, concentration and compliance are also recorded.
- Gait, mobility and functional ability are recorded in a visual way, which enhances the checklist or test results.

Case study 1: Jane

Jane, aged 45 years, lives with eight other clients in a voluntary organisation's residential home. She has myotonic dystrophy and was referred because of problems with gait and falling. A checklist assessment was not able to give an accurate assessment of gait as, although she wants help, she will not comply with any requests to demonstrate her problem. She did walk around the home using furniture to assist and, when not being watched, was able to walk unaided with an exaggerated lordosis and pelvic rotation. She would not walk outside or leave the car if taken out. It was impossible to assess stamina, pain, and gait and the need for assistance. The physiotherapist thought around the problem. Jane loves animals. A trip to the local wildlife park was arranged, Jane left the car to explore and was able to walk around the park using a frame for half an hour before resting.

The trip was videoed. Jane's walking and gait were analysed and a programme of activity was devised with Jane's agreement that aimed at increasing motivation, ambulating and stamina.

STILL PHOTOGRAPHY

Photographs make a permanent current record of:

- position
- posture
- deformity size
- seating
- wheelchairs

(Note that permission must be obtained from the client or advocate before undertaking a video assessment or taking photographs.)

Most physiotherapy services working with people with a learning disability have devised their own form of assessment, a mixture of all the above and based on a plethora of validated assessment forms available, for example: Golding and Goldsmith (1986), Mary Marlborough Lodge (1997, see Appendix B). This is because at present there are few validated assessments that cover all the aspects of a holistic assessment or are able to record minimal change.

Assessments should include, for example:

- *personal details of the individual being assessed: name and preferred name, address, contact telephone number, date of birth, next of kin.*
- *name and addresses of the GP and care manager*
- name and address of day care provider
- *reason for referral, client's/carer's expected outcome*

- previous medical history
- *diagnosis (if available)*
- weight and height
- colour, texture and temperature of the skin and the Waterlow scale reading
- presence of epilepsy, type and degree.
- *medication*
- method of communication (see Chapter 6)
- sensory ability
- current wheelchair and seating, date of provision and name of provider
- current orthotic appliances, date of provision and name of provider
- client's behaviours and tolerance of handling
- functional ability
- range of movement and muscle tone
- posture and deformity
- mobility and gait
- a problem/needs list
- a checklist following referral (ACPPLD standards of good practice – Barnes et al. 1993)

Example

Physiotherapy assessment forms are shown in Figures 7.1–7.7. One client may have a number of assessments carried out by the physiotherapist, for example:

- standard physiotherapy assessment as used in the local service
- assessment for a specific modality for example: riding for the disabled, rebound therapy
- wheelchair assessment: as determined by local wheelchair provider, for example a disabled services centre
- seating assessment, determined as above
- orthotic assessment, in conjunction with orthotic providers
- mobility equipment assessment, often jointly with social service occupational therapists
- manual handling risk assessment (Chartered Society of Physiotherapy 2002)
- team assessments – for example, dysphagia (eating) teams, Down syndrome team, fitness screening

These assessments may not all be part of the standard assessment package but are 'add ons' as and when required and are kept as part of the client's complete assessment record.

As most referrals are based on requests for a maintenance or improvement in function, a clinical assessment is not always the physiotherapist's first priority, although clinical knowledge and assessment underpins all actions by the

PHYSIOTHERAPY ASSESSMENT

Page 1

Name:		
Address:		Sex
		D.O.B
Tel No:	Ethnic Origin:	

G.P. Name:	Date of Initial Assessment:
G.P. Address:	Diagnosis:
G.P. Tel. No.:	Physiotherapist:
Medical Personnel:	

History of Present Condition:	
Past Medical History (including Birth History):	Medication:

Figure 7.1. Physiotherapy assessment, sociodemographic information (form 1).

physiotherapist who uses all the core skills and basic general assessment procedures.

Referrals for specific clinical conditions are assessed in the prescribed way for that condition – for example, low back pain, when a validated musculo-skeletal assessment would be used. The following categories may be used with people with learning disabilities. (Hoffer et al. 1973):

PHYSIOTHERAPY ASSESSMENT

Client Name: **Physiotherapist:**
Date:

Method of Communication, including Communication Aids:	Method of Feeding, e.g. self/assisted
Vision ☐ Normal ☐ Total blindness ☐ Partially sighted ☐ Double vision (etc.) ☐ Glasses (reading/day wear) ☐ Other	**Hearing** ☐ Normal ☐ Complete deafness ☐ Partial deafness ☐ Hearing aid Date of last hearing test:

Behaviour/Concentration Levels:
Activities of Daily Living (e.g. washing and dressing):

Social History

Home Environment (e.g. family members, own home, residential....):
Adaptations (e.g. stair lift, rails, extension.....):

Figure 7.2. Physiotherapy assessment, sociodemographic information (form 2).

1. Community ambulators: walks in and outdoors, may need crutches or braces or both. Wheelchair for long trips.
2. Household ambulators: walks only indoors with apparatus, good transfers, may use wheelchair indoors and for all community activities.
3. Nonfunctional ambulators: walking as a therapy session at home or centre, uses wheelchair for all other activities.
4. Nonambulators: wheelchair bound but can transfer from chair to bed.

form 3

PHYSIOTHERAPY ASSESSMENT   Page 3

Client Name: Physiotherapist:
Date:
Main Carer   Day Centre

Name:	Name:
Address:	Address:
Tel No:	Tel No:

Other Carer   Respite
Facility

Name:	Name:
Address:	Address:
Tel No:	Tel No:

Equipment:

Wheelchair (including make/model, adaptation):

Supplied by: **Date:**   **Review Date:**

Orthotics e.g. footwear, ankle foot orthosis

Supplied by: **Date:**   **Review Date:**

Summary

Figure 7.3. Physiotherapy assessment, sociodemographic information (form 3).

It is advisable to add two further categories:

• Before (1): independent walkers – walking independently under all conditions.
• After (4): entirely dependent – unable to transfer without assistance.

Within those categories there will be a wide variation of conditions and abilities demanding different outcomes and expectations. It is therefore essen-

Client Name: **Physiotherapist:**
Date:

If an activity is performed independently, please mark the corresponding **Yes** box. If assistance is needed or the client is unable to perform the activity, mark the **No** box. Activities performed using a mobility aid (e.g.: *stick*) are independent.

		Yes	No	Comments
In Bed	Turn prone to supine			
	Turn prone to supine			
	Move up/down bed			
	Sit over edge of bed			
	Transfer from bed to chair			
Chair	Move to edge of seat			
	Balanced sitting			
	Transfer from chair to bed			
	Stand up			
	Sit down			
Floor	Get on to floor			
	Get up off floor			
Walking	On level ground			
	On rough ground			
	Slopes			
Stairs	Up			
	Down			
Wheelchair	Adjust sitting position			
	Apply/release brake			
	Propel - forwards			
	- backwards			
	- to left, to right			
	Negotiate - doorway			
	- slope			
	- kerb			
	- transfer to chair			
Fine Motor	Hold a spoon			
	Hold a cup			
	Turn pages of a book			

Figure 7.4. Functional ability.

tial that the physiotherapist assesses the relevant needs of the client in terms of function, quality of life and health gain. A large number of clients present with a multiplicity of needs and it is often necessary to prioritise what can only be addressed by the physiotherapist. The client can then be referred back to the carers to extend this treatment as part of his social and leisure education.

Client Name ....
Physiotherapist ....

PROBLEM / NEEDS LIST

Date identified and signature		Date resolved and signature
.		

Figure 7.5. Problem list.

Date	INITIAL PLAN	Signature
	GOALS	

Figure 7.6. Initial plan and goals.

Case study 2: David

David, aged 43 years, is an independent walker referred by his care manager for deteriorating mobility as a result of painful arthritic hips. He is not very motivated but, after being assessed for level of pain, gait, range of lower limb movement, exercise tolerance, muscle strength, adequate footwear and concentration span he recognised the need for exercise to relieve hip pain. He cannot sustain a programme of exercise because he lives alone. He loves the water and benefits from exercise in a pool. After a few sessions of treatment in the hydrotherapy pool with the physiotherapist who taught exercises to a volunteer carer and David, he was soon joining in a session in a local swimming pool as part of the day centre's leisure programme. He is regularly reassessed in the leisure pool by the physiotherapist with the carer. His motivation and exercise tolerance have increased, gait has improved and pain has decreased.

Client Name: **Physiotherapist:**   **Date:**

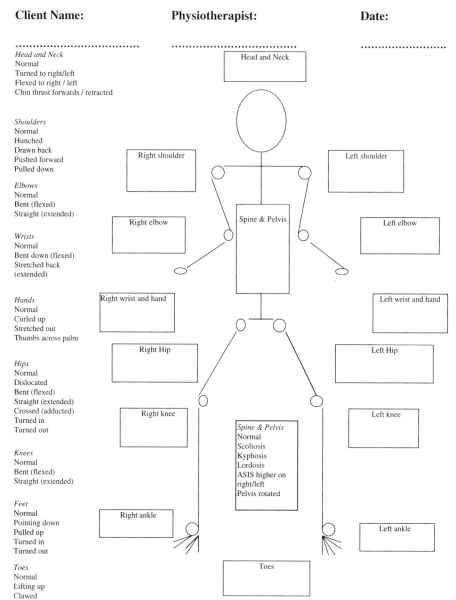

Head and Neck
Normal
Turned to right/left
Flexed to right / left
Chin thrust forwards / retracted

Shoulders
Normal
Hunched
Drawn back
Pushed forward
Pulled down

Elbows
Normal
Bent (flexed)
Straight (extended)

Wrists
Normal
Bent down (flexed)
Stretched back
(extended)

Hands
Normal
Curled up
Stretched out
Thumbs across palm

Hips
Normal
Dislocated
Bent (flexed)
Straight (extended)
Crossed (adducted)
Turned in
Turned out

Knees
Normal
Bent (flexed)
Straight (extended)

Feet
Normal
Pointing down
Pulled up
Turned in
Turned out

Toes
Normal
Lifting up
Clawed

Head and Neck

Right shoulder

Left shoulder

Spine & Pelvis

Right elbow

Left elbow

Right wrist and hand

Left wrist and hand

Right Hip

Left Hip

Right knee

Left knee

Spine & Pelvis
Normal
Scoliosis
Kyphosis
Lordosis
ASIS higher on
right/left
Pelvis rotated

Right ankle

Left ankle

Toes

Figure 7.7. Assessment of deformities, range of movement and muscle tone.

In 1997 the Chartered Society of Physiotherapy with the Association of Chartered Physiotherapists in Neurology (ACPIN) the British Association of Bobath Trained Therapists (BABTT), the Association of Paediatric Chartered Physiotherapists (APCP) and the Association of Chartered Physiotherapists for People with Learning Disabilities (ACCPLD) undertook a study of available assessment and evaluation procedures currently in general use. The brief was to find a method that was sensitive enough to show change in the most profoundly disabled person following physiotherapy treatment. The outcome of the study indicated that TELER, the method devised by A. le Roux (Le Roux 2003), was the most flexible and sensitive.

The TELER method is designed to be a systematic method of clinical note-keeping, not a stand-alone assessment tool. The use of TELER relies on the physiotherapist's underpinning knowledge of pathology, disease, disability and handicap and the ability to carry out an informed assessment as a basis for developing a programme of intervention, goal planning and evaluation. The TELER method is about setting goals, creating indicators for measurement and enabling outcomes to be clearly identified. Examples can be found in Chapter 8.

CONCLUSION

For physiotherapists working with people with learning disabilities there is currently no single assessment method that will satisfy all the needs of the client, primarily because learning disability is not a single medical condition with identifiable boundaries. Physiotherapists therefore have to be flexible in their approach and aware of available resources so that they can undertake accurate assessments upon which to base physiotherapy intervention and measure its outcome. The intervention may, in turn, be part of a multiprofessional programme.

REFERENCES

Barnes, J., Barrell, A., Dennis, C. and Jenkins, J. (1993) *Standards for Good Practice in Physiotherapy Services for People with Learning Disabilities*, Association of Chartered Physiotherapists for People with Learning Disabilities, CSP, London

Bent, N., Tennant, A., Swift, T., Pasnett, J., Suffham, P. and Chamberlain, M.A. (2002) Team approach versus ad hoc health services for young people with physical disabilities: a retrospective cohort study. *Lancet*, **360** (9342), 1264–5.

British College of Occupational Therapists (2003) *Professional Standards for Occupational Therapy Practice*, British College of Occupational Therapists, London

Brown, M. and Rennie, J. (2003) From policy to practice, in *Learning Disability a Handbook for Integrated Care* (ed. Brown M), APS Publishing, Salisbury, Wiltshire, pp. 20–1.

Chartered Society of Physiotherapy (2002) *Guidance in Manual Handling for Chartered Physiotherapists,* CSP, London.

Chartered Society of Physiotherapy (2005) *Standards of Physiotherapy Practice,* Chartered Society of Physiotherapy, London.

Collen, F.M., Wade, D.T., Robb, G.F. and Bradshaw, C.M. (1991) The Rivermead Mobility Index: a further development of the Rivermead Motor Assessment. *International Disability Studies,* **13**, 50–4.

Cyriax, J. (1982) *Textbook of Orthopaedic Medicine,* Vol. 1, 8th edn, Bailliere Tindall, London.

Department of Health (2001*) Valuing People – A New Strategy for Learning Disability for the Twenty-first Century,* Stationery Office, London.

Golding, R. and Goldsmith, L. (1986*) The Caring Person's Guide to Handling the Severely Multiply Handicapped,* Macmillan Education Limited, London.

Hoffer, M., Feiwell, F., Perry, R. and Perry, J. (1973) Functional ambulation in patients with myelomeningocele. *Journal of Bone and Joint Surgery,* **55A**, 137–48.

Kiresuk, T.J., Smith, A., Cardillo, J.E. (eds) (1994) *Goal Attainment Scaling: Applications, Theory and Measurement,* Lawrence Erlbaum, Hillsdale, New Jersey.

Le Roux, A.A. (2003) *The TELER Handbook.* Teler Limited, Sheffield.

Lindsey, M. (1998) *Signposts for Success: in Commissioning and Providing Health Services for People with Learning Disabilities,* Department of Health, London.

Mahoney, F.I. and Barthel, D.W. (1965) Functional evaluation – The Barthel Index. *Maryland State Medical Journal,* **14**, 56–61.

Maitland, G.D., Hergveld, E., Banks, K. and Kay, E. (2005) *Vertebral Manipulation,* 7th revised edn, Butterworth Heinemann, Oxford.

Mathews, D., Hegarty, J. (1997) The OK Health Check: a health assessment checklist for people with learning disabilities. *British Journal for Learning Disabilities,* **25**, 138–43.

McKenzie, R.A. (2003) *The Lumbar Spine, Mechanical Diagnosis and Therapy,* 2nd edn, Spinal Publications, Raumati Beach, New Zealand.

Morris, J. (2002) *Young Disabled People Moving into Adulthood. Foundations 512,* Joseph Rowntree Foundation, York.

Reid, A. and Chesson, R. (1998) Goal attainment scaling: is it appropriate for stroke patients and their physiotherapists? *Physiotherapy,* **84**, 136 –44

Royal College of Speech and Language Therapists (2006) *Communicating Quality 3,* Royal College of Speech and Language Therapists, London.

Russell, D., Rosenbaum, D., Cadman, D., Gowland, C., Hardy, S. and Jarvis, S. (1989) Gross Motor Function Measure, a means to evaluate the effects of physical therapy. *Developmental Medicine and Child Neurology,* **31**, 341–52.

Russell, D.J., Rosenbaum, P.L., Avery, L.M. and Lane, M. (2002) *Gross Motor Function Measure (GMF-66 and GMF-88) User's Manual,* MacKeith Press, Blackwell Scientific Publications Ltd, Oxford.

Scottish Executive (2000) *The Same as You? A Review of Services for People with Learning Disabilities,* Stationery Office, Edinburgh.

Smith, J. (2002) *Smoothing the Transition from Child to Adult Health Care Services for People with Learning Disabilities,* Forth Valley Primary Care NHS Trust, Stirling.

Smull, M. and Sanderson, H. (2001) *Essential Lifestyle Planning: A Handbook for Facilitators,* NWTDT, Manchester.

Wade, D.T. (1992) *Measurement in Neurological Rehabilitation,* Oxford University Press, Oxford.

Wright, J. (2000) *The FIM (TM).* The Center for Outcome Measurement in Brain Injury, New York.

Young, A. and Chesson, R. (1998) Goal attainment scaling as a method of measuring clinical outcome for children with learning disabilities. *British Journal of Occupational Therapy,* **60** (3), 111–14.

8 Interpretation of Assessment Results as a Basis for Intervention and Outcome Measures

ANNELIESE BARRELL

INTRODUCTION

Assessments, as mentioned in Chapter 7, can be undertaken for a variety of reasons and in a variety of ways. The underlying purpose of any assessment is to establish a baseline for further action or intervention.

THE ASSESSMENT REPORT

The assessment report should contain the following:

- the client's name, address and date of birth
- the client's daycare provision
- name and status of the referrer
- initial reason for the referral
- date and result of the assessment
- problems and needs identified
- goals and aims of the intervention
- the intervention plan to include: times, dates, venues, who is involved, an exercise programme (if appropriate) and plans for staff and carer training
- monitoring and review dates, times and venues
- current othortic or mobility equipment

AIMS OF ASSESSMENT:

The aims fall into different categories depending on the reason for the assessment. *The identified needs of the client* could include the following:

- improvement/maintenance of function and ability levels
- development of new skills

Learning Disability: Physical Therapy Treatment and Management. Edited by Jeanette Rennie
© 2007 John Wiley & Sons Ltd

- improvement in quality of life
- reduction in pain
- reduction of spasticity
- improvement in muscle tone
- improvement in muscle strength
- improvement in health status
- increased range of joint movement
- increased concentration
- increased exercise tolerance
- improved motivation

Clients' assessed therapeutic needs do not always coincide with their wishes, therefore the choice of goals will need to take that into consideration. For example, a client may express a wish to walk without pain and without the use of a walking aid but may not be happy to undertake a regular exercise programme aimed at reducing the pain, to increase mobility and improve the gait. The therapist then has to consider all the alternative options to encourage his participation, such as Jabadao, hydrotherapy or a suitable leisure activity adapted to meet his needs (see Part III).

NEEDS OF THE CARER/PARENTS

These cannot be ignored especially for semidependent and totally dependent people with learning disabilities. Dependence on their co-operation is essential in order to achieve any goals or carry out the intervention plan. If the parent is not the main carer there may be differing opinions between carers concerning perceived needs. To address this, there needs to be good communication between the therapist and all concerned with delivering the care to the client. Assessment results and intervention plans need to be very clearly identified, discussed and communicated in order to avoid noncompliance and increased carer stress. The needs of the carer and parents can be identified as the following:

- being able to maintain and or improve their abilities to undertake all that is required to manage the client on a day-to-day basis
- to improve their own and the client's quality of life
- to improve the client's functional abilities
- to relieve and reduce carer stress
- to improve the client's health

SERVICE NEEDS

The provision of any services assessed as being needed by the client is dependent on accurate information in order to do the following:

- Decide how to maximise effective and efficiently delivered treatment based on the best available knowledge, research evidence and current practice.
- Manage resources efficiently. This will include management of staffing levels, provision of modalities such as hydrotherapy and rebound therapy and the provision of therapeutic equipment and treatment bases.
- Plan strategically for future service delivery.
- Develop service and treatment protocols and policies.
- Undertake audit.
- Improve healthcare.
- Improve outcome measurement.
- Ensure client satisfaction.
- Comply with the rights and choices of the individual as laid down in statute and the patient's charters.
- Fulfil health and safety requirements.

INTERPRETATION OF ASSESSMENT RESULTS

Interpreting the assessment results will depend on the following:

- reason for the assessment
- type of assessment
- problems and needs identified
- resources available

A therapist might have been asked to assess a client's position whilst eating. During the assessment for seating and positioning further problems and needs may be identified; for example:

- a medical problem
- a problem of diet
- a problem with the client's swallowing mechanism

These problems will then be referred to the appropriate disciplines or if available to a dysphagia team for further intervention and possible team goal setting.

Assessment results vary considerably and are often completely unexpected. The client has to be *seen* to perform an action not to rely on the opinion of a carer. Clients with learning disabilities constantly surprise therapists by their ability to do something that had previously been thought impossible because of historical and anecdotal data. It is very easy to further disable a client by not being accurate and specific in assessment and by the interpretation of assessment data. However what is *seen* is not always the *problem* or the *need*. Clients with a learning disability have an uncanny ability to mask symptoms and problems; their pain threshold can be high, very low or nonexistent. The therapist has then to enquire further by visiting the day provision or home and consulting the medical file (if it is available and accessible).

- It is common for clients who have always lived in the family home not to have a medical file that is easily accessible to community-based therapists.
- Clients in the community are usually referred by nonmedical personnel (see Chapter 7).
- Clients resettled from long-stay hospitals into the community may have their medical files lodged within the community team base or with the team physician/psychiatrist.

ACTION PLAN

A plan of action is decided once the assessment result has been interpreted – *for example: a worsening scoliosis*. This plan must be discussed and decided by all concerned with the client's care and if possible with the client. Intervention for a scoliosis could involve any or all of the following:

- refer to an orthopaedic surgeon for a baseline
- exercise programme
- positioning advice to carers
- special seating, assessment, reassessment or provision
- hydrotherapy
- rebound therapy
- orthotics, provision of a spinal jacket
- staff/carer training
- surgery

The aim of the therapist's intervention would be the following:

- to prevent further deterioration
- to maintain/improve limb function and trunk mobility
- to maintain an acceptable posture in sitting and lying (and standing if possible)
- to maintain and improve quality of life
- to increase the range of choices available to the client
- to maintain/improve respiratory function

(For more detailed management of scoliosis see Chapter 10.)

Results from the assessment, which are embodied in the action plan, can create real problems for carers and therapists when planning appropriate interventions. These involve time, venue and resources.

TIME

The time taken to enable any intervention to happen can cause the following:

- staffing and staff rota problems
- problems for busy parents
- time of day can create problems for busy community therapists trying to fit in with everyone else's timetable and their own large caseload and workload

VENUE

The venue for the intervention can create problems with the following:

- transport from home or day provision to physiotherapy department, hydrotherapy pool, rebound therapy
- staff available to accompany the client

RESOURCES

The availability of required resources to carry out the intervention plan can be a problem. If they are not available they should be recorded as an unmet need. For example, the unavailability of a hoist or manual handling aids at the poolside or for rebound therapy could restrict the use by the more physically disabled client.

TREATMENT PLAN

Therapeutic intervention requires a treatment plan. Once this has been written further practical questions are raised, which include the following:

- Who is going to be responsible for overseeing the treatment plan in a multiprofessional or multiagency situation? Is there a key worker?
- To whom should the treatment plan be sent?
- Who needs to be taught how to implement the plan?

In a uniprofessional situation the therapist responsible for the client's treatment will be responsible for setting reassessment, review and evaluation dates and times and informing all concerned. In team situations the need for a key or link worker is agreed and a decision is made as to who should assume that responsibility.

Most learning disabilities teams have a strategic policy that gives guidelines to its staff regarding timescales, for example from referral to first contact with the client, from assessment to assessment report being written and sent and to whom. If this is not in place a fair time would be: five working days from receipt of referral to first contact and 21 working days following assessment to the report being written and sent to the client, carers, care manager, medical practitioner and daycare provision.

GOAL PLANNING

The plan of therapeutic intervention – the goal plan – is decided following assessment and discussion between: the client, the carers, relevant therapists and members of the multiprofessional and multiagency team, the care manager and, if relevant, the client's general practitioner who should always be informed of any proposed action. It should be a part of the client's care plan. The advent of the care programming approach to client care takes all of this into consideration making it part of assessment and screening protocols.

Goals are set that will be based on a combination of desired outcomes decided by the client, the carers, the healthcare team, the therapist and the service. Plans for the teaching and training of carers and support staff skills are necessary to enable clients to achieve these goals. They should be decided upon and communicated to the relevant people.

The long-term goal may take a considerable time to achieve. It can, therefore, be broken down into a series of short-term goals. Short-term goals are smaller targets, which should be:

- measurable, achievable, timed and realistic and able to lead towards achieving the long-term goal
- written in language easily understood by all those involved in implementing them
- recorded, monitored and reviewed at regular and stated intervals

---

Example: A household ambulator – Hoffer Scale 2 (Hoffer et al. 1973).
See Chapter 7 for modified Hoffer Scale

Long-term goal: to walk independently.
  Short-term goals:

- to stand independently for a timed period at agreed frequency
- to walk a short measured distance indoors without apparatus, frequency to be agreed
- to walk a short measured distance outdoors with apparatus at agreed frequency
- to walk a short measured distance outdoors without apparatus at agreed frequency
- to walk independently at all times

The method of intervention and monitoring will be decided following discussion with the client and carers.

MONITORING THE INTERVENTION

In Chapter 7, a recent study of assessment and evaluation methods was mentioned which found that the Le Roux method (Le Roux 2003) was sensitive enough for people with profound learning and physical disabilities.

THE LE ROUX METHOD

Goals are written with specific indicators on an ordinal scale of 0 to 5. They can:

- be constantly monitored
- show change
- show the factors influencing change be it: client/carer compliance, change in client health status, change in venue, therapist, weather, time, staffing levels, level of skills of the key staff assisting the client.
- indicate the training needs of the key personnel

In addition the unique method of TELER recording gives an accurate at-a-glance indication of the client's current situation/state.

The TELER method is sensitive enough to indicate minute change or no change, which is very relevant when the desired outcome is maintenance of the healthcare status in cases where there is profound and multiple disability (Chartered Society of Physiotherapy pilot study on the 'measurement of outcome of profound disability' 1997, Chapter 7). This and any other methods of assessment are very dependent on an accurate and informed assessment of need and on sound underpinning clinical knowledge.

Example: moving from supported standing to taking independent steps forward

0 unable to take steps forward unsupported by therapist or carer
1 able to stand supported by apparatus
2 able to stand unsupported but cannot shift balance
3 able to stand unsupported and shift balance for a timed period
4 able to stand unsupported and shift balance all the time
5 able to independently move forward

For each goal the treatment plan would include specific exercises/activities to enable the client to progress.

Goals that are not achieved within the specified conditions should be evaluated for:

- client/carer compliance
- appropriateness
- achievability
- other factors

New goals should be considered taking all the above into account.

It is always possible that some goals may never be achieved for a variety of reasons. The therapist then has to decide if it is time to give up. The decision may be influenced by any of the following:

- healthcare service requirements/policies
- staffing resources
- time
- availability of carer support
- transport

THE MOVE CURRICULUM

The MOVE curriculum (Mobility Opportunities Via Education), which incorporates an as yet nonvalidated method of measurement for functional movement, is increasingly being used with adults in the UK. This educational philosophy was originally used with children in schools in the US. It involves testing, setting goals, task analysis, identifying equipment and measuring prompts required to achieve a task; identifying where a reduction of prompts could be achieved in an agreed duration and planning how to teach the skills for everyday life. It is highly dependent upon commitment to the plan by all carers and staff who work with the clients.

Both the Le Roux and MOVE systems require expenditure before they can be fully used.

MEASUREMENT OF OUTCOME

This should reflect:

- changes in/alteration of function
- changes in health status of the clients
- changes in knowledge or behaviour pertinent to any future health status
- client satisfaction

It can be as simple as :

- nonachievement
- partial achievement
- full achievement

There are many forms of research-based outcome measurements now available to the therapist as shown by Enderby et al. (2006). This brings together valid and reliable outcome measures in a useful format for uniprofessional and multiprofessional working.

The four domains used in this book – impairment, activity, participation and wellbeing – are compatible with the *International Classification of Functioning, Disability and Health (ICF)* (WHO 2001). This states that with ICF it has moved from 'the purely medical model to an integrated biopsychosocial model of human functioning and disability.' It is a model in which the components interact dynamically with each other.

Definitions of the components

- *Body functions* are physiological functions of body systems (including psychological functions).
- *Body structures* are anatomical parts of the body such as organs, limbs and their components.
- *Impairments* are problems in body function or structure, such as a significant deviation or loss.
- *Activity* is the execution of a task or action by an individual.
- *Participation* is involvement in a life situation.
- *Activity limitations* are difficulties an individual may have in executing activities.
- *Participation restrictions* are problems an individual may experience in involvement in life situations.
- *Environmental factors* make up the physical, social and attitudinal environment in which people live and conduct their lives

(WHO 2001)

These components are structured in domains: body function and body structure, activity and participation and environmental factors.

The list of domains is used for classification purposes once 'qualifiers' are introduced.

THE QUALIFIERS

Primary Qualifier

The primary qualifier records impairment of body structure and function and measures its severity on a scale of 0 to 5 (no impairment, mild, moderate, severe and complete).

The activity and participation list of domains uses the *performance qualifier* and the *capacity qualifier* to code information about disability and health.

The Performance Qualifier

This describes how individuals function in their own natural environment and allows the use of their normal equipment and personal assistance.

The Capacity Qualifier

This describes a task or an action carried out under controlled conditions. Individuals carry out the function to the best of their ability.

The difference between capacity and performance indicates the effect of the environment on functional ability.

Further examples of outcome measures that have been adapted for specific modalities and activities can be found in Chapters 11, 12 and 14.

CONCLUSION

Interpretation of assessment results, writing of goals and care plans and the training and teaching of carers, parents and other professionals are dependent upon a variety of circumstances and events, which alter from client to client. The whole process has to be individual to the client's needs but it is also essential that the needs of the carers are included.

The most effective level of service to the client is achieved when good communication between all those involved with delivering the service is accepted as a priority.

Treatment must be monitored and the outcomes of the goals set must be measured to ensure that the intervention is effective and is seen to be effective. To this end methods of measuring outcomes are constantly being developed, tested and peer validated.

REFERENCES

Enderby, P., Alexandra, J., Petheram, B. (2006) *Therapy Outcome Measures for Rehabilitation Professions: Speech and Language Therapy; Physiotherapy; Occupational Therapy,* 2nd edn, John Wiley & Sons, Ltd, Chichester.

Hoffer, M., Feiwell, M.M., Perry, R. and Perry, J. (1973) Functional ambulation in patients with myelomeningocele. *Journal of Bone and Joint Surgery,* **55A,** 137–48.

Le Roux, A.A. (2003) *The TELER Handbook.* Teler Limited, Sheffield.

WHO (2001) *The International Classification of Functioning, Disability and Health,* World Health Organisation, Geneva.

III Practical Treatment and Management

9 Postural Care

JOHN GOLDSMITH AND LIZ GOLDSMITH

SECTION 1: DEVELOPING A SERVICE TO PROVIDE POSTURAL CARE AT NIGHT

INTRODUCTION

People who are unable to move well may be at risk of developing distortions of body shape over a period of time. Fulford and Brown (1976) identified destructive positions as a cause of this and called for therapeutic intervention. The development of a postural care service will seek to allow individuals to enjoy life while providing them with supported symmetrical postures in sitting and lying, with standing being included if appropriate, over most of 24 hours a day to protect body structures.

Since the mid-1960s therapists and manufacturers have combined to develop symmetrical support in sitting and standing. Seating systems to control upright functional sitting include stabilisation of the upright posture, which can be tolerated for limited periods (Mulcahy 1986), while multiadjustable armchairs with tilt-in-space facilities cater for the need to provide symmetrical supported postures during the hours that must be spent relaxing (Medical Devices Agency 1995). In one variety, the facility to use the chair for side lying, prone and postural drainage offers the individual changes of position and function with one piece of equipment. Moulded seating interfaced with a wheelchair offers support for mobility for people whose body shape cannot be accommodated in more conventional wheelchairs (Nelham 1984). Pressure relief is provided by a variety of foams, gels and flotation cushions (Young 1992; Lowthian 1997). Standing frames offer the opportunity to progressively bear weight from prone to upright for those who are able (Green et al. 1993).

The routine application of support and protection of a growing body in the lying posture is a concept that is acknowledged (Bell and Watson 1985) but is only gradually being generalised within community services. The distorting effect of gravity on body shape of young babies has long been recognised and their need for supported positioning to counteract abnormal tone has been developed (Fulford and Brown 1976; Bellefeuille-Reid and Jakubek 1989;

Learning Disability: Physical Therapy Treatment and Management. Edited by Jeanette Rennie
© 2007 John Wiley & Sons Ltd

Turrill 1992; Hallsworth 1995). These principles logically extend to the motor-impaired child and adult and it is suggested that abnormality of tone and movement with the critical factor of resultant loss of extension at hips and knees causes individuals to lie in destructive postures for long periods at night from a very young age; these habitual lying positions very often become recognisable as the pattern of fixed distortion of body shape as the person grows. Therapeutic skill lies in recognition and correction of seemingly innocuous deviations from symmetry before damage to skeletal structures occurs. Evidence on which to base clinical practice is plentiful and readily available by investigating habitual lying postures and analysing the consequent body shapes in adults.

Recently, equipment has been developed that allows for comfortable, versatile adjustment of support and control in any lying posture, for any shape or size of user. Short-term results of use indicate significant benefits, even for those with established problems and it is considered that accurate therapeutic positioning at night offers an important opportunity to influence body shape for the following reasons:

- The time available for application of corrective forces is in the region of 10 hours per night offering periods of stretch in excess of the six hours frequently accepted as being necessary to maintain muscle length (Tardieu et al. 1988).
- During sleep, with the comfort of supported positioning, the perverse influences of abnormal tone are reduced allowing more correction than is available during the day.
- At night there are no other demands being made on the individual, so that therapy can be carried out without inconvenience.
- Associated improvements in sleep patterns and wellbeing ensure that parents are continuously motivated to carry out the therapy consistently in the long term.

Section 1 of this chapter will reflect the experience of provision of this care by therapy services in Mansfield, Nottinghamshire. Feedback has been extracted from a study involving 31 families who have been offered Symmetrisleep night positioning equipment.

IDENTIFICATION OF THOSE IN NEED OF POSTURAL CARE

The Mansfield Checklist of Need for Postural Care

Provision of a postural care service requires acknowledgement of need and cooperation from all those involved in the individual's care, including management and hands-on carers. These factors have therefore been expressed in nonmedical terms to increase accessibility:

- Does the individual tend to stay in a limited number of positions?
- Do the knees seem to be drawn to one side? . . . or outwards? . . . or inwards? . . .

- Does the head seem to turn mainly to one side? . . . to the right? . . . or the left? . . .
- Does the body tend to flex forwards? . . . or extend backwards? . . .
- Does the trunk tend to bend to the right? . . . or the left? . . .
- Is the body shape already asymmetric? . . .

DEVELOPING A REGISTER OF PEOPLE IN NEED OF POSTURAL CARE

It is suggested that minimum data collection for each individual on the register would include the following:

- An estimation of the dominant distorting tendencies within the body using the Mansfield checklist.
- Photographic evidence of the individual's unsupported and supported postures in lying. (It has been found that photographs taken from the end of the bed tend to give a useful perspective.)
- An estimation of lying and sitting ability using the Chailey scales (Mulcahy et al. 1988; Pountney et al. 1990).
- Measurement of body symmetry (Goldsmith et al. 1992).
- X-ray analysis.

This register and minimum data collection would form the basis of educational material to alert clinical and financial management to the need for postural care within a community and also to work with individual parents, carers and clients.

PROVIDING TRAINING AND SUPPORT FOR CARERS

Analysis of time spent in daytime occupation and with parents and carers reveals that most time is spent at home (Table 9.1).

Providing good postural care as a routine domestic habit may require behavioural change within the family. To initiate that change, a high level of training, support and efficient equipment provision is needed in the early stages. The younger the individual is when carers are introduced to the principles of postural care, the easier it is.

Table 9.1. Breakdown of time spent during a year

Hours in the year	8760
Daytime occupation, for example:	
9.00 a.m. until 3.00 p.m. × 5 days	1440
a week × 48 weeks	
Hours at home	7320
Hours in bed, for example:	
10.00 p.m. until 8.00 a.m. × 365 days	3650

Support for carers is provided in the following ways:

- good training and preparation
- regular phone calls during the first weeks
- individual practical sessions
- follow up clinics in which carers set up the positioning so that effectiveness can be checked and changes made if necessary
- home visits

The aims of training are that the carer will understand the destructive effect of static asymmetric postures, be able to identify joints at risk and to correct the individual's posture effectively. The following strategies are used in this programme:

- individual teaching
- demonstration
- diagrams
- photographs
- keeping a postural care diary
- group family workshops

'Postural Care: Family Workshop'

These formal workshops provide a theoretical basis for the carer's developing skills. The text of the family workshop contained in a slideshow and booklets (Goldsmith and Goldsmith 1996; Goldsmith et al., 1998) includes the following concepts:

> Therapy has two halves: (1) postural care; (2) development and mainte-
> nance of function.

Development and maintenance of function has tended to be a high-profile aspect of therapy, perhaps because it offers the possibility of short-term rewards. Unfortunately, without systematic provision of supported postures in sitting, standing and lying, short-term gains can be lost in the long term by developing distortion of body shape. Postural care, offering long-term protection of body shape, should become the foundation of therapy. On this foundation individuals can be encouraged to function according to their natural condition.

> What is postural care?
> Protection of body shape by supporting the body in a straight and com-
> fortable position both in the day and at night.

Carers are empowered by the assurance that providing postural care is a common-sense, practical skill, akin to packaging any vulnerable object.

Does the person I look after need postural care?

The Mansfield checklist is used to allow carers to identify for themselves that they may need to provide postural care.

Working together

It is stressed that there is a need to work together with therapists in an ongoing relationship, constantly changing strategies as the individual grows and changes.

Once carers are skilled in positioning they are able to continue providing postural care despite changes in therapy personnel and service provision.

The following three terms are used when talking about postural care: (1) destructive postures; (2) supported postures; (3) postural moulding.

A basic vocabulary needs to be established, which is often simplified to such terms as 'bad postures' and 'good postures' once they have been identified and photographed in individuals.

What are destructive postures? Postures in which the body may be damaged by being left unsupported. While in these postures some of the joints may be stressed.

Carers need to be aware of the damage that can occur when individuals are left in destructive postures. To date some therapists may be unaware of these destructive postures, often occurring at home and in the night, negating hands-on therapeutic effort when traditionally the therapist's remit has been to provide input during the day. When parents are uninformed and without the necessary equipment these postures can act as an unacknowledged threat to the body shape and abilities of the individual. The prospect of their young children not growing into a conventional human shape is a notoriously hard concept for parents to accept but it needs to be stressed that early intervention is necessary as it is easier to maintain symmetry than to correct damage and distortion.

> What are supported postures?
>   Postures in which the natural shape of the body is protected and all joints are supported in a neutral, comfortable position.

The key to provision of a postural care service is that individual work is done to devise, equip and photograph supported postures for each person. The implications of informing parents of this need is that a service must be integrated to provide the equipment necessary. To date, service provision has not become fully integrated, resulting in the continuation of haphazard and all too often unsuccessful aspects of care in much of Britain.

> Symmetrical support is needed in sitting, standing and lying.

Very often the possibilities of providing supported standing reduce as the individual grows larger and handling becomes more difficult. However, support in symmetrical sitting and lying should continue throughout adult life. For many adults who have not had the benefit of postural care the aims are to increase comfort levels, reduce tone and gradually to coax the body into a less destructive position.

> What is postural moulding?
>   The use of posture to allow the force of gravity, as it presses down, to mould the body to the shape you want.

This can be explained with particular reference to the chest, it is demonstrated that if the chest is positioned in lying with the sternum directly above the spine, gravity as it presses down will flatten the chest in a symmetrical manner. Lateral support will reduce the flattening spread of the chest. If the chest is positioned with the sternum to one side the flattening effect will tend to distort the chest and spine asymmetrically.

Night time is the best time to provide postural moulding because:

1. Muscle spasms are reduced when the individual is asleep.
2. The body is lying down flat so that gravity can be used to straighten the body.
3. At night there are long periods of time during which no other demands are made of the individual.

The benefits of successful postural care:

1. Protection of body shape.
2. Improved function.
3. Reduced long-term need for surgery.
4. Reduced need for expensive, complex equipment to cater for future problems in body shape.
5. Health gain for the individual, improved quality of life, improved sleeping patterns and reduced pain.
6. Resultant health and emotional gain for all the family.

Postural Care Leaflets

To explain the concept that habitual static night positions will have an influence on the individual's shape and ability to develop and maintain function in the day, the following lighthearted illustrations and simple text are used.

THE ASSESSMENT PROCEDURE

SLEEP AND THE FAMILY

All assessments must be carried out with hands-on participation by the carers. Before assessing the physical support that is needed it is important to have an understanding of sleep processes (Ferber 1986) and gain an insight into the established sleep behaviours of the individual.

It has been acknowledged that individuals with multiple neurological disabilities associated with distortion of body shape often have disturbed sleep, which does not respond easily to treatment. Polysomnographic evidence

Lying squint can cause problems

Lying with legs to one side makes it difficult to sit straight

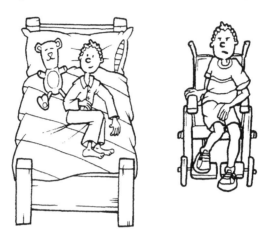

Lying with knees out to the side makes it a problem to bend in the morning

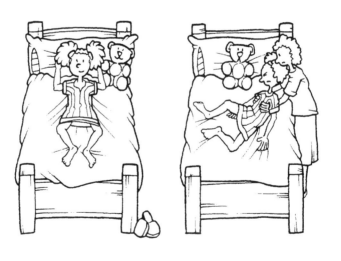

Figure 9.1. Lying squint can cause problems.

Lying with knees together makes it hard to sit and stand

Lying with backs bent makes it hard to sit straight in the day

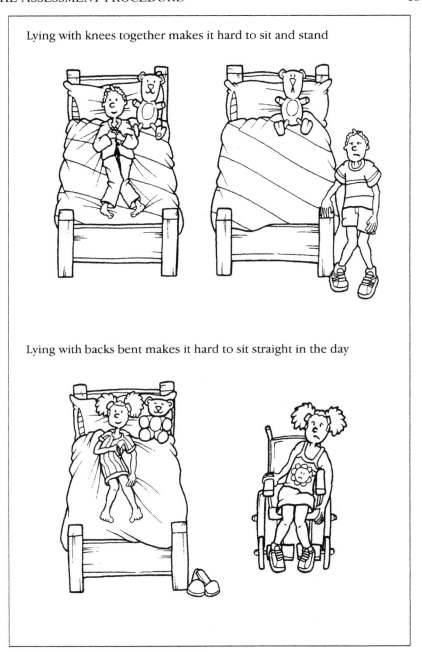

Figure 9.1. *Continued*

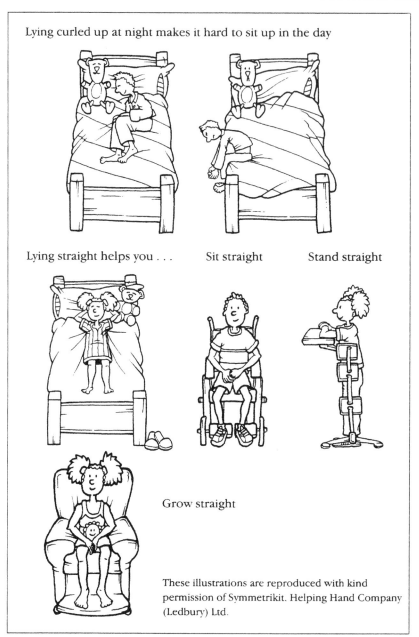

Lying curled up at night makes it hard to sit up in the day

Lying straight helps you . . .   Sit straight   Stand straight

Grow straight

These illustrations are reproduced with kind permission of Symmetrikit. Helping Hand Company (Ledbury) Ltd.

Figure 9.1. *Continued*

reveals increased apnoea of central and obstructive origin, decreased ability to change body position and epileptiform discharges in the sleep of people with severe cerebral palsy (Kotagel et al. 1994). Circadian rhythms may be disturbed (Okawa et al. 1986), and the behavioural approach, sedation and analgesics may have been tried but found to be ineffective with this group (Jan et al. 1994). In these circumstances the physician may be presented with an exhausted individual, unable to communicate adequately, possibly suffering from chronic pain of uncertain origin, accompanied by a desperate family with no simple answer to their problems. Careful consideration should therefore be given to any potential solutions that may offer some help to this small minority of people who find themselves providing care in the community under almost intolerable circumstances. It has been suggested that melatonin may be helpful in the management of individuals whose main presenting problem is interruption of circadian rhythms and who are unable to respond to other interventions (Jan et al. 1994).

As sleep behaviour will have a profound effect on the family, it is a subject that must be addressed in a tolerant, sensitive and generous manner. Therapists who do not enjoy working closely with all kinds of families will not find this area of therapy rewarding.

Physical assessment will be carried out over a period of time, with some individuals adapting immediately to the intervention and some requiring a period during which both the position and equipment used are adjusted. There may also be a need for time spent 'getting used' to the equipment and a willingness to 'give up' for a time and to 'try again' when the family feels ready. The 'aches and pains' experienced in the initial stages of even slight alterations to sleeping positions must be allowed for. Many people find that positioning is best applied after the individual has settled into bed and has become drowsy; there is no need to apply positioning the moment the individual goes to bed. In general, simple solutions are more likely to be accepted by families than complicated arrangements. The long-term benefits of 10 hours therapy a day are worth every effort to establish a successful habit, although most mistakes are made in the introduction of too much change, too soon, with insufficient training and support.

Feedback from the 31 Mansfield families illustrates the variations in time taken to establish a night positioning habit, with some taking to it 'instantly' and one needing 12 months to establish the correct position and become used to it.

Detailed results of the study have been written up (Peters et al. 1998) and are encouraging, with benefits described in reduction of high tone, improvements in sleeping patterns and with users sleeping as shown in Table 9.2.

POSITIONING AT NIGHT

It has been recognised that individuals with severe movement problems do not move from one position to another during the night as able-bodied people

Table 9.2. Benefits from the Mansfield study

In a much straighter position	19
In a straighter position	5
About the same	5
In a less straight position	0
In a much less straight position	0
Could not answer	2

do. Kotagel et al. (1994) observed that, in a group of nine disabled people, there were only three significant changes of position during a night, compared with 59 changes in position in an able-bodied control group. Assessment will begin from the habitual position and seek to reduce the destructive tendencies of the position. The equipment, patented as 'Symmetrisleep', allows for infinite variations of support and control for these habitual static positions. It comprises a Velcro sheet attached to the mattress to fix the positioning components, which are a variety of brackets, pads and cushions. An 'overmantel' of foam or sheepskin may be used to cover the supporting structures and is in turn covered by a stretch sheet.

A Symmetrisleep Knee Cosy is used for those individuals who need control to maintain a particular hip posture in association with total body control. Temperature sensitive foams of various consistencies are adjusted within zipped compartments to offer the support and control that is needed.

POSITIONING EXERCISES

Therapists and carers can experience the sensation of changes in body position by using the equipment themselves although they will probably be habitually too mobile to tolerate restriction overnight. Use of strapping to simulate loss of hip and knee extension will enable them to experience the obligation to lie in typical windswept, adducted or abducted postures when in prone or supine.

SAFETY CONSIDERATIONS

Considering the vulnerability of this group, care should be taken when assessing risk. The following factors need to be considered when thinking about introducing subtle change to night positioning habits:

- breathing
- reflux
- epileptic fits
- temperature control

Breathing

Individuals with fixed distortion of body shape may have a very limited repertoire of breathing patterns and therefore extreme care should be taken to ensure that changes of position do not compromise ventilation. An oximeter may be useful in these cases. Some will suffer from apnoea of obstructive or central origin as a result of their condition, resulting in alarms and positive pressure breathing equipment being in use. Positioning of the head and neck must be carefully monitored in these individuals.

Reflux

Individuals who suffer from reflux must be positioned in such a way as to ensure that airways are not compromised should this occur during the night. Position as it affects tube feeding using percutaneous endoscopic gastrostomy (PEG) should be considered.

Epileptic Fits

As people with multiple disabilities have an increased tendency to suffer from epilepsy and fits may occur during the night (Kotagel et al. 1994), care must be taken to investigate the type and severity of fits and advice should be sought as to the implications of control of posture at night.

Temperature Control

A variety of equipment can be selected to ensure that temperature can be regulated to suit the individual. With use of an overmantel the moulded shape created will decrease the amount of air circulating over the skin surface and will therefore tend to beneficially increase body heat for those who tend to be cold. For those with a high body temperature, brackets and pads, sometimes combined with the use of sheepskins, allows for efficient positioning without an increase in body temperature. These strategies, along with alterations in the quilt, blankets and sheets used over the top will allow for temperature to be regulated in association with protection of body shape.

ANALYSIS OF DESTRUCTIVE AND SUPPORTED POSTURES

The following section, illustrated with an individual with normal movement, is included to sensitise therapists to the innocuous early stages of deviation from symmetry. In each position destructive and supported postures are identified, and the need to control the whole body must be recognised as control of one segment will often result in abnormality of tone transferring to another part. There are typical destructive postures that are often adopted, with typical, easily identifiable results. Observation of the body shape of adults will often betray the habitual lying posture which will vary in detail according to the individual but may be because of the downward force of gravity working in combination with four main factors:

- lack of physical support
- abnormality of tone associated with loss of extension at hips and knees
- habit
- the flattening effect of the weight of bedclothes

Side Lying Position

Although often identified as a functional position for during the day, particularly for people who tend to extend, unsupported side lying is potentially an extremely destructive position to sleep in. When an individual is asleep extensor tone is reduced and function is not so relevant, the factors influencing the choice of side lying at night should therefore be recognised as very different from those influencing the individual during the day. Choice of side lying will be influenced by an established positional habit, often with associated limited repertoire of breathing patterns and the need to protect the airway for individuals who suffer from reflux or fits.

Destructive Postures in Side Lying

When in side lying the underneath shoulder will inevitably be moved either forwards or back, introducing rotational distortion into the chest, which combined with the weight of the top arm will effectively flatten and twist the thorax. Typically, the shoulders will be pushed upwards and inwards with the scapulae migrating around to the sides. The pelvis will be pulled either forwards or back by the weight of the top leg compounding rotational destruction, stressing the hip joints and establishing gross asymmetry of the leg posture. It is very difficult to balance the chest and pelvis in a true side lying position. As illustrated in Figures 9.1 and described in Fulford and Brown (1976), as soon as an individual becomes asymmetric the moulding effect of gravity quickly distorts both the chest and pelvis. This pattern often becomes recognisable as the pattern of fixed distortion as the individual gets older and attempts are made to seat the rotated pelvis and support the scoliotic chest.

Supported Postures in Side Lying

Supporting side lying symmetrically is difficult. Attempts must be made to shape the supporting surface to accept the underneath shoulder; taking the weight of the top arm will reduce its flattening effect on the chest. The head, neck and waist need shaped support in order to keep them in line. The weight of the top leg needs to be completely supported to prevent it from tilting or rotating the pelvis. Although this can be done it has been found that devices to support the top leg adequately can be difficult for the user and family to accept.

Prone Position

For those who like to sleep in a prone position, it is often a strong and comforting habit and it can be difficult for a person who habitually sleeps prone to be able to adapt to an alternative position, although the destructive patterns can be extremely perverse.

Destructive Postures in Prone

When lying unsupported in prone the head will be turned to one side to breathe, introducing rotation to the chest. An asymmetric lordosis is typical in this group.

There are three main categories of destructive posture affecting the legs and pelvis in prone

- Windswept prone. To accommodate hip flexion contractures, evident in many subjects, the body is often moved into a semi side lying position with the legs rotated to one side and the knees drawn up. Typically a windswept body shape results, often with severe internal rotation of the underneath leg.
- Prone with legs turned out. This group are those who lie with the knees out to each side. Frequently anterior dislocation of the hips leads to associated severe difficulties with sitting and subsequent spinal problems.
- Prone with legs turned in. This group will often start with a seemingly innocuous internal rotation at the hips but as loss of extension increases at the hips and knees an extremely perverse pattern emerges with leverage of the lower leg creating severe internal rotation at the hips.

Supported Postures in Prone

If the chest is raised with a small wedge the individual may be able to turn the head with less rotation travelling into the chest.

For those who are 'windswept' packing under the hips to accommodate hip flexion enables the pelvis and legs to be moved to a more neutral position. Lateral support combined with a pommel shape will help to support the legs.

For those whose legs turn out, hip flexion combined with lateral support may reduce the severity of external rotation combined with extension at the hips.

For those who internally rotate, correction is relatively easy in the early stages with a pommel and lateral supports, becoming more difficult once the lower leg is raised from the supporting surface when the hip is in a more neutral position.

For all categories, packing to support as small an amount of knee flexion as possible will help to allow the feet to remain plantargrade.

Supine Position

This is the easiest position in which to reduce destructive tendencies in the body and to provide symmetrical support. Persuading an individual to sleep in supine may be introduced very gradually, perhaps introducing the position for periods in the day to start with and then for short periods at night. Achieving a symmetrical supine sleeping position will have significant beneficial impact in the long term.

Destructive Postures in Supine

Although the chest will often rest relatively symmetrically in supine, lateral trunk flexion may occur and the chest will tend to flatten. There are three main categories of destructive posture of the legs and pelvis in supine, resulting from loss of extension, as in prone.

- Windswept supine. In this posture the legs are frequently drawn or fall to one side with the result that the knees flatten to the ground and the pelvis drops backwards on the opposite side.
- Supine with legs turned out. In this posture the extreme external rotation at the hips may cause anterior dislocation and create problems with hip flexion and resultant spinal problems.
- Supine with internal rotation at the hips. The natural tendency of some individuals to adduct at the hips combines with hip and knee flexion to lever the hips into increased internal rotation.

Supported Postures in Supine

Minimal support to provide enough knee flexion to give comfort, combined with lateral boundaries, will maintain hips, knees and pelvis symmetrically without increasing hip and knee flexion contractures. Any device that introduces more hip flexion than necessary will merely increase the disability of the individual.

Lateral boundaries at the hips and sides of the chest can be used to maintain trunk symmetry. Support for the feet can be provided with cushioning or soft AFOs.

SECTION 2: POSTURAL CARE SKILLS PROGRAMME: EMPOWERING FAMILIES AND CARERS

INTRODUCTION

Section 1 of this chapter described postural care at night. Section 2 describes 24-hour postural care, which is a gentle, respectful approach that enables individuals with movement difficulties to grow and/or stay as straight, independent and comfortable as possible. Good physical care is fundamental to wellbeing and has a profound beneficial effect on quality of life for the individual and all those who care for them. A course called the Postural Care Skills Programme (PCSP)© provides a qualification for families and carers, to give them the knowledge and skills to successfully self manage this therapeutic approach. 'Given enough information and the chance to talk things over with peers ordinary people (in this context non-medical people) are more than capable of understanding complex issues and making meaningful choices about them' (Suroweicki 2004).

CURRENT PROVISION, CULTURE AND VALUE BASE: THE MEDICAL MODEL

A seminal article by Fulford and Brown (1976) identified position as a cause of what was then termed 'deformity' and called for physiotherapeutic intervention and yet in 2005 the medical model has not delivered relevant National Standards and services to provide this care are still inadequate. Many services routinely fail to provide either structured training or a reliable source of equipment and label the family's difficulties with making changes in care routines as 'noncompliance'. The terminology employed by professionals subscribing to the medical model reveals a culture in which families are expected to do as they are told and includes the terms 'assessment' and 'prescription' without including families and carers in that assessment process. Lack of 'compliance' is then cited as a major problem, when in fact families and professional carers have encyclopaedic knowledge and experience of living with chronic complex needs. The difficulties in producing scientific evidence in relation to these multifactorial physical, behavioural and social issues are used as an excuse to discredit common-sense solutions to obvious problems and, as a result, individuals are left to lie and sit in easily avoidable destructive postures which result in damage to body structures and muscle tone.

CULTURAL CHANGE: THE SOCIAL MODEL

When searching for solutions to these problems the option of employing enough therapists to provide 24-hour care for all those in need is clearly impractical and it is suggested that a social model of empowerment to raise widespread knowledge and skill must be considered (Carpenter 2000; Samuel and Pritchard 2001). When considering the timings involved it is clear that postural care has to be applied by families and carers on an ongoing basis:

- there are 8760 hours in the year
- typically an individual will spend approximately 1140 hours at school or 1440 at day care, 7320 hours with family and 3650 hours in bed

The key to providing successful postural care is to empower families and carers. Valuing people with profound multiple learning disability (PMLD) requires family and professional carers to have access to high-quality specialised training to provide the best possible care. At present many individuals are responsible for providing complex care but are left without the understanding, training and equipment required. By empowering and valuing carers through quality assured training, we value people with movement problems.

The terminology of those subscribing to the concept of postural 'care' includes 'empowerment through education', 'collaboration' and 'support'. The PCSP acknowledges, enhances and formalises the already existing, vast skill of families and professional carers. They are taught therapeutic principles, carry out their own risk/benefit analyses and make their own plans as to how theory can be applied to the complexities and reality of their situation. Within the social model PCSP tutors may come from many different backgrounds but demonstrating genuine respect for the rewarding but demanding role of both family and professional carers is a fundamental requirement. The highly structured nature of the course enables tutors to acquire the necessary clinical skills. Tutors provide high-quality training, collaborate to access appropriate equipment and then give ongoing support.

THE NEED

The vast range of existing skills of both family and professional carers needs to be enhanced and formalised so that the following principles become common knowledge:

- Identification of need. This section covers how and why the body distorts. It involves identification of destructive postures and conversely the supportive symmetrical postures, which protect body shape (Symmetrikit Postural Care Pathway 2002).
- Pain and consent. This section contains analysis of pain-related and non-pain-related behaviours leading to the development of a baseline score so that pain can be monitored and managed. As the approach is founded on gentleness and the development of relaxation and confidence this also allows the individual's level of consent to be identified and respected.

- Achieving thermal comfort. The concepts in this section cover understanding of the complexity of achieving thermal comfort when both the reflex and behavioural components of thermal regulation may be compromised. Learners apply routine monitoring of core temperature and application of appropriate thermal care.
- Therapeutic positioning at night. The topics covered introduce an understanding of the behavioural complexities, physical dangers and disturbances of sleep behaviour in those with neurological impairment, as described in Section 1. Students learn about application of therapeutic positioning at night in a safe, humane manner. Night positioning has been found to be effective in preventing/reducing distortion of body shape as it typically accounts for approximately 4000 hours per year at a time when the body tends to be relaxed and susceptible to gentle supportive forces (Goldsmith 2000).
- Use of equipment. This covers use of postural care equipment effectively, safely and humanely.

THE PROGRAMME

The highly structured course to provide this training is a nationally recognised qualification, quality assured through the Open College Network at Warwick University, and an independent education provider, PCSP (UK) Ltd (see Appendix B).

Implementation of the course consists of investment in existing personnel by training postural care tutor/managers to deliver the general skills course to family and professional carers. In this way postural care skills can be introduced over a wide variety of services including residential and family homes, day services and schools.

The process takes 1 year for the tutor/manager and 6 months for the general skills learners. The general skills course is flexible but can be carried out over six four-hour long tutorials with project work to be completed in between.

OUTCOME MEASURES

Self-assessment learner skills profiles can be completed prior to the course and on completion to illustrate either individual skills or consolidated team profiles and manage progress.

CONCLUSION

Controlled and comfortable symmetrical lying postures at night have been demonstrated to have significant benefits for people with movement problems. This provision should be seen as complementary to postural care in the day.

An integrated service to provide training and support for all hands-on carers and efficient provision of equipment is considered to be essential for the success of this intervention.

The present expensive but haphazard system, in which individuals attempt to fit into the different agendas of service providers and seek equipment from a variety of uncoordinated sources including health, social services, education and charities, represents a waste of resources with inevitably unsuccessful results. Although pioneering therapists are encouraged by results within individual services, they are discouraged by lack of uniformity of provision across areas and the difficulties in providing support services after the individual leaves school (Thomas et al. 1987; Greig 2005). Until a consistent service is provided it must be recognised that therapists cannot fully investigate the efficacy of this therapy.

It is felt that it would be cost effective for a single authority, however resourced, to be responsible for provision of a reliable, integrated postural care service that covers sitting, lying and standing, over the age ranges, in daycare and home settings. Once reliable, long-term postural care has been established longitudinal studies in this context will be needed to monitor the long-term effects of this therapy.

REFERENCES

Bell, E. and Watson, A. (1985) The prevention of deformity in cerebral palsy. *Physiotherapy Practice*, **1**, 86–92.

Bellefeuille-Reid, D. and Jakubek, S. (1989) Adaptive positioning intervention for premature infants: issues for paediatric occupational therapy practice. *British Journal of Occupational Therapy*, **52** (3), 93–7.

Carpenter, B. (2000) Sustaining the family: meeting the needs of families of children with disabilities. *British Journal of Special Education*, **27**, 135–44.

Ferber, R. (1986) *Solve Your Child's Sleep Problems,* Dorling Kindersley, London.

Fulford, G.E. and Brown, J.K. (1976) Position as a cause of deformity in children with cerebral palsy. *Developmental Medicine and Child Neurology*, **18**, 305–14.

Goldsmith, S. (2000) The Mansfield Project: postural care at night within a community setting. *Physiotherapy,* **86** (10), 528–34.

Goldsmith, J. and Goldsmith, L. (1996) *Symmetrical Body Support: A Carer's Guide to the Management of Posture,* The Helping Hand Company, Ledbury.

Goldsmith, E., Golding, R.M., Garstang, R.A. and Macrae, A.W. (1992) A technique to measure windswept deformity. *Physiotherapy*, **78** (4), 235–42.

Goldsmith, J., Goldsmith, L., Peters, A. and Hewitt, L. (1998) *Postural Care Workshop for Families,* The Helping Hand Company, Ledbury.

Green, E.M., Mulcahy, C.M., Pountney, T.E. and Ablett, R.H. (1993) The Chailey standing support for children and young adults with motor impairment : a developmental approach. *British Journal of Occupational Therapy*, **56** (1): 13–18.

Greig, R. (2005) *Valuing People. The Story So Far . . . A New Strategy for Learning Disability for the Twenty-first Century,* Department of Health Publications, London.

Hallsworth, M., (1995) Positioning the preterm infant. *Paediatric Nursing,* **8** (1), 18–20.

Jan, J.E., Espezel, H. and Appleton, R.E. (1994) The treatment of sleep disorders with melatonin. *Developmental Medicine and Child Neurology,* **36** (2), 97–107.

Kotagel, S., Gibbons, V.P. and Stith, J.A. (1994) Sleep abnormalities in patients with severe cerebral palsy *Developmental Medicine and Child Neurology,* **36,** 304–11.

Lowthian, P. (1997) Notes on the pathogenesis of serious pressure sores. *The British Journal of Nursing,* 6 (16), 907–12.

Medical Devices Agency (1995) Upholstered chairs for children: a comparative evaluation. *Disability Equipment Assessment,* **A16.**

Mulcahy, C.M. (1986) An approach to the assessment of sitting ability for the prescription of seating *Occupational Therapy,* November, 367–8.

Mulcahy, C.M., Pountney, T.E., Nelham, R.L., Green, E.M. and Billington, G.D. (1988) Adaptive seating for motor handicap: problems, a solution, assessment and prescription. *British Journal of Occupational Therapy,* **51** (10), 347–52.

Nelham, R.L. (1984) Principles and practice in manufacture of seating for the handicapped. *Physiotherapy,* **70** (2), 54–8.

Okawa, M., Takahashi, K. and Sasaki, H. (1986) Disturbance in circadian rhythms in severely brain damaged patients correlated with CT findings. *Journal of Neurology,* **233,** 274–82.

Peters, A., Hewitt, L., Goldsmith, J. and Goldsmith, S. (1998) Provision of postural care at night within a community setting: a feedback study. Available at www.helpinghand. co.uk/docs/290.pdf

Pountney, T.E., Mulcahy, C. and Green, E. (1990) Early development of postural control. *Physiotherapy,* **76** (12), 799–802.

Samuel, J. and Pritchard, M. (2001) The ignored minority: meeting the needs of people with profound learning disability. *Tizard Learning Disability Review,* **6** (2), 34–44.

Suroweicki, J. (2004) *The Wisdom of Crowds,* Abacus, New York.

Symmetrikit Postural Care Pathway (2002) The Helping Hand Company, Ledbury.

Tardieu, R., Lespargot, A., Tabary, C. and Bret, M.D. (1988) How long must the soleus muscle be stretched each day to prevent contractures. *Developmental Medicine and Child Neurology,* **30,** 3–10.

Thomas, A., Bax, M. and Smyth, D. (1987) *The Provision of Support Services for the Handicapped Young Adult,* Department of Child Health and Charing Cross and Westminster Medical School, London.

Turrill, S. (1992) Supported positioning in intensive care. *Paediatric Nursing,* May, 24–7.

Young, J. (1992) The use of specialised beds and mattresses. *Journal of Tissue Viability,* **2** (3), 79–81.

10 An Approach to Treating and Managing Severe Physical Disability

ANN FINDLAY

INTRODUCTION

A significant number of learning-disabled clients referred for physiotherapy have congenital neurological deficit. Others have one of a variety of 'syndromes' or chromosomal disorders. The vast majority of clients with a neurological deficit present with abnormal tone, movement and posture, which are the primary cause of contractures and deformity. Central brain damage is compounded by resultant muscle and bone growth disparity and change of muscle properties (O'Dwyer et al. 1989; Gage 1991; Croal 1999).

When working with clients who have learning disability, therefore, the approach must be holistic in nature. Therapy intervention is also likely to be extended to include parents/carers or staff, ensuring a consistent approach to the physical management and care of these clients.

Along with the learning disability comes a variety of levels of handicap and impairment, but all have multiple problems. This needs to be fully understood by all clinicians, as awareness of all physical, sensory and communication problems as well as any challenging behaviour is necessary to ensure effectiveness of treatment.

It is not, therefore, that therapists working with clients who have learning disability differ significantly from others, and they do not perform magic with clients. It is the broad base of knowledge learned earlier and a change in approach to the client that prove important when working within this field. A desire to work in the field is also vital, together with an understanding that change may not be dramatic, and a variety of methods for measuring change may be required for one individual (see Chapters 7 and 8). Many of the skills used when working with learning disabilities are identical to those used in

Learning Disability: Physical Therapy Treatment and Management. Edited by Jeanette Rennie
© 2007 John Wiley & Sons Ltd

neurology, general medicine, orthopaedics, and so forth, but with a totally different approach.

GENERAL OVERVIEW

When working with individuals who have learning disability, the broad aims of physiotherapy management and intervention are as follows:

- to assess the needs of the client and carers
- to maintain the good general health of the client
- to prevent or minimise contractures and prevent fixed positional deformity
- to maximise the client's functional movement, ability and independence
- to share specialist knowledge and skills with clients, carers and relatives

Achieving these aims of good physical management can assist clients to maintain and improve their quality of life.

In general terms, an eclectic approach to treatment will be used, with therapists considering more than one specific method of treatment to achieve even the smallest change. However, due to the neurological nature of the deformity and impairment, the Bobath approach is often used as a basis for treatment and will be considered later in this chapter.

Brief mention should be given to electrical equipment and electrotherapy techniques. Although occasionally used with clients with learning disabilities, use is not common. This is primarily due to the fact that many clients cannot give a reliable response. Physiotherapists may decide that their client would benefit substantially from certain modalities and on occasions choose to use modalities such as Flowtron, ultrasound, transcutaneous electrical nerve stimulation (TENS) and laser. All of these would need to be supervised by the physiotherapist. Commonly, Flowtron is used for treatment of oedematous limbs. Some physiotherapists have found that it can be used for clients with a limb contracture to maximise extension with good effect. Laser is not available in all areas, but has been used successfully in the treatment of varicose ulcers, diabetic sores, infected wounds and various pressure areas. This is usually carried out in association with a clinical nurse specialist to enable the best use to be made of dressings. Laser therapy and the correct effective dressing can undoubtedly speed up the healing rate of wounds but must be used in conjunction with the dressings that are most effective and not simply the cheapest. Neuromuscular electrical stimulation (NMES) has not been tried with clients with learning disability. Research has so far tended to be undertaken with patients who can respond reliably. Clients with 'moderate to severe cognitive impairment' or 'severe, frequent epilepsy' fall into the excluded category (Croal 1999).

When using TENS, Flowtron and ultrasound, the exclusions applicable to clients without a learning disability would also apply.

INDIVIDUAL TREATMENT

Individual treatment can be broadly subdivided into the categories of 'hands-on' treatment, education, seating and equipment and acute treatment. An individual may dip into any or all of these sections when receiving physiotherapy intervention. What is vital is that it is a client-centred, needs-led approach, respecting individuals' needs and opinions and including their participation, where possible, in any intervention and decision making.

'HANDS-ON' TREATMENT

Hands-on treatment incorporates all physiotherapy techniques and exercise, either passive, active or active-assisted. Depending on the setting, hands-on physiotherapy may be undertaken on a therapy ball, floor or plinth. This involves the facilitation of normal movement. As long ago as 1943 the Bobaths observed that muscle tone was an alterable state and they have shown that muscle tone is influenced by handling and positioning. The Bobath concept aims to change/influence postural tone and then to enable the client to experience normal movement. The concept looks at groups of muscles and the patterns of movement that their activity creates. It looks at the contractures and deformity often seen in cerebral palsy as secondary to the condition and aims to make patterns of normal movement possible.

No standard treatment is available, all clients have their own treatment regime. As Bobath and Bobath (1984) wrote of their treatment,

> It is not a 'method' as it is neither rigid or standardised. It takes into account that CP and allied conditions comprise a group of symptoms in which there is great variety, therefore treatment has to be flexible and adapted to the many and varied needs of the individual child. No standard set of exercises will be adequate to the needs of all children.

An in-depth knowledge of normal movement and the process of normal development is essential when working with adults with a congenital neurological deficit.

Water-based activities also fall into this category. Again, decreasing tone and facilitation of normal patterns of movement in hydrotherapy would be common when working with this client group. All other benefits of hydrotherapy are also evident. For the more able or mobile client, the Halliwick method may be used. (See Chapter 11.)

EDUCATION

Education in the use of equipment, orthotics, seating and 24-hour physical management for each individual is essential. This may involve a number of people, including parents, carers, hospital staff, social work staff and private providers, to name but a few.

Good communication is vital in the field of learning disability and involves a broad spectrum of people. If treatment for these clients is to move forward, close liaison with other professionals is paramount. Clients with learning disabilities must not be denied access to services such as medical consultants, surgeons, orthotists and bioengineers for financial reasons or otherwise. However, it is important that any such professionals are aware of the complex problems of the client, and the difficulties which may arise from their handling or care. Physiotherapists can play a lead role in education and management of other staff should the need arise. Uniprofessional support should also be given to colleagues not so familiar with the learning disability client group. This is particularly important with relatively newly qualified staff who may find the varied and challenging work in learning disability difficult initially and offputting if appropriate support is not available. Many staff from the social services and independent sectors such as resource centres, adult training centres and small group homes will look to physiotherapists to lead them in aspects of an individual's physical management.

SEATING AND EQUIPMENT

Postural care/management

Postural care/management is a term used to describe the use of specialist equipment to achieve good positioning, known as a physical management programme, and worked over a 24-hour period. This programme must be designed to meet individual needs, maximising strengths, personality and uniqueness. Regular change of body position is essential for everyone, both for comfort and prevention of deformity. Good basic positioning is also the foundation of all useful movement. This is discussed further in Chapter 9.

Seating

Assessment, provision and maintenance of specialised and adapted wheelchair seating and indoor seating is required to provide an appropriate degree of comfort and postural control. This involves a lengthy process from assessment to delivery. Wheelchair and seating systems have become some of the most important positioning devices available and clients are very dependent on them. Positioning within a seating system is the foundation upon which an effective therapy or physical management programme can be built. Many professionals share this complex area and the lead role varies from area to area. Either a physiotherapist or occupational therapist usually takes it and both must liaise closely to achieve the best outcome for each individual.

Each area also has different financial restraints and therefore seating is not consistent between different areas of the country. This can be a source of great frustration for all concerned and so clear boundaries should be clarified before assessment is carried out, particularly if parents are involved, in an effort to prevent disappointment. Often carers may have seen a chair, which they deem to be suitable at an exhibition or demonstration, which may not be within the financial boundaries of the providers. It is easier if this is clarified at an early stage to enable alternatives to be sought.

Equipment

This includes provision, maintenance, renewal and ongoing assessment of equipment used in the physical management programme. Orthoses such as ankle foot orthoses, footwear, splints, epileptic helmets and spinal jackets also require provision and maintenance, as well as mobility aids of various types. This equipment will not always be used when the physiotherapist is present but it will remain their remit to oversee and monitor the use of all equipment and orthoses and to ensure its safety and suitability for its purpose. Many physiotherapists within the learning disability service refer clients to the local orthotics or podiatry department but also have access to an orthotics clinic specifically for clients with learning disabilities. This is useful as it gives the time necessary to fully assess and discuss the very individual needs of the client. Where clients are part of a generic clinic, adequate time must be provided and allowance made for the more noisy or disruptive. Some system for trialling new equipment should also be in place as often clients may not be able to tolerate the orthotic device provided, or may take a longer period to adjust to it than is anticipated by the orthotist.

Acute treatment

Acute conditions are usually classified as problems that need to be responded to within a period of 24 hours. They may be associated with seating, orthotics or more medical problems such as chest infections, pneumonia, asthmatic attacks, fractures, or inability to bear weight, to name but a few. Acute conditions may also arise as a result of a psychiatric problem. If clients are already on the caseload of a physiotherapist, and remain in their own home, then treatment is often undertaken by that physiotherapist. If it is a problem requiring specific techniques (such as mobilisations) liaison with the generic services is advisable. On occasions this may result in a joint visit. Learning-disabled clients must not be denied their right to access generic services if appropriate but often it is a physiotherapist from the learning disability service who can respond more quickly, or can achieve the best result because of the clients' and carers' recognition of them and of their knowledge of the client.

Physiotherapists working in learning disability can often be used as a screen by carers looking for advice in an acute situation. They may be the first line of call for carers (barring 999 situations) and can often prevent precautionary hospital admission. The skills gained before specialising are never forgotten and are frequently used. Mobility problems, gait problems and chest problems often result in a telephone call from a general hospital or generic physiotherapy service to the learning disabilities physiotherapy service. In turn, physiotherapists working in learning disability need to know their limits clearly and when to call upon the skills of the generic services. Physiotherapy staff discharging clients from hospital wards should also ensure that an adequate hand-over has been undertaken and sufficient information has been supplied to facilitate ongoing treatment of the client.

ENSURING CONTINUITY OF MANAGEMENT

The clients described in this chapter have complex needs and can be very vulnerable. The requirement for 24-hour postural management continues in various settings. This may include respite care, holiday accommodation, hospital admissions and clinic appointments, or a transition in life, such as moving from child health to adult services, or moving into a residential unit. If contractures are to be contained, pressure care maintained, and lifelong deformity prevented, postural management must be continued in all of these settings. Complications also arise between staff in group homes or nursing homes, where not all staff are in regular contact with the physiotherapist, or due to staff changes common in such establishments, and there is liable to be a delay before new staff can be individually trained by a physiotherapist.

A 'communication passport' produced for each individual is one example of a way to alleviate these problems:

- it is tailored to meet the individual needs of each client
- it is user friendly for all staff, family members, carers and other professionals
- it can be multiprofessional

- it provides accurate information and photographs, which allow continuation of care in any setting and in any area of the country
- it provides immediate information on admittance to a general hospital, which often makes a considerable difference to the management of a client admitted, preventing deterioration in condition, either medical or physical, while appropriate information is sought

It may also be used to show the ideal positions that can then be incorporated into daily living tasks. This may be of particular importance for a client showing a challenging behaviour where therapeutic intervention may not be tolerated or be very limited. The same movements built into daily tasks may pass unnoticed by these clients but carers have a constant reminder of the necessary movements and can compare various tasks and positions with the 'wanted' and 'unwanted' positions.

Communication passports are best in a small format such as A5, allowing the information to be easily carried in a handbag or bag on the back of a wheelchair. Ring binders have proved successful, allowing sections of the passport to be removed if necessary, depending on which appointment or visit is being undertaken. This may be particularly important if confidential information such as drug history is contained within this passport. It is *not* intended that this passport should replace vital letters such as hospital discharge letters and full therapy assessment reports, and it must be remembered that information contained within the passport will be freely available to a variety of people.

Each passport will be personal, reflecting the lifestyle and personality of the individual. If the passport is to work effectively then the client's needs must also be reflected in this document and the amount of help required.

The case study at the end of this chapter is presented as a modified version of a communication passport. It shows postural management (Figures 10.1 to 10.11) and describes the physiotherapy needs of a client written in the first person. This amount of information from a single profession would not generally be required in the passport but this example was used as an aide-mémoire by the care staff in the small group home where this young man lives. Information not required can be removed when visiting hospitals or holiday locations, where all the equipment would not be used.

Please note that this is an example only, and various versions, formats and ideas can be incorporated (McEwen and Millar 1993); for instance a young woman with autistic syndrome disorder carries one to groups that she participates in around the city.

Case study in form of communication passport

Communication passport

Page 1 | Page 2

HELLO

My name is Alan. I have Cerebral Palsy which affects my trunk and all four limbs. This means that although I have some movement, which should be encouraged, my movements are limited and I have difficulty controlling my limbs for doing purposeful activities. This means that I require a lot of help with most aspects of my daily life.

Unfortunately I am unable to speak, although I can answer yes and no. I have a good understanding of what people are saying, so I am able to let you know how I feel or what I need. My nonverbal communication is also good.

So, PLEASE give me the chance to communicate with you. Just give me plenty of time to answer, and keep your questions simple! I'd be happy for you to communicate with me all day – I hate being ignored.

In general I am a very sociable person, but I do get a bit cross if no one is giving me any attention. Well, would YOU like to sit in one position for hours on end without any stimulation or conversation?? I particularly enjoy music and

One way of maximising what I do is through physiotherapy treatment and postural management. This communication passport is designed to briefly explain what these physiotherapy sessions involve, and how YOU can help me out with physiotherapy. It will also mention some of the equipment that I need to use. I hope it will give you an idea of what I can do for myself, and in what ways you can help me.

people singing and I am a Jambo! (Oh, sorry – this means a Hearts FC Fan if you are not educated properly!)

Continued

Page 3

This jacket has been specifically designed and made for me to keep my trunk in a good position and to prevent my spine from deforming further. It also helps me to maintain good posture, as without it I would not be able to sit up straight. Although the jacket looks hot and uncomfortable, it is important that I wear it almost all the time during the day. A close fitting T-shirt underneath the jacket makes it more comfortable. Getting the jacket on properly may take practice, so please ask my key worker or physiotherapist to show you the first time.

Page 4

The chair I sit in is my own 'Symmetrikit' chair. I should always use this chair when sitting as it gives my whole body support and keeps it in the best position. To benefit I must be correctly positioned in the chair. Firstly get my bottom as far back in the chair as possible. The back cushion should be puffed up, so that I'm not slouching. An 'Edinburgh Harness' is in place to stop me from sliding down. The straps should always be kept at the same length, and should not be adjusted or I am not safe and secure. My feet then need to be strapped in place and a pommel is placed between my knees to keep my legs well positioned. This method of positioning is also followed when I am in my wheelchair.

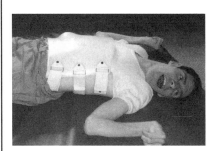

Figure 10.1. I'm wearing my jacket.

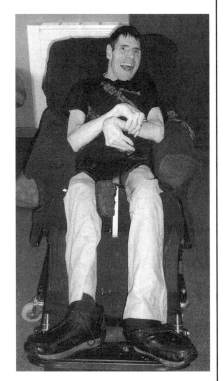

The shoes that I wear are also specially made and help keep my feet and toes well positioned.

Figure 10.2. Sitting in my Symmetrikit chair.

Page 5

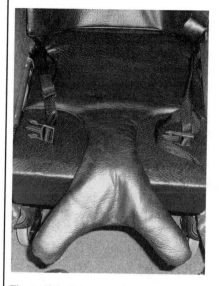

Figure 10.3. This is my Edinburgh harness.

Figure 10.4. Here I am sitting in my wheelchair.

Page 6

During my physiotherapy sessions I spend some time lying on the mat without wearing my spinal jacket. The physiotherapist is trained to do stretching exercises to help maintain the range of movement in my arms and legs. I also do bridging and rolling exercises to maintain the flexibility of my trunk. These exercises should only be done by the physiotherapist, as there is a risk of damage to my bones and tendons. However, this does not mean that I cannot enjoy lying on the mat outside physiotherapy sessions – there are lots of other things we can do!

Lying on the mat gives me freedom to move myself safely without my spinal jacket. You can't imagine how good that feels! My legs can be positioned in an 'E-BLOCK'. If music is playing I am encouraged to move independently and I enjoy this very much!

It is also a good position for relaxing. I need two people to help me from my chair to the mat and back again, and if I'm not too tired I can manage to take a few steps.

Continued

Page 7

Page 8

The next photographs show me lying on my front on what is known as the prone 'lyer'. This is my least favourite position, but it is a good way of straightening my body, especially my hips and knees, preventing them from fixing in a chair shaped position. It also gives my spine a stretch and relieves pressure from areas I've been sitting on. I normally stay on the prone lyer for about half an hour, and it is much more enjoyable if you stay and keep me company. For example, I enjoy drawing with help while in the lyer.

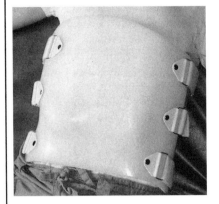

Figure 10.5. My spinal jacket is about to be taken off for my physiotherapy exercises.

Figure 10.6. Lying quietly on the mat.

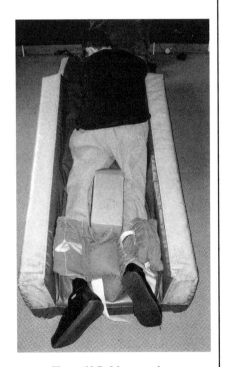

Figure 10.7. My prone lyer.

Page 9

Figure 10.8. I do smile in this position.

Page 10

Another useful piece of equipment for me is the EasyStand frame. As I am unable to stand unsupported, this frame allows me to experience weight-bearing which has many benefits. It stimulates sensation in my feet and legs and helps prevent osteoporosis (a bone disease) from occurring. Standing is good for other parts of the body including bladder and bowel function and circulation, and it stretches the leg muscles which may become tight from frequent sitting. It also allows me to be the same height as other people, and in this position there are more activities I can do, such as playing with a ball, drawing or painting. Frequent standing in the frame will also help maximise my ability to stay upright when transferring, e.g. from my chair to bed, bed to chair etc, which hopefully in turn will help YOU my carers!

Positioning is a big part of my care plan and it makes a huge difference to my long-term quality of life. Remember I need to be positioned 24 hours a day, 52 weeks of the year! It is better if my own equipment is used as it has been set to suit my individual needs. At night I sleep in a special system called a 'Symmetrisleep'. This keeps me in a good position but allows me to be turned during the night by my carers. They will show you how this system works so please ask.

To position me in the standing frame first make sure that the frame height and knee pads are set correctly for my height, then bring my chair as close between the bars as possible. Place my feet, using the straps provided. A wooden block goes under my right foot, as my right leg is shorter than the left. Two people can assist me forwards (don't lift) and once I am leaning against the frame the back support can be positioned and tightened, to keep me upright. My elbows can rest on the table,

Continued

Page 11

with a pillow for comfort if I'm not involved in an activity. I stand in the frame for half an hour each day, but must be wearing my spinal jacket to keep me upright.

Page 12

The following diagram shows the ARROW walker. It is a gait trainer that allows me to take a few steps by myself. Its wheels have locks that can limit the movement of the wheels in different directions. Again two people are required to get me onto the seat, and the walker is set just for me. Leaning on the front pad and holding the rail, I can use my legs to propel myself but need help steering. The walker is best used outside where I have more room to move about without knocking something flying.

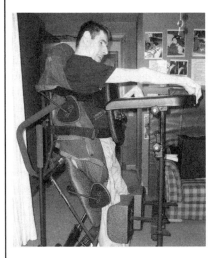

Figure 10.9. Me standing in my 'EasyStand' standing frame – from the side.

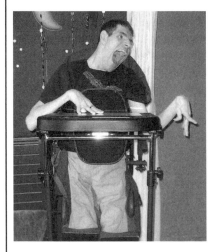

Figure 10.10. Me in my 'EasyStand' standing frame – from the front.

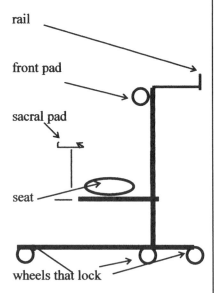

rail

front pad

sacral pad

seat

wheels that lock

Figure 10.11. This is just a diagram of my ARROW walker.

Page 13

My weekly physiotherapy session also includes a hydrotherapy session. The physiotherapist does similar stretching exercises to those on dry land, and the warm water is excellent for relaxing my tight muscles, allowing my arms and legs to move more easily. I am even able to take a few steps with support from the physiotherapist. Floating mats are sometimes used, giving me the security to relax while my exercises are done. Hydrotherapy is something I LOVE – it gives me freedom to move without my jacket. Please don't take me swimming in colder water – I can't cope with that.

Page 14

I hope you have found this booklet useful in giving a brief overview of my physiotherapy management. All of the things mentioned have been designed to maximise my abilities and help with the things I'm not so good at. They are necessary to give me the best quality of life both now and in the future. This booklet is not long enough to detail everything, but my carers and physiotherapist, who know me well, will be happy to demonstrate for you how to do something.

Thank you for taking the time to read about me and for helping me to help myself to get the very best out of life

CHEERS!

CONCLUSION

Due to the ongoing, lifelong problems associated with a neurological deficit, treatment will also be lifelong. There is very little benefit from a physiotherapy session lasting half an hour once or twice weekly, without the consistent associated management from *all* other persons involved in the life of the client. Although this is generally more prevalent in the child health services, there is no reason why it should not also be the case with adults. It is only through a dedicated multiprofessional approach that deterioration in condition and worsening of contractures resulting in deformities and diminished quality of life can be slowed or prevented.

The problems associated with abnormal muscle tone, posture and movement are always present and it is only through a combined effort by all that normal movement can be encouraged. This does not mean, however, that physiotherapists expect all this work to be carried out by others; they must remain the link between all parties if success is to be achieved. It should not be the intention of the physiotherapy service to 'medicalise' the problem of a learning disability. The aim must be to maximise the physical potential and facilitate function so that disabilities do not become handicaps and people can live their lives in the way they find most fulfilling.

REFERENCES

Bobath, K. and Bobath, B. (1984) *The Neuro-development Treatment*, Bobath Centre for Children with Cerebral Palsy, London.

Croal, I. (1999) Effects of neuromuscular electrical stimulation (NMES) on spastic and nonspastic muscle of children with cerebral palsy. *Association of Paediatric Chartered Physiotherapists Journal*, **90**, 34–48.

Gage, J. (1991) *Gait Analysis in Cerebral Palsy*. MacKeith Press, London.

McEwen, C. and Millar, S. (1993) *'Communication Passports' Augmentative Communication in Practice: Scotland*. Collected Papers: Study Day, CALL Centre, University of Edinburgh.

O'Dwyer, N.J., Nelson, P.D. and Nash, J. (1989) Mechanism of muscle growth related to muscle contracture in cerbral palsy, *Developmental Medicine and Child Neurology*, **31**, 543–52.

11 Hydrotherapy

PATRICIA ODUNMBAKU AUTY

INTRODUCTION

Hydrotherapy is the treatment of disease or disability in heated water using its properties of buoyancy and thermal assets to relieve pain, promote relaxation and foster confidence and independence. It has long been recognised as an effective treatment method for rehabilitation of physical injury and physical disability and can also provide an aquatic recreational activity for those whose physical musculature could not tolerate cold water.

This chapter does not cover the whole subject of hydrotherapy. Its objective is to combine information about pool therapy and learning disability to demonstrate expansion of the properties of water to allow for risk taking, experiential learning, tactile and body awareness training and guidance of behaviour prior to use of public pools.

Care must be taken to distinguish between the therapeutic/rehabilitation aspects of hydrotherapy and recreational activities in water: each requires different skills. Both water-based activities are beneficial but the physiotherapist's role is predominantly in therapeutic aspects of hydrotherapy (Reid Campion 1997; Chartered Society of Physiotherapy 2006). The role of training carer/support staff in water safety is smaller but equally valuable part of the service: it ensures the future safety of the client when in the water. Where resources and skills allow, therapists can be the instigators of water-based sports. Participation in activity holidays could be one consequence of using the hydrotherapy pool to build confidence in water and instil an understanding of risk and safety in the client.

FACTORS INFLUENCING PROVISION OF HYDROTHERAPY

1. The clients
   - The number of children or adults requiring hydrotherapy.
   - The complexity of the clients. Their physical disability, sensation loss, pain factor, cognitive ability, behaviour that challenges.

Learning Disability: Physical Therapy Treatment and Management. Edited by Jeanette Rennie
© 2007 John Wiley & Sons Ltd

- The clients who have minimal dysfunction and require pre-public pool experience
2. The staff. The staffing resources available, their level of skill and provision for updated training practice.
3. The pool
   - Its shape, size and depth.
   - Its surroundings/environment.
   - Its accessibility.
   - The equipment available.

When acting as a consultant to introduce clients to public pools, prior visits to these establishments are important to discover any potential risks and, where possible, to reduce these areas of risk. Clients and staff should be encouraged to familiarise themselves with the pool and its facilities to enable a smooth and successful introduction. This familiarisation may not be necessary for children.

CLIENTS

More children and adults with multiple complex disabilities are entering the paediatric and adult services than ever (Chapters 1 to 3 and 7). Added to this, parents', carers' and clients' expectations have grown so that hydrotherapy is seen as an essential part of their intervention. Despite this there is a continued loss of many hydrotherapy pools in conjunction with the closure of the last few long-stay hospitals and financial restraints within the NHS Primary Care Trusts and local authorities' budgets. Most clients with complex needs have some degree of cerebral palsy, treatment of which is described in many books (Reid Campion 1991; Cogher et al. 1992). One condition that requires special consideration, however, is epilepsy (see Chapter 2 and Chadwick 1997).

At one time epilepsy was listed as one of the contraindications to hydrotherapy. If such a group were to be excluded, 90 % of people with complex needs and learning disability would be affected – the very people who benefit from this modality. Epilepsy is now accepted as one of the risk factors to be accommodated and planned for.

Safe guidelines can be provided only if the type and duration of seizures, the recovery period of the individual and any medication required are known. The carer/support worker will be responsible for providing the medication and its administration. It also helps to know if there are any precipitants and warnings. These must be noted and taken into consideration when recording risk assessments and emergency procedures for both inside and outside the pool.

Further problems are encountered with clients who have eating and drinking difficulties and who are known to aspirate. Some may have percutaneous endoscopic gastrostomy (PEG) inserted. How do we manage a programme for them and should we? This is a difficult decision for some services as the risk may be considered high. It will depend on the medical advice, the skill of the individual therapist and the outcome of the risk-taking meeting around the client. Once the decision is taken that hydrotherapy outcomes would outweigh the risk factors, protocols are then developed to suit this need. Rules of conduct are required for the staff team and support staff/parents so that, should the client go into stasis, everyone knows what to do and follows the recorded action plan. It was easier to deal with such incidents when a pool was on a hospital site; community placements have added more difficulty and risk, requiring ambulances to be called in case of an emergency. An established protocol must be written and all staff trained in whatever procedures are established by the providing service. As long as these procedures are established and followed there is no need to exclude such clients from hydrotherapy.

It is not only the clients with complex needs who require hydrotherapy. There are many clients with minimal physical dysfunction who have a need for confidence and esteem building, and in some cases assistance with aspects of their inappropriate sexual behaviour, in preparation for introduction to public pools.

Many clients may be tactile defensive and the close proximity of the therapist may increase their tension or fear. Their resultant behaviour could interfere with support provided, the planned programme or even safety; thus specific knowledge of the client is essential. Each service will establish its own basic information requirements based on the CSP Core Standards of Practice on documentation, and the employing Health Service Protocols. These must be within reach at the session (Figure 11.1).

Contraindications include:

- Infections.
- Cardiac conditions.
- Extreme high or low blood pressure.

Care must be taken regarding:

- Sensation level.
- Urinary and bowel incontinence – there is no solution but it is important to be aware of the local pool procedures in case of an accident. See an example of a letter sent to GP to ensure that there are no unknown contraindications (Figure 11.2)

STAFF INVOLVEMENT

In many areas, clients live in community houses with support staff. It is important that the staff are aware of their clients' strengths, skills and requirements when they bring them to a hydrotherapy session. Parents must also be and feel involved in the young person's therapy.

PHYSIOTHERAPY SERVICES

HYDROTHERAPY INFORMATION

NAME:	D.O.B.
Address:	
	Tel.

Tel. No. for contact ....

REASON FOR REFERRAL:

RELEVANT CLIENT INFORMATION e.g. disability, specific requirements,

GP NAME & ADDRESS

HAS GP BEEN INFORMED?   YES/NO   DATE

ANY AREAS OF CONCERN?/ RISK ASSESSMENT (Movement & handling)
Equipment e.g. hoist, sliding board

CARER INVOLVEMENT

SIGNED: **DATE:**

Figure 11.1. Example of hydrotherapy information sheet developed by Lewisham and Southwark ALD physiotherapy services.

In sessions provided by some services, support staff are expected to work alongside therapists in the pool. Training must be arranged to acquaint them with the purpose of the intervention and the most appropriate holds for their client (taking into consideration the Knowledge and Skills Framework (NHS

Dear Dr.

Your patient ...... is being seen by the physiotherapy service
for people with learning disability.

We feel that a course of hydrotherapy would be greatly
beneficial to this patient. I should be grateful if you would let
me know if there is any reason why your patient would not
benefit from this form of treatment.

Yours sincerely,

Physiotherapist

NB: *The word patient and not client is used deliberately in this context.*

*There are legal implications in ensuring correct information about the clients'
ability to receive hydrotherapy intervention. It is therefore important to ensure
that the GP receives this letter.*

Figure 11.2. Example of letter to GPs developed by Lewisham and Southwark ALD
Physiotherapy Services.

KSF) and the Development Review Process). This enables them to position,
facilitate and support clients correctly in the water. Parents should also be
encouraged to participate, but there is a need to be sensitive as to how much
one can expect from overstressed parents. There are many older parents who
have never been in a pool and it would not be right to expect this type of
involvement. Cultural issues must also be considered for the client's staff and
parents. Some cultures would not wear European swimwear for modesty and
religious reasons and other dress must be accepted.

If we want this type of involvement, it is incumbent upon us to provide
training and update this training at appropriate intervals. Everyone must know
what we aim for, what objectives we want to achieve through both short-term
and long-term treatment.

The movement and handling directive and all health and safety legalisation
must be complied with. When clients arrive for their session, the information
pertaining to their individual requirements should already be recorded on the
hydrotherapy information sheet and must be followed. Support staff should
also understand the movement and handling regulations. Advice around this
may be necessary. It is sometimes difficult to persuade parents to comply with
these procedures. If so this must be recorded. However, they should be shown
a safe method of movement and handling for the young person.

It is essential that whoever is present at the poolside understands and is aware of the safety and emergency procedures. It is helpful if resources allow the presence of a colleague on the poolside who can observe and offer advice.

THE POOL

Most people with learning disabilities now live in the community and receive the services that they require within their locality. Many local authorities can now provide public pool facilities, which can be heated to correct temperatures so that clients can receive a hydrotherapy service within this public environment. This excellent trend increases physiotherapists' responsibilities and risks because they no longer have the added protection of a hospital site or institution. They have to learn different pool protocols or influence the establishment of them. The equipment may not always be suitable and risk assessments can be problematic. However, every opportunity should be taken to influence any building of pools to gain the best facilities for those who have a disability.

The physiotherapy service for learning disability in Southwark cooperated in the design of a community hydrotherapy pool. It was designed with a hydraulic variable depth facility. This allows increased opportunities for freedom and independence and less touching/handling from the therapist. As part of a community facility, with enabling equipment, it allows clients with complex needs to access the pool and assists in community integration.

Pool equipment

The responsibility for supply and maintenance of essential equipment to allow clients access to the facilities – for example, height-adjustable beds, hoists and rails – will be the duty of the provider of the hydrotherapy pool.

However, it is the responsibility of the therapists using the pool to check the date of service on this equipment so that they know that it conforms to all the legislation on equipment. Anomalies should be reported immediately to the managers of the pool.

INFORMATION REQUIRED BEFORE COMMENCING SESSIONS

1. Client
   - Essential information (Figure 11.1).
   - Aims and objectives for six-week period of hydrotherapy (Figure 11.3).
   - At each session an achievable goal should be set that is integral to the six-week plan.
   - At end of period: evaluation outcomes (Figure 11.4).

HYDROTHERAPY

Air Temp:
Water Temp:

DATE	AIMS	PLAN	OUTCOMES	PHYSIO	SS

Figure 11.3. Example of hydrotherapy aims, plan and outcome developed by Lewisham and Southwark ALD Physiotherapy Services.

HYDROTHERAPY EVALUATION (AUDIT)

Client/Therapist	Aims & Objectives	Health/Support	Client Participation	Handling Skills	Outcomes

Signature ....

Date ....

Figure 11.4. Example of hydrotherapy evaluation developed by Lewisham and Southwark ALD Physiotherapy Services.

2. Environment
  - The pool and service-specific protocols.
  - Risk assessment of pool facilities.
  - Available equipment, which complies with EC Directives.
  - The water condition and temperature.

A six-week period had been selected for the hydrotherapy following results from a project undertaken to evaluate and cost hydrotherapy in the Lewisham Disability Service (Odunmbaku Auty 1990). Part of the project aimed to establish the optimum number of sessions required to:

- maintain range of movement
- maintain the client's learning curve
- improve and maintain function
- maintain carer/support worker involvement and enthusiasm

The results showed that the optimum number of sessions was six weeks, with the option of starting another six weeks following a rest period of six weeks.

For clients with pain, burns or recent injuries, session times would need to be revised. Many such clients are treated in the acute sector but it is often in their best interest to be treated by the specialist therapists who understand learning disabled clients and their specialist needs.

The loss of a number of hydrotherapy facilities and lack of staffing resources in some areas is of constant concern to physiotherapists who find it increasingly difficult to provide hydrotherapy let alone the optimum number of sessions for their clients.

THERAPY IN THE POOL

ADJUSTMENT TO WATER

Children may find this easier than older clients. Previous experience of hydrotherapy will have been recorded in the client's notes. However, time must be taken to allow for both mental and physical adjustment to the medium. It is important to allow for adjustment because clients may fear water or even experience dizziness. As verbal communication for most of the clients is difficult or nonexistent, the reaction to this may be to push the therapist away or become aggressive. This may be misinterpreted as challenging behaviour, a difficult label to lose. Time, therefore, is well spent in allowing adjustment to occur and confidence to grow.

EFFECT OF WATER

The physical properties of water, its weight, specific gravity, density, buoyancy, refraction, hydrostatic pressure and viscosity must be taken into consideration when planning a programme.

People with musculo-skeletal fragility will react to the pressure of water and may experience breathlessness.

The density of the body changes with age; children and young people on the whole carry less adipose tissue than those in middle years. It is more difficult for clients who have little muscle bulk or fat to float. Many clients with a complex disability have difficulty in eating or drinking and are often underweight, and consequently may be undernourished and therefore carry very little muscle bulk or fat. The energy expenditure of these clients must be monitored.

It is difficult to find the point of balance in water with clients who have severe deformities and asymmetrical bodylines. Observation must be acute to detect the moment of balance so that only the required minimal support is given.

Refraction of the water can cause extra difficulties to those who already have perceptual difficulties and poor body image and visual impairment. The intervention should be modified to take this into consideration.

Turbulence can be used to assist and resist movement in the pool. Care must be taken not to allow unintentional turbulence emanating from therapist's movement to interfere and prevent the client performing an activity: this is a particular problem when trying to teach clients cause and effect.

CLIENT MOTIVATION

Clients with learning disabilities often have little or no motivation or it may be hidden deep within them. Learning disability services offer a range of interventions to clients from babyhood to elder care, adjusting the modality to suit individual needs. It requires knowledge, training in the therapeutic aspects of pool therapy, skills in assessment and handling, ability to pass on those skills to support staff and carers and above all the personality and the particular ability to motivate clients to achieve success.

None of the above can be obtained without the cooperation and participation of the client. This cooperation requires staff to have the ability to motivate, empower and modify a client's behaviour.

Expectations of children and adults must always be high but realistic, otherwise there will be no achievement. It is especially important in learning disability where clients' motivation is frequently low and when little has been expected of them.

It is essential that the learning curve of individuals is understood so that teaching is adjusted to allow them to achieve their aim. An appropriate way should be selected which gives them the ability to comprehend, respond, attempt or initiate the desired activity, enjoy it and succeed. To be successful, the following areas require attention:

- communication
- task analysis of activity

- aims and objectives of assessment or intervention
- preset outcome measures
- evaluation of outcomes

PROGRAMME

There are different approaches and methods of treatment, each of which has merit. The therapist should select the appropriate methodology for each client be it Bad Regaz, Halliwick techniques (Kelsey 2006) or an individualised method for that client, based on the principles and properties of water.

Support staff and carers should be encouraged where possible to participate within the pool.

The aims and objectives of hydrotherapy may be the same for a child as for an adult, these being closely related to the disability or disease. The differences will be the way in which the physiotherapist communicates and conducts the session. Children learn best through play. Age-appropriate music and singing can be of assistance to facilitate smooth gentle motion or more rapid excitable movement. It is often at this stage where cultural differences, though not insurmountable, are difficult to overcome due to lack of knowledge of other cultures' music and songs.

Programmes for clients are individualised and the client receives one-to-one attention in the water. This may be from the therapist for only part of the programme; the parent or support worker will also be involved. Traditional rehabilitation programmes can be adjusted to suit the individual's cognitive development. Assumptions cannot always be made about clients' understanding of their body or spatial awareness. This must be taken into account as part of the assessment for the pool.

Holding the floating clients in the supine position with minimal support and effort in the water, encourages them to move and promotes the development of their body awareness. If they lift their heads, their feet will go down. If they put their heads back into the water, their feet will rise. The therapist can encourage these movements until clients realise that they can initiate these movements purposefully. It takes patience and skill to hold the client as he moves his head in different directions. If the client is in a floating position and makes a movement with hand, arm, foot or knee then the therapist assists the action by moving the client through the water for a proportional distance. Once the client ceases to move, the therapist stops. This assists the client to learn cause and effect. It is difficult to stand still in the pool waiting for the next tiny movement but it is essential to do so.

The following may be incorporated within the programme:

- body/spatial and perception awareness
- learning of cause and effect
- stretching of spine or limbs

- relaxation of muscle spasm and body tensions
- beginnings of independent floating
- non-weight-bearing walking, or weight-bearing walking
- what the client wants to do and achieve
- fun

Each part of the programme must be interchangeable to adapt to the client's initiative. Observational concentration is an essential part of the therapist's skills and repertoire so that no part of the learning curve initiative of the client is missed. A client floating on his back may turn his head to follow a sound or person. The therapist can then facilitate the body to follow the turn. It would be frustrating for the client and wrong to miss his first attempt at initiating movement for swimming. At times it is necessary to judge when to interrupt the learning curve for the sake of safety; for example how do you learn not to put your head into the water and breathe if you do not know it is an unpleasant experience?

It is important to note that one of the effects of hydrotherapy is that clients' vocalise more in the pool, not only with increased volume but also with changes of sound. This interesting outcome should be encouraged and contact with the speech therapist can add professional knowledge, so that specific sounds can be encouraged within the session for the clients' benefit.

The sessions may last 20 to 30 minutes depending on the client's condition and the temperature of the pool (Skinner and Thompson 1983). Therapists must be aware of their own energy expenditure and time their input appropriately. Davis and Harrison (1988) accepted that two hours was possible but this depends on the complexity of the clients within each session.

POOL FLOATS AND EQUIPMENT

'To use or not to use?' This question must be decided by each service. Equipment can be used to support clients completely, to allow them to experience nonpersonal support and freedom – an unusual experience for complex disabled clients.

Floats can be used:

- to assist buoyancy
- to resist buoyancy to strengthen muscle
- to support one area of the body while the therapist concentrates on another
- for recreation

The hydrotherapy service for adults in Lewisham and Southwark does not use floats. The rationale is that people who already have difficulty learning would have to learn all the sensations of pool therapy using floats and relearn them when they are removed. The aim is to foster as much independence as possible and to disengage from the client as soon as feasible. This can be achieved if physical support is given, which can be instantly monitored by touch and finely controlled. When the aquatic programme is recreational then all pool equipment can be used to increase enjoyment.

OUTCOMES AND EVALUATION

Each session should have a preset outcome, which will be part of the overall six-week plan. Notes of each session must be recorded within the code of practice timescales. Photographs or videos provide a helpful record. Permission for these must be obtained from the client (or parent if the person is under age or cannot understand and give consent) if they are to be used beyond their private file.

At the completion of the interventions, the outcomes are evaluated and a rating may be given. Each service may have its own outcome rating, be it TELER (Chapter 8) or the Goal Attainment Scale (GAS) (Brown et al. 1998). Table 11.1 is an example of a simplified outcome rating system.

It is important to continue research into hydrotherapy and to evaluate the evidence collected and to allow this evidence to be used to inform and improve future practice.

RECORDING

Clear, concise, accurate records must be kept so that should there be a change-over of staff, continuity of programmes can be promoted.

The personalities of the therapist, parents and staff will also influence the outcomes. This is an undisputed dimension and must be understood and noted in the outcomes.

DISCHARGE

If the original referral was for an introduction to water with the intention of using public pools discharge can be completed once that has been achieved.

Table 11.1. A simplified rating system

Rating	Outcome
−1	The presenting difficulty has increased, skills have been lost, opportunities narrowed since the start of intervention.
0	The presenting difficulty or skill level has remained the same. No or minimal change.
+1	Objectives are partly achieved, some progress has been made, there has been a moderate reduction in difficulty, skills have increased somewhat, although not as much as was aimed for.
+2	Objectives have been almost or totally achieved. There is the aimed-for reduction in difficulty, increase in skill.

CONFIDENTIAL

**PHYSIOTHERAPY SERVICE FOR ADULTS
WITH LEARNING DISABILITIES**

DISCHARGE SUMMARY

NAME:

D.O.B:

ADDRESS:

DATE OF REFERRAL:

REASON FOR REFERRAL:

SUMMARY OF INTERVENTION:

FURTHER ACTION TO BE TAKEN:

Signed ....   **Date** ....

Figure 11.5. Example of discharge summary developed by Lewisham and Southwark ALD Physiotherapy Services.

However, more complex clients can continue with hydrotherapy for many years with the required break in between sessions because the benefits of this modality have been well documented and noted and outweigh other forms of treatment. On their return, new programmes will be devised building on previous outcomes, progress and new objectives for further achievement (Figure 11.5).

For the best results, continuity of therapists and carer in the pool is preferable so that the understanding of the individual's learning and achievements is continued and allowed to flourish.

CONCLUSION

Hydrotherapy is sometimes seen to be an expensive modality and has high resource implications for staffing but it is not always seen as the positive pain-relieving, muscle-relaxing, rehabilitation and clinical modality that it is. The project on the evaluation and costing of hydrotherapy showed it to be cost effective. The survey of the clients and the carers showed that they appreciated and understood its benefits and limitations but all agreed that it was effective and successful. It is therefore important to keep in mind that in these days of scarce resources, hydrotherapy is a clinical- and resource-effective intervention.

CASE STUDIES

MOLLY

Molly is a woman in her mid-thirties with right hemiparesis as a result of Sturge-Webber syndrome. She has extensive haemngiomas. She uses a wheelchair but can stand and transfer herself. She wears a caliper on one leg. She was referred to hydrotherapy as a safe environment in which to work towards swimming for leisure and to be encouraged to use and mobilise her right side.

She challenges the service because she is noisy, bites her left hand and has been known to hit out at people when frustrated or distressed, especially over unfamiliar activities. If cut she bleeds profusely. She has seizures.

Molly is self-conscious about her appearance, which requires a sensitive approach. It was decided to overcome this problem by suggesting that she, and all the staff who work with her, wear a T-shirt over their swimwear.

An understanding of her needs and how to work through her challenging behaviour was obtained from her physiotherapist, challenging needs worker and staff. A consistent approach to her behaviour was undertaken and guidelines written in her hydrotherapy notes.

She was given a six-week course of hydrotherapy. The short-term aim was to encourage activity in the pool and to work towards swimming. The long-term goal is to enable use of a public swimming pool. The same care worker and therapist always worked with Molly in the pool.

A risk-taking assessment was undertaken and followed throughout her sessions; contingency plans were made in case she were to have a seizure or bleed in the pool.

The first session was used as an introduction to the pool environment and water. This proved, in the beginning, to be difficult and ground rules of acceptable behaviour were set. Molly was supported in the pool so that it was difficult for her to bite her hand. She was encouraged to experience and enjoy the sensation of water. The therapist and carer were careful in positioning themselves so as not to encourage poor behaviour. The first session was short and ended when the client was enjoying the session. It was important never to take her out of the pool when she was not enjoying it.

Over the six-week period, Molly became accustomed to the consistent routine and began to enjoy the session. By the end of six weeks, she was lying on her back supported by the therapist and beginning to have confidence in the floating position. She had begun to lie on her front and glide towards the wall bar. Her confidence had grown to being able to hold onto the bar on her own and beginning to let go while needing only minimal support.

Action

1. The outcomes were evaluated and it was decided that another session was required to build on her confidence and to introduce more people into the pool to allow Molly to adjust to public pools after this session.
2. To assess the public pool near her home and to set a date for a swimming pool session with Molly and her carer.

ADAM

Adam is a wheelchair-dependent man in his forties who has spastic quadriplegia. He is able to express his needs and participate verbally in his programme planning.

He was referred for hydrotherapy because of acute pain in his right hip and very limited mobility. He was very anxious and fearful of pain increasing movement. He was awaiting hospitalisation for surgery to his hip. He presented almost lying in his chair in extension as a result of spasticity and limited hip movement.

The reason for hydrotherapy was explained to Adam, his support staff and worried family. A six-week course of hydrotherapy was agreed upon. His GP was notified and the date set.

Transfer from wheelchair to changing table and pool trolley was stressful and painful and required careful movement and handling. A hoist was used. Adam was introduced to the water carefully, allowing time for adjustment while verbally reassuring him. He was supported under his shoulders while the plinth was lowered, and buoyancy assisted him to float off the plinth. He was rigid and fearful so he was also supported around his hips.

Gentle side-to-side movements (weaving) were used and the thermal aspects of the water given time to work. Movements were smooth and gliding and no other turbulence was allowed. Gradually Adam relaxed and, as the experience became pleasant, some reduction of pain was achieved.

The main area of concern was how to get Adam out of the pool, dressed and seated with as little pain as possible so as not to negate the relaxation achieved.

The support staff had been very well prepared before the session so that they would be aware of the necessity to hold and move him gently and smoothly. They therefore understood the difficulties and had realistic expectations of the session.

The aims of the session were to achieve relaxation of muscles, relieve pain and increase joint movement.

Over the six-week period the outcomes achieved were relaxation of muscles, which led to pain reduction and greater willingness on Adam's part to move and experiment a little in the pool. By the end of his session he was looking forward to further hydrotherapy.

The carers learnt to move and handle Adam in a more appropriate way so as not to exacerbate pain. They enjoyed the hydrotherapy and were pleased with the pain reduction and Adam's ability to sleep after these sessions.

Action

To continue hydrotherapy until Adam was admitted to hospital.

REFERENCES

Brown, D.A., Effgen, S.K. and Palisano, R.J. (1998) Performance following ability – focused physical therapy intervention in individuals with severely limited physical and cognitive abilities. *Physical Therapy,* **78** (9), 934–50.

Chadwick, D. (1997) The Encyclopaedia of Epilepsy (2nd edition). Alden Colour, Oxford.

Chartered Society of Physiotherapy (2006) *Guidance on Good Practice in Hydrotherapy*, CSP Publications Unit, London.

Cogher, L., Savage, E. and Smith M.F. (eds) (1992) *Cerebral Palsy – The Child and Young Person*, Chapman & Hall Medical, London.

Davis, B.C., Harrison, R.A. (1988) *Hydrotherapy in Practice*, Churchill Livingstone, Edinburgh.

Kelsey, B (2006) The Halliwick Concept, *Aqualines*, **18** (1), 4–7 [see also www.halliwick. org.uk]

Odunmbaku Auty, P.M. (1990) *Hydrotherapy – Evaluating and Costing a Physiotherapy Intervention (Modality) in the Service for People with Learning Disabilities using Hydrotherapy as an Example. Is it a Cost Effective Resource?* Chartered Society of Physiotherapy, London.

Reid Campion, M. (1991) *Hydrotherapy in Paediatrics*, 2nd edn, Butterworth Heinemann, Oxford.

Reid Campion, M. (ed.) (1997) *Hydrotherapy Principles and Practice*, Butterworth Heinemann, Oxford.

Skinner, A.T., Thompson, A.M. (eds) (1983) *Duffield's Exercises in Water*, 3rd edn, Bailliere Tindall, London.

12 Riding for Disabled People

ALYS WATSON

INTRODUCTION

Riding for the disabled in UK could be said to date from the initiative of a physiotherapist, Olive Sands, who took her horses to the hospital where she worked during the 1914–18 war for men wounded in France to ride as part of their rehabilitation.

By the 1950s and 1960s, a handful of pioneers were exploring the possibility of riding for all types of disability. These pioneers included occupational therapists and physiotherapists. By 1969, the Riding for the Disabled Association (RDA) was founded. It developed more as a recreational and group activity than one with any specific therapeutic aims. Unlike the German and Swiss models, it lacked the structured educational standards and a clearly defined treatment approach necessary to attract healthcare professionals, other than in an advisory capacity.

Now, physiotherapists through their clinical interest group, the Association of Chartered Physiotherapists in Therapeutic Riding (ACPTR), formerly the Association of Chartered Physiotherapists in Riding for the Disabled, have developed a three-part accredited course, 'The Horse in Rehabilitation'. This provides a nationally and internationally recognised qualification, encouraging systematic study and research and emphasising treatment. Successful completion of the course requires the physiotherapist to have demonstrated appropriate riding and horse-handling skills, a knowledge of equine anatomy and psychology and an awareness of the risks inherent in a riding situation. The most significant requirement is the ability to analyse the horse's movement, assess each rider and select an appropriate horse to obtain the maximum therapeutic advantage.

This chapter offers an introduction to horse riding and the use of the horse as part of a treatment programme for people who have learning disabilities and associated physical disabilities. It includes RDA classifications, criteria for selecting riding as a treatment method and contraindications and special precautions. It is illustrated by four case studies.

Learning Disability: Physical Therapy Treatment and Management. Edited by Jeanette Rennie
© 2007 John Wiley & Sons Ltd

CLASSIFICATIONS WITHIN THE RDA

- *Hippotherapy.* This is treatment using the movement of the horse, based on the principles of neuromotor function and sensory processing and is entirely reactive, the horse through his movement influencing the rider. It is carried out by an appropriately qualified physiotherapist working with a horsemaster. Back riding, a highly skilled technique, is included under hippotherapy. Here a suitably qualified physiotherapist either sits behind the client on the horse, or supervises another back rider, to achieve therapeutic aims not possible from the ground. Baker (1993) emphasises the careful selection of clients for back riding.
- *Therapeutic riding.* Riding is taught. The rider becomes proactive and starts to influence the horse. The physiotherapist assessing the rider, and with the instructor plans a riding programme and monitoring progress.
- *Recreational riding.* Although this chapter deals primarily with treatment and is more concerned with the first two classifications, recreation using the horse has an acknowledged therapeutic input.

The classifications are not watertight compartments and there is considerable overlap between the three.

All riders are encouraged to progress through these classifications as far as their disabilities allow, gaining the maximum stimulation and enjoyment from the experience.

Treatment on the horse depends on the horse's ability to move the rider's pelvis and trunk through three dimensions: laterally, anteroposteriorly and rotationally. The response is automatic, with no cortical input, demanding balance and sensory integration to remain centred and upright on this moving base – a base that at the same time is being carried forward through space.

There are striking similarities between a human pelvis when walking and when being moved by a walking horse. Fleck (1997) has shown that linear displacements of a rider's pelvis walking and riding differed only in magnitude, not in timing or sequence.

An average human walk is 110 to 120 steps per minute; that of the average horse 100 to 120 steps per minute; this stride length provides a rate of movement at which the rider's pelvis and trunk can learn to accommodate. In 10 minutes, at 100 steps per minute, the rider experiences 1000 displacements to which she must respond.

Riede (1988) maintains that the overall treatment goal of hippotherapy is automatic postural stability in alignment with the centre of gravity. To illustrate how this occurs, Table 12.1 analyses the horse's walking pattern and the rider's response. The horse's walk is a four-beat sequence. Rider response comes mainly from the hind limb movement. Table 12.2 gives the rider response to variations of stride and direction.

Mandel (1984) states that 'Without doubt, the best sitting posture is obtained on horseback.' It encourages a position optimally aligned for balance. Where

Table 12.1. Rider Response to Walking Horse

The rider's pelvis and thighs form an interface with the horse. Proprioceptive receptors from here signal disturbance of this sitting base when the horse walks and require a response from the rider for balance to be maintained. Having correctly identified the disturbance, there is a need for an adaptive response in the rider's trunk to realign his body in answer to his pelvic movement, keeping it upright and facing forwards.

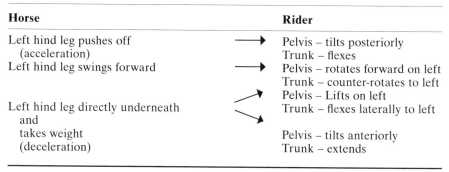

Horse	Rider
Left hind leg pushes off (acceleration)	Pelvis – tilts posteriorly Trunk – flexes
Left hind leg swings forward	Pelvis – rotates forward on left Trunk – counter-rotates to left
	Pelvis – Lifts on left Trunk – flexes laterally to left
Left hind leg directly underneath and	
takes weight (deceleration)	Pelvis – tilts anteriorly Trunk – extends

This sequence repeats for the right hind leg.

Table 12.2. Variations in stride and direction

Walking horse	Rider response
Work in straight lines	Flexion and extension of pelvis and trunk
Stride lengthening and shortening	Greater demand to follow movement
Halt to walk to halt transitions flexion/extension	Biggest challenge to flexion/extension control
Upward transitions (halt to walk)	Flexor truncal response
Downward transitions (walk to halt)	Extensor truncal response
Work on circles	Weight shift to outside, with trunk elongation to that side (Citterio 1985)

correct alignment is achieved, a plumb line dropped from the rider's ear passes through shoulder, hip and heel (Figure 12.1(a)). The small degree of hip flexion encourages an upright pelvis. This is posturally important but also allows maximum transference of movement from horse to rider. A familiar deviation from this, sacral sitting, with a posteriorly tilted pelvis and increased hip flexion, blocks movement and reduces the horse's therapeutic input (Figure 12.1(b)).

In planning a therapy programme the most important consideration is the horse's movement. The stride should be rhythmic and regular but variations such as stride length, smooth gait with little rider disturbance or 'big' movement requiring maximum rider response will be considered by the physiotherapist in selecting an appropriate horse.

Optimum posture

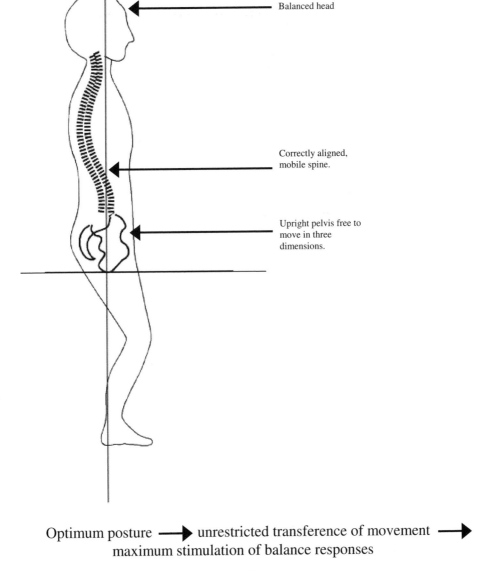

Optimum posture ⟶ unrestricted transference of movement ⟶
maximum stimulation of balance responses

Figure 12.1a. Optimum posture.

<u>Sacral sitting</u>

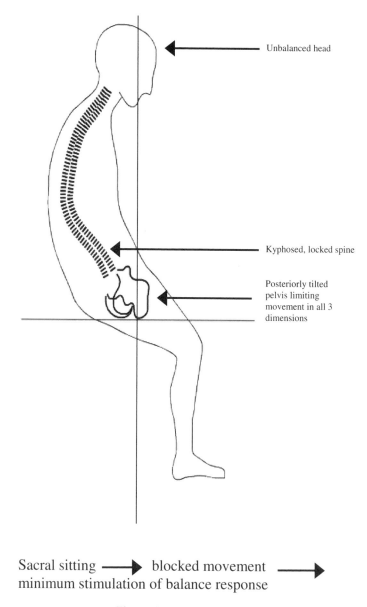

Unbalanced head

Kyphosed, locked spine

Posteriorly tilted
pelvis limiting
movement in all 3
dimensions

Sacral sitting ⟶ blocked movement ⟶
minimum stimulation of balance response

Figure 12.1b. Sacral sitting.

Other factors to be considered in planning a therapy programme are:

- *Height of horse.* The average horse provides the optimum movement but, in selection, the amount of assistance needed from the side-helpers, who must be able to reach their riders, must be considered.
- *Width of horse.* This should be narrow for clients with tight adductors although broad may give a better base for balance.
- *Psycho/social factors.* This includes the relationship of horse and rider and the integration of horse and rider within a group
- *Special equipment.* This is usually advised by the physiotherapist, and used to enhance the therapeutic input.
- *The team.* This consists of a leader competent in horse handling, and side-helpers especially trained in mounting and handling riders.

CRITERIA FOR SELECTING RIDING AS A TREATMENT METHOD

The most significant factor in using the horse in rehabilitation is the influence of his movement on improving neuromotor function and sensory processing. The following disabilities should benefit the most:

- neurological motor dysfunctions
- problems of sensory integration
- difficulties with perception and coordination

CONTRAINDICATIONS

- Uncontrolled epilepsy. Clients with controlled epilepsy are welcomed but those where it is uncontrolled could be a hazard to themselves and others in the riding situation.
- Arthritis in the acute phase, including Still's disease.
- Multiple sclerosis in the acute phase.
- Unhealed pressure sores.
- Behavioural problems that cause a safety hazard to the client, horse or staff.
- Severe allergies or asthma exacerbated by the horse or his environment.
- Clients who are too heavy, either for the horse or to be safely mounted and dismounted.
- Clients who, after a suitable trial period, clearly do not wish to ride.

SPECIAL PRECAUTIONS

- Monitoring of clients with sensory loss for pressure sores, not only over the ischial tuberosities, but over the inner surface of lower limbs.
- Careful fitting of riding helmets where a shunt is situated behind the ear.

- Regular information exchange between clinical, care and riding teams on relevant medical and general management.
- Ongoing reassessment of clients by the riding team to allow for the considerable changes that may occur with riding therapy.
- Riding for the Disabled Association health and safety guidelines relating to assistance with mounting recommend:
  - assessment of the task (risk assessment); where the rider's weight exceeds the recommended limits, it may be necessary to refuse to allow that rider to ride
  - full use of mounting blocks and wheelchair ramps
  - instruction of those involved in mounting in correct lifting
- Education, health and social work staff assisting at riding sessions should seek insurance from their employing authorities.

The following four case histories illustrate the practical application of using the horse as part of a rehabilitation programme.

CASE STUDIES

CASE STUDY 1: PETER

Peter was a 14-year-old boy with spastic quadriplegia and profound learning disabilities. He had bilateral cataracts leading to the loss of sight in his right eye and eventually to total blindness. He had no speech but showed recognition of familiar voices and sounds, responding to simple commands. He indicated pleasure by smiling.

Until then, physiotherapy and good management at school and at home had maintained his functional ability, movement range and posture but the onset of total blindness had resulted in a steady deterioration. He stopped rolling independently and moving around in his walker. He was less ready to turn to sound or explore with his hands. The school staff reported increasing difficulty in positioning him upright in his chair and standing frame because he slumped to the left, with increasing reluctance to raise his head or respond to stimuli. This limited his involvement in and benefit from all classroom activities. Over six months, hip abduction decreased by $20°$ (bilaterally) and he developed a scoliosis concave to the left, a flattened lumbar curve and increased thoracic kyphosis. He stopped using body tilt reactions to maintain sitting balance, substituting excessive, disruptive parachute responses.

The concern over this deterioration led to consideration of alternative therapy and hippotherapy was proposed.

The following assessments were made at the start of the programme:

- posture and balance on the horse
- body-tilt reactions in sitting, off the horse

- mobility, using a standard functional mobility chart
- range of hip movement
- reports from mother and school staff on general alertness and wellbeing

Peter rode on a sheepskin, giving a soft, warm sitting surface, allowing an unimpeded transference of movement from horse to rider that is not possible with a saddle.

Despite tactile and verbal prompting, Peter remained in sacral sitting throughout the 20-minute session. It was therefore decided to use back riding at the next session. The aim was to correct Peter's pelvic position sufficiently to allow the movement from the horse to stimulate his balance responses.

A bigger, specially trained horse was used to accommodate the two riders. The back rider's hands over Peter's pelvis facilitated antero-posterior pelvic movement in rhythm with the movement of the horse's hind legs. As Peter's pelvis became more upright, he started to straighten his spine, lifted his head – and smiled.

By the fourth week, Peter's pelvis was following the movement input from the horse with minimal facilitation from the back rider. He was also responding to verbal cues to 'sit tall' and of 'head up'. During the next two sessions, accelerations and decelerations at the walk were introduced to facilitate anteroposterior trunk control.

By the seventh week, Peter rode without a back rider. Initially he relapsed into a degree of sacral sitting. This time, tapping his lumbar spine and repeating 'sit tall and head up' produced a positive response. If the horse maintained an active walk, pelvic and adaptive trunk responses occurred and Peter laughed and clapped his hands. If the walk slowed he relapsed into posterior pelvic tilt. Reestablishing the active walk again produced an upright pelvis, correctly aligned spine and head – and pleasure from Peter.

From the start, the commands 'walk on' and 'halt' were used to the horse to allow Peter to anticipate, prepare and make the appropriate response to these movements. As DeLubersac (1985) has pointed out: 'The rider is able to anticipate an action that is already familiar.' Peter now started to show a feed-forward response, a mechanism for postural control discussed by Carr and Shepherd (1987), anticipating and staying with accelerations and decelerations without loss of balance.

After 12 weeks Peter had made good progress. Figures 12.2 and 12.3 record his posture and balance and he showed an increase in hip abduction of 10° bilaterally.

A report from his school reads:

Peter returns from riding animated and happy. At first, his improved response level only continued into the afternoon, but we now recognise an overall improvement throughout the week. We have noticed real progress in his posture since he started riding, both in the classroom and going out in his wheelchair. If he slumps to the left, he will now usually correct his position on request and he has again started to

Hippotherapy assessment

Name: Peter   **Assessor:** AW

Horse: Eddie   **Equipment:** Sheepskin

	Date: 1st Week	Date: 2nd Week	Date: 6th Week	Date: 12th Week	Date: 24th Week
Maintains position					
At Halt	C1	A3	B5	D4	E6
At Walk	C1	A6	B6	D6	E6
Acceleration /Deceleration at Walk.	C0	A0	B2	D4	E6
Halt to Walk to Halt Transitions.	C0	A0	B1	D3	E4
Comments	Uncorrected sacral sitting blocking movement and balance responses	Head lifted and smiled	Good posture stimulated by walk	Showed pleasure at response to active walk	Greater response to verbal cueing

Poor Posture (PP)   means sacral sitting, flexed spine, head not erect OR uneven pelvic weight-bearing with spinal and/or head asymmetry.

Good Posture (GP)   means upright, level pelvis with centred head and spine.

Coding:

A = Backrider – maximum facilitation   0 = Unable to perform

B = Backrider – minimum facilitation   1 = PP 30 seconds, unreliable performance

                                           2 = GP 30 seconds, unreliable performance

C = Side helpers only, stabilisation at knee and ankle

D = Side helpers only, stabilisation at ankle only   3 = PP 1 minute, variable reliability

E = No stabilisation   4 = GP 1 minute variable reliability

                                           5 = PP 5 minutes, greater reliability

                                           6 = GP 5 minutes, greater reliability

                                           7 = PP indefinitely, complete reliability

                                           8 = GP indefinitely, complete reliability

Ideal score = E8

Figure 12.2. Hippotherapy assessment.

move around in his walker. He is turning to sound and reaching out to locate various objects placed on his table. We feel that he is now adapting to his loss of sight and starting to use his other senses to compensate for his lack of vision.

The innovative element of using the horse and the powerful impact that he has on his rider may, as in Peter's case, provide the catalyst to move the whole rehabilitation process forward again.

Assessment of body tilt reactions using vestibular board and tiltmeter

Patients Name: Peter_____   Assessor: AW_____

		1 Week pre-riding	After 12 weeks riding
Angle	10°	No response	No response
of Lateral	20°	No response	Delayed response
Tilt	30°	Loss of balance with lateral parachute	Some body tilt response preceding lateral parachute
Angle	10°	No response	Minimal response
of A/P	20°	Increased flexion	Correct body tilt
Tilt	30°	Loss of balance	Correct body tilt

Patient in cross- legged sitting

Figure 12.3. Assessment of body tilt reactions using vestibular board and tiltmeter.

CASE HISTORY 2: DAVID

Wade et al. (1986), among others, now recognise stroke patients as having disturbances of concentration and learning. While acknowledging that stroke patients are not usually included in the caseload of those working entirely in the field of learning disability, it is hoped that the following case history will be of value. Readers will recognise familiar problems and be able to relate them – and the problem solving – to some of their own clients.

David was a 64-year-old ex-army officer who suffered a right-sided stroke two years before coming to the RDA. Before his stroke he had been very active and enjoyed physical challenges. With such a temperament, his physical and learning disabilities were a shattering blow to his morale. He was very depressed and was looking for a suitably demanding and stimulating physical activity. Riding appeared a possibility to fulfil this need, at the same time helping with his therapy requirements.

At his preriding assessment, he walked with a circumduction gait using a tripod stick and wearing a right ankle foot orthosis (AFO). He had limited right-shoulder movement, could grasp and release an object if placed in his right hand, but had a tactile astereognosis.

He had problems of right-left discrimination, concentration and memory and his expressive aphasia led to frustration and tension. Physiotherapy was no longer available, but he had regular speech therapy. A prime aim of riding was to promote midline symmetry with prospective carryover into standing.

Riding Eddie, David sat as he did at home, with a left lateral pelvic shift, weight bearing predominantly on the left with a compensatory right trunk and head side flexion and retraction of his right pelvic and shoulder girdles. Johnstone (1987) emphasises the need in stroke rehabilitation for meticulous positioning of the base in weight bearing and for lateral transference of weight over the affected side to achieve this. The principles of riding therapy agree with this – that the first requirement, where asymmetry exists, is correction to midline.

Initially David was not expected to hold the reins and Eddie was led. We used a sheepskin rather than a saddle, allowing David to focus his attention on attaining a symmetrical sitting base. By keeping his hands on his thighs he facilitated right shoulder girdle protraction.

Leading Eddie on a 20-metre circle to the left gave the centrifugal effect of transference of weight to the outside (right) seat bone, with trunk lengthening on the right (Citterio 1985).

Using the riding school mirror, we asked David to correct his position at halt, and then asked him to make the same corrections with Eddie walking towards the mirror. Berquet (1977) found using a mirror essential in correcting postural dysfunction.

David was encouraged to give verbal commands to Eddie and we liaised with his speech therapist, listing the words relating to the horse, his equipment and the riding lesson.

Exercises were introduced, all performed at a walk, giving the unique benefit of an underlying continuum of three-dimensional movement throughout. These encouraged the postural responses to external perturbations, in this instance the walking horse, as well as the postural adjustments preceding voluntary limb movements and centre of mass displacements described by Horak (1987). Reaching across with his left hand to touch successively his right hand, knee and then slide down towards his right foot served the double purpose of weight transference to the right and cross facilitation. Right rotation transferred weight to David's right seat bone, whereas left rotation gave right pelvic and shoulder girdle protraction, so rotations in both directions were practised. By introducing variations in the horse's stride length and direction, use was being made of the theory that motor learning requires repetition in a variety of settings to assist learning.

David was now starting to appreciate the greater freedom with which Eddie moved when the rider's weight was centred and used this as a feedback to check for his correct position. With midline symmetry now established, a saddle was introduced. David's posture remained symmetrical and he was given adapted reins, allowing him to place both hands on the reins. By doing this, symmetry and visual and tactile awareness of the right side were encouraged.

David could now start controlling his horse and steering around a course, following demonstrated instructions to turn left or right.

A year after starting to ride, David was riding independently in the school, as part of an adult class, following right/left commands. He could trot and achieved an unscheduled but successful canter, which he described as 'marvellous'!

His confidence had returned and his horizons widened. He had taken up swimming again, was dinghy sailing and was no longer reluctant to go out and meet people.

Functional progress was assessed using a timed walking test with an ABAB design. This simple test has been shown to have both validity and reliability. It provides multiple information, as Goldfarb and Simon (1984) have shown that gait speed relates strongly to cadence and stride length and Bohannon (1989) that it also relates to balance. See Figure 12.4.

Riding, for David, had helped his motor and cognitive learning but perhaps the greatest benefit for him had been psychological.

CASE HISTORY 3: GEORGE

George, aged 32 years, lived at home with his parents and attended a day centre. He had learning disabilities and a moderate ataxia but walked independently both indoors and out. His understanding was good but speech was limited. He lacked motivation and confidence, had difficulties with sequencing and had spatial problems.

Timed walking test

Name: David   **Assessor:** AW

Test	Time in Seconds			
	A	B	C	D
Walking 5 m and return (total 10 m)	24.16	18.07	19.53	16.30

A = 1 week preriding   Using Tripod
B = After 8 weeks riding.   Using stick
C = After 8 weeks no riding.   Using stick
D = After 8 weeks resumed riding   Using stick.

Figure 12.4. Timed walking test.

His typical posture was sacral sitting with flexed spine and head, making eye contact difficult and interaction with his associates at the day centre very limited.

With his history of being withdrawn, with little interest in his environment, it was encouraging to note his positive reaction when introduced to his horse, Dandy, patting him, talking to him and examining his saddle and bridle.

George's saddle had a cover with adjustable sacral pad and anterior thigh rolls to correct his sacral sitting. With his good understanding, it was possible to ask George to sit tall and look at the rider ahead, at the same time asking him to check if this rider was himself sitting tall. This produced a postural response in George of a correctly aligned spine over his now more upright pelvis and at the same time encouraging him to raise his head and relate to the other rider.

As his sitting balance and manipulative skills were reasonably good, he started by holding the reins, but with a leader in attendance.

Although receiving individual attention where necessary, George rode in a group lesson. The advantages for him were that it provided a more interesting social environment, gave him an opportunity to copy and learn from the other riders, and later provided the possibility of developing social skills of one rider helping the other.

Initially, George had difficulty in judging distances and adjusting Dandy's pace before he either bumped into the leading pony or left a yawning gap, with the rest of the ride bunched up behind. The safety reasons for keeping a correct distance were explained, and the problems caused for the other riders when this didn't occur. George had already demonstrated his ability to control Dandy's pace and was now given the responsibility of showing how well he could do this to get his spacing right. To help him, it was decided to vary the approach, turning the activity into a game and providing more group interaction. The ponies were halted at intervals round the school. George, on Dandy, walked forward and, on reaching the correct distance from the pony in front, George called 'walk on' to that rider, both riders and ponies then walking on towards the next pony where the sequence was repeated until the whole ride was moving, correctly spaced. George's anticipation and judgement of distance started to improve and he even reproved a rider for not walking on immediately!

Another of George's problems, poor sequencing, gave rise to difficulties with mounting and dismounting. To dismount, George would drop the reins and try to dismount with both feet still in the stirrups, often before Dandy had stopped moving. Asking George to verbalise his intention as he performed the task proved helpful. Thus:

'Halt. Reins in left hand' [assistant touching his hand].
'Both feet out of stirrups' [assistant checks].
'Right [indicated by touch] leg back and over. Dismount.'

Unvarying repetition improved his performance, which over eight weeks became increasingly reliable.

Praise for success in this task, as recognised by McGibbon (1994), was invaluable in building George's self-esteem and confidence.

Correct sequencing during games brought the reward of successful completion of the activity and, to everyone's surprise, George started to prove himself quite competitive.

Taking a coloured ring, selecting a matching coloured bucket in the arena, riding to it, halting and dropping the ring in the bucket required colour matching, judgement of distance, steering and controlling the pace of the pony and sequencing – for example, halting the pony before releasing the ring. Performed as a team game, this called for awareness of the team members and of other competitors. Taken together, these activities demanded a combination of motor, cognitive and social skills.

There was no doubt about George's progress in the riding class, but it was important to his quality of life that there should be carryover into his daily living activities. After 12 weeks of riding, there was the following response to questions relating to his everyday life, noted and recorded both at the day centre and at home:

- improved interaction with his peers
- increased verbal communication
- a marked change in his general interest and confidence
- improvement in activities involving correct sequencing

George had been able to demonstrate the transfer of learning skills acquired during riding to his everyday life and this assured us that his learning had become more secure.

His father felt that it was the motivation of the whole riding situation that had produced results so far not achieved by other means.

CASE HISTORY 4: WAI KWAN

Wai Kwan, a small Asian girl aged 7 years, came with her special school to ride with the Hong Kong RDA.

Horses are seldom seen in Hong Kong, except on the racecourse, and Wai Kwan's mother was very doubtful about allowing her to come to ride.

Although able to walk indoors, Wai Kwan did not use this as a purposeful activity and staff used a wheelchair for all community outings because she had a tendency to fall and objected to having her hand held. She had periods of hyperactivity, alternating with total passivity, and she rocked her body and bit her hands when distressed. She had very poor sensory discrimination, tactile defensiveness, and an aversion to handling. She had no speech and her understanding was difficult to assess.

Our aims for Wai Kwan were to use the constant sensory input provided by the rhythmic, repetitious movement of the pony to facilitate sensory discrimination. So far she had not developed the ability to sift through and suppress irrelevant sensory information and produced inappropriate responses to incoming information.

Although a small pony made it easier for the side-helpers to reach the child, its shorter, choppier gait in this case provided too much stimulation, so a larger pony with a longer stride and smoother movement was chosen.

Wai Kwan's tactile defensiveness gave her an aversion to touching fur, so a smooth cotton fitted rug was used to cover the pony. She would not tolerate a riding helmet but as the session was to be conducted by a physiotherapist we were able to start without one.

Her teacher walked on one side and acted as interpreter for the English-speaking physiotherapist.

Wai Kwan body-rocked violently, closing her eyes and biting her hands. She resisted any attempts to steady her balance, so a rather nerve-racking policy of 'hands off but eyes on' was pursued. After 10 minutes, she tried to throw herself off the pony but her teacher reassured her and the session continued. After 20 minutes, she had opened her eyes but continued to body rock and bite her hands at intervals. We agreed to continue for a further two sessions to see if there was any improvement.

The second session started as the first but, half way through, she lay back spontaneously on the pony and we continued to walk with her lying quietly in supine with her head in midline and her arms relaxed by the pony's sides, and this pattern was repeated at the next session.

This amount of progress justified a continuation of the riding programme. With subsequent sessions, we allowed her to continue to choose her position following the principle advocated by Ayres (1972) of allowing the child to direct her own actions. She moved between supine and sitting with eyes open and hands relaxed, without body rocking or hand biting, as long as we remained in attendance only, without touching her

By the sixth session, she spent the entire time sitting, propping forwards on open hands and getting movement from the pony's shoulders through her own upper limbs and shoulder girdle. She now tolerated a riding helmet, if it was fitted once the ride had started.

Riding had so far been in a sheltered indoor arena. To test her progress we moved into the adjoining outdoor arena. It was breezy and sunny, with some noise from the neighbouring school. Wai Kwan reverted to her body rocking and we realised that we were trying to move too fast, the smallest change in sensory input generating a disproportionately large effect with which she still could not cope. Fortunately, returning to the original arena allowed her to recover and we finished the session without noticeably having lost ground.

Eight weeks of hippotherapy produced the following results:

- She sat quietly on the pony for a 20-minute ride, tolerating a degree of handling from the side helpers to correct her balance.
- She accepted a riding helmet throughout the ride.
- Provided the ride started in the more sheltered school she was now able to cope with the outdoor arena in calm weather.
- By folding back the front of the rug, she was able to place her hands directly onto the pony's shoulders and tolerated this as long as the pony was moving. This correlated with the findings of Fisher et al. (1991) in their treatment of tactile defensiveness. The moving pony provided the controlled vestibular-proprioceptive stimulus, facilitating the appropriate interpretation of tactile sensory input.

Her achievements to date led us to hope that progress would continue and that there would eventually be measurable carryover into her everyday life.

Her mother's amazement, on coming to the RDA, in seeing what her daughter could achieve provided ample justification, even had there been no other, for continuing her hippotherapy.

CONCLUSION

Riding for disabled people has become increasingly valued throughout the world because, as Hamilton (1997) wrote: 'The traditional treatment setting has no modality to match the versatility of the horse. This alive and moving "apparatus" provides a multitude of stimuli to treat a variety of diagnoses. The horse can assist the client in attaining motor skills that would be difficult or slow in coming in the clinic.'

REFERENCES

Ayres, A.J. (1972) *Sensory Integration and Learning Disabilities*, Western Psychological Services, Los Angeles.

Baker, E.A. (1993) Back-riding techniques in therapy, in *Therapeutic Riding Programmes*, (ed. B. Engel), Omnipress, Maddison WI, pp. 558–62.

Berquet, K.H. (1977) Maskulare Kreuzschmerzen bei Haltungsschaden, in *Lumbalgie und Ischialgie*, (ed. H. Junghanns), Stuttgart, Hippokrates-Veil, pp. 27–8.

Bohannon, R.W. (1989) Correlation of lower limb strengths and other variables with standing performance in stroke patients. *Physiotherapy Canada*, **41**, 198–202.

Carr, J. and Shepherd, R. (1987) *Movement Science: Foundation for Physical Therapy in Rehabilitation*, Aspen Publishers, Rockville MD.

Citterio, D.N. (1985) The influence of the horse in neuromotorial evolution. *Proceedings of the Fifth International Congress on Therapeutic Riding*, ANIRE Association, Milan, Italy.

DeLubersac, R. (1985) The psychomotor mechanism, riding and the horse. *Proceedings of the Fifth International Congress of Therapeutic Riding*. Milan, Italy.

Fisher, A., Murray, E. and Bundy, A. (1991) *Sensory Integration: Theory and Practice,* F.A. Davis & Co., Philadelphia.

Fleck, C.A. (1997) Hippotherapy: mechanics of human walking and horseback riding, in *Rehabilitation with the Aid of the Horse: A Collection of Studies* (ed. B. Engel), Therapy Services, Durango CO.

Goldfarb, B.J. and Simon, S.R. (1984) Gait patterns in patients with amyotrophic lateral sclerosis. *Archives of Physical Medicine and Rehabilitation,* **65**, 61–65.

Hamilton, K. (1997) An introduction to treatment with the use of the horse, in *Therapeutic riding 11. Strategies for rehabilitation* (ed. B. Engel), Omnipress, Maddison.

Horak, F.B. (1987) Clinical measurement of postural control in adults. *Physical Therapy,* **67** (12), 1881–5.

Johnstone, M. (1987) *Restoration of Motor Function in the Stroke Patient: A Physiotherapist's Approach,* 3rd edn, Churchill Livingstone, Edinburgh.

Mandel, A.C. (1984) The correct height of school furniture. *Physiotherapy,* **70** (2), 48–53.

McGibbon, N.H. (1994) Motor learning: the common denominator. *Proceedings of the Eighth International Therapeutic Riding Conference,* New Zealand, pp. 94–6.

Riede, D. (1988) *Physiotherapy on the Horse.* Translated and edited by G. Tebay, Delta Society, Washington DC.

Wade, D.T., Parker, V. and Langton Hewer, R. (1986) Memory disturbance after stroke: frequency and associated losses. *International Rehabilitation Medicine,* **8**, 60–4.

13 Rebound Therapy

SALLY SMITH AND DEBBI COOK

INTRODUCTION

Rebound therapy is becoming well established as a treatment modality in the field of learning disability. Many physiotherapists working in this area use trampolines in day centres, leisure centres, or schools to establish rebound therapy.

The trampoline was invented by a French neurologist who called it the 'trampolino' and used it to treat brain-injured children. In the UK, the trampoline was originally used for sports and recreation in schools and leisure facilities. By the early 1980s its use as a therapeutic tool was becoming more obvious.

Bhattacharya et al. (1980) published results of studies undertaken for NASA, which showed that jumping on a trampoline was less stressful to the neck, back, and ankle than jogging on a treadmill for an equivalent oxygen uptake. In fact the conclusion was that 'any activity on a rebound unit is more efficient than a treadmill running at any speed'.

Peterson (1981) described studies undertaken at UCLA in California on the use of the rebounder. She quoted Frost who stated that 'it improves the performance of the heart, lungs and lymphatic system. It improves circulation and muscle tone and challenges the skeletal muscles to increase stamina without any of the jarring associated with other aerobic activities.'

This study also claimed that 'children who had learning problems were found to have a 70 % improvement in co-ordination and balance after some months of rebounding.' The alternating movements – such as slapping the right knee with the left hand were the ones that most quickly improved coordination. Addy (2006) also used the trampoline as part of a movement programme to treat developmental coordination disorder.

At the same time as these studies were being carried out in the US, Eddie Anderson MCSP RGRT – then headmaster of Springwell Special School in Hartlepool – started using the trampoline with children with physical and learning disabilities. His aim in introducing them to the equipment in an integrated movement programme was to give the children a full range of movement experience. This led to the regular use of the trampoline with children

Learning Disability: Physical Therapy Treatment and Management. Edited by Jeanette Rennie
© 2007 John Wiley & Sons Ltd

for specific therapeutic outcomes according to the needs of the individual child: 'rebound therapy'. Through the early to mid 1980s these techniques developed by Eddie Anderson were adopted by physiotherapists and remedial gymnasts, and expanded and adapted for use with adults with learning disabilities. Today they have been consolidated and are now in regular use by therapists in the field of learning disability.

Rebound therapy has taken its place as an established treatment modality alongside the more familiar components of a whole movement programme such as hydrotherapy, fitness training and horse riding. It is still growing and developing as physiotherapists gradually become more skilled at assessing and formulating programmes for this equipment and other therapists, carers, teachers and day-centre staff become equally skilled at working with people on the trampoline.

USE OF REBOUND THERAPY

Rebound therapy can be used for people with a range of disabilities from mild physical and learning disability to profound and multiple learning disabilities. There is a wide range of starting positions, from lying to kneeling, sitting or standing. These can be graded according to the person's ability.

It is used in a strictly controlled manner by a skilled therapist or operator. The idea of using a mobile, unstable surface to activate movement is not new to physiotherapists: gymnastic balls and wobble boards have been used for many years.

Rebound therapy for adults, as for working in water, can assist in the training of movement by using the power and lift in the trampoline bed to initiate or energise movement, where on 'land' this may be very difficult or impossible. Like any other modality, rebound 'should not be used in isolation but should be integrated into weekly programmes and should be viewed not as a substitute for existing therapies but as a complement to them' (Smith and Cook 1990).

SCREENING AND CONTRAINDICATIONS

There are very few people who would not be suitable for rebound therapy (ACPPLD Rebound Working Party 1997). Any person who is to participate should be screened for:

- cardiac or circulatory problems
- respiratory problems
- vertigo, blackouts or nausea
- epilepsy
- spinal cord or neck problems

- spinal rodding
- open wounds
- any recent medical attention
- brittle bones
- osteoporosis
- friction effects on the skin
- unstable/hypermobile/painful joints
- severe challenging behaviour
- gastrostomy/colostomy bags
- herniae
- joint replacement/implant surgery
- reflux
- stress incontinence
- prolapse

There are only three absolute contraindications for taking a person on a trampoline. These are:

- detaching retinae
- atlanto-axial joint instability (Ali et al. 2006)
- pregnancy (seek medical advice) (Kinect Australia 2006)

Any therapist considering starting rebound should refer to the Chartered Society of Physiotherapy information paper *Safe Practice in Rebound Therapy* (Chartered Society of Physiotherapy 2007). This states that:

> 3.1 Physiotherapists should confine themselves to the use of therapeutic strategies that they are able to apply safely and competently (Rule 1, CSP 2002)
> 3.2 To ensure safe practice the physiotherapist should gain practical experience by attending a course in Rebound Therapy.

The physiotherapist should also have knowledge of the physical properties of the trampoline and the physiological effects and perceived therapeutic benefits on the body.

Before commencing treatment, the operator should have the following skills and be competent and confident about using them.

- getting on and off safely and enabling the client to do so
- bouncing in a stable position
- killing the bed, which means absorbing all energy from the bed so that it stops moving completely
- kipping the bed, which means transferring kinetic energy from operator to client by depressing the bed beneath the client's feet as he or she bounces
- damping the bed, which means absorbing some of the energy from the bed so that the client can maintain a controlled bounce

- riding the bed – it is essential that the operator stays in contact with the bed to enable him or her to maintain a stable position
- emergency stop

The operator should also be able to perform the following manoeuvres safely:

- half turn
- star jump
- tuck jump
- straddle jump
- pike jump
- seat drop

PHYSIOLOGICAL AND THERAPEUTIC EFFECTS

Rebound therapy has been found to have the following observable physiological and therapeutic effects.

PHYSIOLOGICAL EFFECTS

Cardio-Respiratory System

There is a high demand on muscles to support the body against the increased gravitational effect and in the control of movement required when acceleration takes place. This causes the heart and respiratory rate to increase and, as a consequence, venous and lymphatic drainage increases. Constant muscle work to maintain position and balance increases the demand for oxygen.

Muscle Tone

The effect on muscle tone can be observed in people with physical disabilities. Application of the right level of bounce is critical; too much can increase spasticity and too little under-stimulate.

Vigorous bouncing can cause an increase in tone by stimulating the sensory systems, for example the stretch receptors in muscles and proprioceptors in joints. Gentle bouncing can reduce high tone/spasticity by having a shaking effect on the muscle spindles.

Postural Mechanism

By creating a dynamic movement situation that challenges balance mechanisms, observable improvement can be made. This is particularly relevant when working with adults where a dynamic balance situation can be difficult to create in lying, sitting or kneeling.

Kinaesthetic Awareness

By multiple stimulation of joints, pressure stretch receptors, skin and muscles, kinaesthetic awareness is improved, leading to improved body image and spatial awareness.

THERAPEUTIC EFFECTS

Movement

- Movement can be facilitated at different stages of the bounce. The most active movement takes place at the top of the bounce where acceleration of the body equals the down-thrust of gravity to allow a momentary 'gravity-free' zone.
- By using good positioning and gently bouncing, relaxation can be achieved easily.
- The lowering or raising of muscle tone enables active movement to take place.
- Anticipation of movement occurs because of the effects of timing and rhythm imposed by bouncing.
- Balance and equilibrium reactions can be achieved through stimulation of postural mechanisms. Protective and saving reactions can also be developed.
- Small, impoverished body movements can produce larger movements than on land when a bounce is correctly applied because of the ability of the trampoline springs and their recoil to amplify the movement.
- Momentum and rhythm can be used to help teach new movement skills and energise movement.

Perception

- Body image, body-part awareness and positional sense are enhanced through tactile compression and joint sensation.
- Increased perception of body image and spatial awareness combined with rhythm and movement develop concentration.
- The experience of being free in space and falling is important for stimulating postural reflexes and saving reactions.
- Sensory input is increased via tactile, proprioceptive, auditory and visual channels.

Communication

- Cardio-respiratory effects and excitement may increase vocalisation, leading to exclamations and gasps.

- Eye contact tends to be increased as the client and operator are in close face-to-face contact. Establishing better eye contact leads to better concentration.

General Health and Social Benefits

- It can be used to develop fitness.
- It improves chest condition by shaking the lungs and stimulating the cough reflex.
- It increases flatulence by creating gaseous movement in the body.

Use of the trampoline is a valued activity by the population as a whole and rebound therapy allows people with a learning disability to access this for its physical, social, emotional and recreational aspects.

PRACTICAL APPLICATION OF REBOUND THERAPY

Rebound therapy always starts with a full physiotherapy assessment and medical information must be gained from the appropriate source.

Following this, the client's strengths and needs are noted and documented and an individual programme is devised. A number of care factors must be taken into consideration before treatment commences. Care factors are directly related to starting positions.

The following information should not be used without the operator having undertaken formal training on a recognised rebound therapy course.

CARE FACTORS

When a client is placed in any one of the starting positions, which may range from lying through to standing, the therapist/operator must always check the safety and comfort. This must never be left to an assistant or carer.

For example, if individuals are placed in prone (on the stomach) over a wedge, the operator must ensure that they have sufficient head control to maintain a safe head position. It is also essential that the amount of bounce put into the trampoline does not cause unnecessary whiplash due to poor head control. The operator should also check that the client is bearing weight correctly through shoulders and elbows. Fingers should be checked that they are not through the holes (webbing) of the trampoline and female clients should have a pillow underneath them to protect their breasts.

Finally checks must be made to toenails to ensure that they are protected from the surface of the trampoline.

The operator must ensure that, as he moves around the trampoline, his body weight does not unintentionally disturb the balance of the person on the wedge. This is because the wedge raises the person off the bed thus making him or her more vulnerable. For any starting position, the therapist must run through a similar process to ensure continued comfort and safety.

The operator in charge of the session is also responsible for the training, attentiveness and positioning of the spotters. These are people placed around the trampoline whose job it is to maintain the safety of those upon it. If the client is able to stand and walk the spotters need to be very alert, particularly if the person has poor balance. The operators need to move around the bed with extreme care. They must take more care with those who have tight Achilles tendons and cannot put their heels down flat and they must be prepared for any client to sit down unpredictably. It is dangerous to try to attempt to hold them up.

THERAPEUTIC USES

Each starting position has its own different therapeutic value and use. An example of this is side lying. A client can be placed in this position for the following therapeutic effects:

- Reduction of tone. The client should be supported on pillows and gentle continual bouncing should continue until tone reduces.
- Stretching of trunk and hips – an ideal position to stretch a scoliosis.
- Relaxation: continual gentle bouncing, client lying on a variety of textures such as silk, cotton and fur. This can be accompanied by quiet music. Use different smelling oils under the bed (position these before placing person on trampoline). Place parachute/scarves/silks over person whilst bouncing. (Refer to Chapter 16 on complementary therapies.)
- Increase sensory input: use of vibration or scratching/tapping on the bed.
- Teaching rolling or using rolling as a sensory activity.

Slow Rolling

The client is approached from behind. The operator places one hand on the client's hip to prevent an uncontrolled roll. The client is placed on one side, lying, facing away from the operator, at one side of the bed. The head can be supported by pillows or by another operator on the bed. The operator places one foot at the client's hip level and one at shoulder level. One hand is placed on top of the hip and the other on the shoulder. Small gentle bouncing is started. The operator slides his or her feet backwards one at a time and guides the client as he rolls towards the operator down the slope created by the operator's body weight. Feet are kept apart when moving backwards. A spotter must be positioned directly behind the operator.

Fast Roll

The position is as for a slow roll. Gentle bouncing is started. The client is then pulled towards the operator as he runs backwards with feet still apart. The client will follow down the slope. A spotter must be positioned directly behind the operator. Fast rolling should only ever be attempted with someone with good head control.

A more able person sitting on a soft play roll would gain therapeutically in the following ways:

- Improvement to balance: gentle rocking side to side, or forwards and backwards, using two operators. The closer the operator is to the client the more the balance is stressed.
  - Operator sitting in front of client on roll, each facing the other, operator's hand on client's shoulders. Progress to forearm and hand holds.
  - Operator standing in front of roll, supporting client with shoulder, holding forearm or hand.
  - Operator standing in front of roll, second operator sitting behind the client with hands on shoulders or hips.
  - Operator standing in front of roll, second operator standing behind the roll, client unsupported.
  - This can be progressed further by client placing hands on head and shoulders. Further progressions include playing 'pig in the middle' with a ball and two operators or throwing ball to and from an operator.
- Improving posture: work person's abdominals by operator bouncing behind person.
- Improve weight bearing through legs/feet by gentle bouncing.
- Stretching muscles: by sitting astride the roll and by gently bouncing to work the Achilles tendons and hip adductors.
- As a precursor for horse riding: various degrees of bouncing with client either supported or sitting free on roll.
- Improving exercise tolerance: people with very good balance can 'ride' the roll around the bed or can be kipped while 'riding' the roll.

Progression or alternatives include using a shaped roll, a physio ball, or a soft play block. The following are the therapeutic uses for someone who is learning or is able to stand or jump:

- To improve balance: progress from just standing on unstable surface with support of two people, to walking along or around bed, to jumping with support of two people then one person, then independently.
- To experience being free in space: being kipped by two operators, progressing to one, then independently.
- To improve circulation: gentle jumping by client works the soleus muscles and produces a pumping action on the underlying venous system.

- To improve eye contact and concentration: operator at front uses 'look at me' commands.
- To improve fitness and exercise tolerance: gradually increase length of time a client bounces.
- To stretch Achilles' tendons: gently bounce the person in standing. The operator at the back can stand closer to the person to create slope so that the heel is lower than the toe.

In any of the starting positions a variety of equipment can be used as described in Tables 13.1 to 13.4.

Table 13.1. Positioning equipment

Equipment	Use of equipment
Wedge	Positioning in prone, supine or for leg support.
Roll	Sitting astride, side sitting, supported sitting together with an operator (or two), or for initiating hands and knees position over the roll.
Soft play blocks	Sitting on, supporting.
T Rolls	Supporting legs, shoulders and head or trunk.
Thin mats	To protect knees from webbing when working in hands and knees and high or half-kneeling position.

Table 13.2. Sensory equipment

Equipment	Use of equipment
Parachute	Visual, auditory and tactile stimulation. Those with profound and multiple disabilities can be wrapped and supported in it and those who are ambulant can do seat drops into it.
Music	To assist timing and rhythm, for relaxation or motivation and confidence giving.
Bells/drums	Bells can be tied to springs to assist rhythm or in the centre of the trampoline to assist people with visual impairment locating the centre. Drums can be beaten for rhythm.
Sheepskin/fur coat/ Sheet/Sari silk	All can be used to lie on for tactile stimulation. Sari silks can be used for visual stimulation as they float when air goes into them.
Scented oils	These can be burnt for olfactory stimulation. (Refer to Chapter 16 on complementary therapies.)

Table 13.3. Coordination equipment

Equipment	Use of equipment
Ball/skittles/hoops/balloons	Throwing/catching/holding/targets, etc.
Symbols/photographs	Provide visual reinforcement for a physical move.

Table 13.4. Handling and moving equipment

Equipment	Use of equipment
Slidesheets	Transferring people into centre of trampoline.
Moving and handling belt	A comfortable support for operator to use as a safety and teaching tool.

CASE STUDY MR X

Mr X is a 37-year-old community ambulator (Hofferscale). He has cerebral palsy and is able to walk independently, with a step through gait of the right leg and a step to gait with the left leg, around his day centre and out of doors (on flat terrain).

This gentleman had no concept of crawling or kneeling up and could not stand up from a long sitting position. To get up from the floor he would have to push up on his elbows in reverse on to a low chair and then stand up. Communication was by a short vocabulary of Makaton signs and his own adapted signs. He spoke with no clear words.

The following shows the progressions made in his physical ability and his communication and interaction with staff on and off the trampoline during a 27-month period of rebound therapy:

January, Year 1

- He had no concept of moving from long sitting to standing.
- A physiotherapy roll was introduced but he required maximum assistance to stand up via high kneeling while using it.
- He could only work in long sitting, bouncing forward and backward. He managed this independently.
- He required two-handed support in standing. Maximum assistance required to stand up.
- He tried assisted rolling but was very resistant.
- His willingness to cooperate on the trampoline was very variable.

October, Year 1

- He is now turning in long sitting.
- He sat astride a roll and initiated bouncing for the first time.
- Standing by transferring his weight forwards.
- Walking forwards, backwards and sideways on the trampoline with one person's support. He occasionally walks independently but is very unsure.

November, Year 1

- Now starting to make choices about activities on the trampoline.
- Improved posture noted in standing with less trunk flexion. Working on independent standing with one operator doing gentle bouncing while client maintains an upright posture.

January, Year 2

- He attempted to move onto his hands and knees via side sitting but unable to achieve this.

February/March Year 2

- He displayed good walking forwards, backwards and sidewards with minimal assistance of one operator and increased confidence.
- Now progressing to jumping with two-handed support pushing through operator's hands, knees extended, however; using arms more than legs.

April Year 2

- Narrower standing base of support noted with improved standing posture.

May, Year 2

- He started to work in high kneeling with two operators assisting him into this position. Used building bricks (Mr X's preferred activity) to reach for them.
- His high-kneeling posture was very poor with increased lumbar curve, wide base, flexed hips needing full physical assistance to achieve both this and side sitting.
- He was precarious in both of these positions.

June, Year 2

- He starting to initiate movement from side sitting to high kneeling, although he did not achieve the movement.
- He was adopting the side-sitting position by choice and reaching from this position.

July, Year 2

- He was making choices of direction and indicating that he wished to walk around the trampoline.

- Now once he is in a high kneeling position he needed very little help to maintain it.
- Improved communication was noted, with 'me' stated clearly.

September, Year 2

- He achieved the hands and knees position (unable to crawl).
- He was starting to attempt to stand from sitting by putting hands down in front of him but was unable to do so and fell back into side sitting.
- He maintained high kneeling independently.
- He communicated 'no' clearly and, as the session was cut short because of his refusal, he demonstrated that he was sorry.

October, Year 2

- He displayed good reaching in high kneeling.
- Was unable to go from a standing position into a crawling position on a crash mat.
- Crawling was achieved.
- He assumed high kneeling independently with good weight transference in this position.
- He is now able to stand with a member of staff crouching in front and assisting him to bring his weight forward, and then Mr X stands up virtually independently.
- Able to stand from kneeling position into standing with one hand supported by operator and pushing up from mat with the other hand. It took several attempts but it was achieved. He was using Makaton signs for 'brick' and 'lie down'.

November, Year 2

- He is moving independently from long sitting to side sitting to high kneeling with verbal prompt and demonstration.
- He is able to move into high kneeling from four-point kneeling with verbal prompts and demonstration.
- He is showing good reaching when high kneeling and counterbalancing with arms.
- He stood up from his hands and knees on the second attempt but with poor quality of movement.
- Able to move into standing then to hands and knees then into sitting before getting off trampoline.
- Now able to jump with one operator giving one hand support and doing gentle kipping.

December, Year 2

- An attempt was made to improve the quality of the sitting-to-standing move with work on half-high kneeling to encourage more weight transference to the right side.

- He is standing and jumping with two-hand support and is now bending knees and joints in the jump.
- He was making more attempts at Makatan signing and said the word 'bricks'.

January, Year 3

- His jumping whilst standing improved. The operator was almost able to release one hand support once jumping started. He was jumping with good rhythm.

February, Year 3

- He achieved 20 independent jumps with stability.
- Independence in jumping was increasing with every session.

March, Year 3

- Crawling.
- He made a good attempt at moving from standing to being on his hands and knees whilst on the trampoline – but still needed assistance.
- Independent jumping.

April, Year 3

- Attempting to initiate bounce in standing.
- Able to damp bed when he chooses to.
- He was not scared of falling onto bed and will choose to sit if not wanting to comply.

CONCLUSION

The use of the trampoline is an activity that is valued by the population as a whole and therapists have discovered that the combination of the physical, social, and emotional aspects of rebound therapy has an extraordinarily therapeutic value for people with learning disabilities.

REFERENCES

Addy, L.M. (1996) A multiprofessional approach to treatment of developmental coordination disorder. *British Journal of Therapy Rehabilitation*, **3** (11).
Ali, F.E., Al-Bustan, M.A., Al Busairi, W.A., Al Mulla, F.A. and Esbaita, E.Y. (2006) Cervical spine abnormalities associated with Down Syndrome. *International Orthopaedics* **30** (4), 284–9.

Bhattacharya, A., McCutcheon, E.P., Sharvtz, E. and Greenleaf, J.E. (1980) Results from a NASA supported study. *Journal of Applied Physiology*, **49** (S), 881–7.

Chartered Society of Physiotherapy (2002) *Rules of Professional Conduct*, 2nd edn, Chartered Society of Physiotherapy, London.

Chartered Society of Physiotherapy (2007) *Information Paper, Safe Practice in Rebound Therapy*, Chartered Society of Physiotherapy, London.

Kinect Australia (1996) Health and medical information sheet (Victoria Government) www.betterhealth.vic.gov.au/bncu2/bncarticles.nsf/pages

Peterson, V. (1981) *Variations on a G Force*. Article received from 1240, East 800 North, Utah 84097.

Smith, S. and Cook, D. (1990) A study in the use of rebound therapy for adults with special needs. *Physiotherapy*, **76** (11), 734–5.

14 Group Work

JEANETTE RENNIE, LUCY CLARK AND HELEN HOLME

INTRODUCTION

In everyday life people of all ages live and work in groups and frequently choose to spend at least part of their recreational time participating in group activities such as parties and nightclubs, further education classes, team sports and exercise groups at a gym.

Chapter 6 described the necessity for people with learning disabilities to learn to build relationships and to be able to participate with people who were not learning disabled, individually and in group activities.

Much of the group work undertaken by speech and language therapists, occupational therapists and learning disability nurses is specifically designed to improve relationships. Groups often have to consist of people with similar needs, such as sign groups and groups for symbol work. Communication skills frequently need to be consolidated in a familiar setting before the speech and language therapist can transfer a group to a community setting to encourage communication in context. Nurses undertake personal development groups and assertiveness groups designed to help people with learning disabilities understand sexuality and how to express their emotions appropriately. In these groups they may liaise with psychologists or occupational therapists (Bruce 1988). Nurses and occupational therapists frequently work with dieticians and physiotherapists with groups that promote a healthy lifestyle.

This chapter looks at group work primarily as a way of improving physical ability. It describes a range of therapist-led groups that can be undertaken in homes, centres or the community. They can be used as treatment sessions or therapeutic recreation in their own right or as a precursor to activities, sport and outdoor pursuits with the general population.

Physiotherapists have long recognised group work as a way of encouraging individuals to progress from directed individual treatment to taking more responsibility for their own exercise and for developing beyond the 'patient' attitude of being set apart because of disability (Gardiner 1971). Gardiner also regarded peer support and mild competition and the stimulation of activities

Learning Disability: Physical Therapy Treatment and Management. Edited by Jeanette Rennie
© 2007 John Wiley & Sons Ltd

as valuable aids to recovery, as did Thow (2006) in her development of Glasgow's community fitness and cardiac rehabilitation groups.

In 1970 Cotton, referring to group work in relation to conductive education, wrote that '...it is important as it is stimulating and makes the children ambitious.'

The idea of making some children, and adults, more ambitious has led to criticism of group work by people who regard it as a way of encouraging a feeling of failure in the rest of the group. (The advantages and disadvantages are explored more fully in Chapter 15.) In practice it has been found that clients who have learning disabilities enjoy encouraging each other and express delight at the feeling of achievement when they learn something new and are told that they are improving.

Clients are frequently referred to physiotherapists for a specific symptom but are subsequently found to be polysymptomatic. This reflects the trend in the general population demonstrated by results of a study undertaken with patients referred by general practitioners to primary care physiotherapists for a programme of group exercise (Crook et al. 1998).

REASONS FOR SELECTING GROUP WORK TO IMPROVE PHYSICAL ABILITY IN PEOPLE WITH LEARNING DISABILITIES

- To maintain and improve general fitness.
- To monitor physical ability and transfer to individual treatment if necessary.
- To encourage working together.
- To improve communication.
- To improve concentration.
- To engender a feeling of achievement.
- To have fun.

    Group work involves the participants in

- observing
- listening
- learning
- working together
- improving skills
- appreciating achievements

The structure and predictability of the group builds up expectations for each client. The participants can relax within this structure and learn to cope with any small changes that may be made.

Groups tend to be of long-standing duration as continuity is an important factor. If the complexity of activities in the group increases clients may participate for several years. It is essential, therefore, to keep careful records to ensure that aims are being met and reviewed.

Figure 14.1 is an example of a weekly record sheet that is used as the basis of assessment using an individual six monthly report form (Figure 14.2).

PRECAUTIONS

- Individual assessments should be undertaken to ascertain individual health needs and problems.
- The specific group must be appropriate for the client – for example dancing is unacceptable to some cultures.
- Carers and daycare staff should be consulted about the compatibility of group members.
- The number of group participants should be appropriate to the activity and complexity of clients' conditions.
- The number of staff and their experience should be appropriate to the size of the group, the complexity of the clients' conditions and the activity being undertaken.
- Any group held in a home, social services or community centre will be integrated into the timetable and needs to be flexible enough to accommodate fluctuating staffing levels.

EXAMPLES OF GROUP WORK

Groups may consist of the following:

- groups performing recognised exercises, which are sometimes undertaken as individual physiotherapy but where the element of working as part of a group enhances the treatment
- composite groups, which include recognised exercises but also use activities that cannot be undertaken individually
- specialist group activities used primarily with people with learning and physical disabilities
- group activities used by the general public but utilised to achieve physiotherapy goals with a group of people with learning disabilities

It is rare for any group to be taken by a physiotherapist alone. Some groups require a contribution from different professionals and specific teaching from the physiotherapist. In all groups participants require individual encouragement from members of staff as well as their peer group. People with challenging behaviour or special toileting needs will require the support of their own support worker (usually social services or voluntary agency staff).

v = participated o = did not participate A = did not attend (s) = seconds   Date:

Name	Sit. Ex.	Comments, Observation	Stand Ex.	Comments, Observation	Slalom (s)	Comments, Observation	Dance	Comments, Observation	Obstacle (s)	Comments, Observation	Relax
E	v	Keen. Sustained knee extension with hip abd. And adduction	v	In circle . Good balance kicking forwards.	12	Independent, slightly breathless	vvv	All 3 dances with another client (L, S)	37	Independent. No one near when stepping onto mat	v
S	v	Participated in all – verbal and physical assistance	v	In circle - poor side stepping, turned in direction of movement	32	Followed staff – lot of verbal encouragement	v	Both dances with staff	78	1 hand support over inclines and roll. Verbal help.	v
V	v	Not in room	v	Not in room	7	Independent – not breathless – ran out of room	o	Not in room	11	Independent –ran out of room	o
L											
J											

Signature-------------

Figure 14.1. Mobility/fitness group – weekly record.

Name   Date   Physiotherapist

General health (note any change)

Individual Aims

Activity	Physical Objectives A: Reduce assistance B: Improve co-ordination C: Improve speed	Rating scale	General Objectives A: Improve participation B: Improve communication C: Improve sequencing	Rating scale
Sitting exercise				
Standing exercise				
Slalom course 12.5 m				
Dances				
Obstacle course 16m				

Rating scale

Rating	Outcome (Speed averaged over participating weeks)
−1	Participation in activity has decreased, or more assistance is required, or where a speed element is involved this has decreased >5%
0	No or minimal change <5%
+1	There has been some increase in participation, or less assistance is required, or where a speed element is involved this has increased a little >5%
+2	Participation has increased, or little or no assistance is required, or where a speed element is involved this has increased >10%

General comments

Figure 14.2. Physiotherapy mobility/fitness group – six monthly progress.

RECOGNISED EXERCISES

KEEP-FIT AND WEIGHT-REDUCTION GROUP

The help of a physiotherapist and dietician was sought by a centre manager to improve the health of overweight and obese clients by running a class at the centre.

Place

A room in the centre is used for this group.

Participants

There are eight adults who are community ambulators (Hoffer scale 1) (see Chapter 7) and have mild learning disabilities. All are overweight or obese. The majority presents with Down syndrome.

Staff

This includes one physiotherapist who gradually delegated the routine leadership to a physiotherapy technician. It also included one dietician and members of the social work centre staff.

Programme

The following are the aim of this class:

- improve mobility
- improve stamina
- increase aerobic activity
- reduce weight

The Keep-Fit (Exercise) Class

This includes:

- warm-up exercises in standing
- stepping, running on the spot
- exercises in long sitting including pelvic rocking, pelvic lifts, touching toes
- exercises in lying including pelvic tilting, straight leg raise and back extension
- slow stretches in standing

Discussion on Diet

Members of the group discuss what they have eaten for breakfast and lunch and what are healthy foods. They may have a tasting session.

Dietician

The dietician weighs each client once a month. Weight loss ranges from 0.5 kg to 4 kg in one month.

GET FIT GROUP

Patients in a learning disability and forensic ward were starting to participate in walks and cycle rides at weekends with members of the nursing staff. The physiotherapist was asked to undertake a baseline fitness assessment with the patients. After the initial assessment it became apparent that they were extremely unfit.

Discussion took place with the proposed participants as to the value of becoming fitter and a regular weekly fitness group was established.

Place

The ward dining room is used for this group.

Participants

The original four men were aged between 25 and 50 years. Participants had mild to moderate learning disability and were community ambulators (Hoffer scale 1) (see Chapter 7). Individual participants presented with the following: minimal rheumatoid arthritis, cerebral palsy, genetic abnormalities, challenging behaviour, psychiatric illness.

Staff

One physiotherapist, one or two nurses and a physiotherapy student on placement.

Programme

The exercises that are undertaken are appropriate to the type of movement required when walking up hills and over rough ground:

- sufficient time is allowed for participants to organise themselves and prepare mentally for participating in a group requiring physical effort and concentration
- warm-up exercises and stretching in standing
- lower limb strengthening exercises in standing
- shuttle run
- aerobic sequence
- slalom course running around cones timed over a measured distance
- modified hurdle course jumping over 15 cm high objects timed over a measured distance
- press-ups – individually modified and counted
- abdominal exercises – individually modified and counted
- cool down

Fitness was monitored regularly. Over a period of one year the degree of difficulty and the distance run or walked, both in the exercise group and during the weekend walks and expeditions, had measurably increased.

At the end of the year three patients and three male nurses walked the West Highland Way (96 miles rough walking) over a period of 7 days. Another male nurse drove their support vehicle carrying overnight equipment.

The fitness group and week-end country walks became a regular part of the wards programme for subsequent appropriate patients.

COMPOSITE GROUPS

GENERAL MOBILITY AND FITNESS GROUP

A day centre for adults with learning disabilities has a preponderance of members who require regular monitoring and encouragement from a physiotherapist to prevent rapid deterioration of mobility and to improve their general fitness. Most do not need individual physiotherapy.

Place

A large room in the centre is used for this group.

Participants

These are 18 adults aged between 22 and 50 years. All participants have moderate to severe learning disability and their physical ability is level 2 or 1 on the Hoffer scale or fully independent (see Chapter 7). Individual participants present with the following: Down syndrome, cerebral palsy, spina bifida, progressive neurological disorders, challenging behaviour, severely limited vision and poor hearing.

Staff

These include one physiotherapist, four of the centre staff, one volunteer, and nursing, therapy and social work students.

Programme

- Warm-up exercises in sitting and standing, which also increase range of movement and improve coordination specific to individuals participating.
- Slalom course, running/walking around cones, timed over a measured distance.

- Country dancing: three country dances, modified by Claire Dennis and taught by her to members of the ACPPLD at their 1994 conference. The aim of these dances for this group is to
  - improve stamina
  - improve coordination
  - improve ability to work with a peer group partner
  - improve ability to work in a team
  - improve ability to follow others
  - learn a useful activity
- Obstacle course: run/walk up and down two large wedges, over a roll, through a roll, onto and off two mats and between two cones. Timed over a measured distance. The aim is to
  - improve stamina
  - improve range of movement
  - improve movement repertoire
  - improve balance and coordination
  - improve turn taking
- Final stretch and relaxation sitting in chair.

The additional aim of this group is to encourage group participation, interaction and peer support, spontaneous conversation between clients, ability to choose a partner.

USING A PUBLIC LEISURE POOL FOR A PHYSIOTHERAPY GROUP

A number of adults with learning disabilities from two day centres and an inclusion project have progressed beyond the need for hydrotherapy in an especially heated pool. However, they benefit from exercising in warm water and using its property of buoyancy to assist and resist movement and for the opportunity it gives for risk taking and experiential learning (see Chapter 11). Additionally, use of a public pool fulfils the aims of the inclusion project, which are that clients should mix with non learning-disabled people by using community facilities.

Place

A public leisure pool concurrently used by members of the general public and other disabled people present. It is relatively quiet during term time and very busy during school holidays.

Participants

These are adults with moderate to severe learning disability; one is fully independent. The physical ability of the others is level 2 or 3 on the Hoffer scale (see Chapter 7). Individual participants present with the following: cerebral palsy, minimal cerebral palsy, progressive neurological disorder, limited vision, challenging behaviours.

Staff

One physiotherapist and five daycare staff.

Programme

- The physiotherapist, one daycare staff member and two participants travel together and are the first to arrive.
- Daycare staff member and one participant join in a community aquarobics group for people who are not learning disabled to improve clients' coordination, general fitness, concentration and confidence with women who are not disabled.
- The physiotherapist works one-to-one with each participant as they arrive using exercises appropriate to the individual (see Chapter 11) and using the facilities of the pool for physiotherapeutic aims.
- Pool facilities appropriate for this group are:
  - variety of textures of pool surround, steps and inclines to improve balance
  - varying depth of water to improve balance
  - fast-flow channel to improve balance, by walking both with and against the flow, and to improve coordination, walking pattern and muscle strength by using resisted walking against the flow
  - waves: to improve balance, coordination, posture and muscle strength
  - fountains to increase balance and confidence
  - walking between other swimmers: to improve balance, coordination and confidence
  - Jacuzzi pool for relaxation
- Daycare staff work with physiotherapist to use the pool facilities as appropriate for the participants.
- All join in a group based on the Halliwick principles (Martin 1981), which include:
  - standing in circle, each participant walking under a human arch made by other participants and staff (disengagement)
  - arms linked in a circle floating supine – backfloat (vertical rotation – balance restoration)
- All continue using pool facilities.
- All shower and dress, or help to dress, themselves.

SPECIALIST GROUP ACTIVITIES

JABADAO

The name Jabadao is the name of a company and charity, which is a UK national development agency for dance/movement work (see Appendix B). It undertakes training and project work and is developing resources to establish dance/movement as an ordinary part of being human and as a medium for learning and growth.

Jabadao's work is informed by the world of dance therapy, psychology (particularly the work of Abraham Maslow in the US), and other body therapies – for example, the Alexander technique, Bartenieffs fundamentals, Laban movement analysis, authentic movement principles, and contact improvisation and group therapy.

Basis

The work of Jabadao is based on the concept that an understanding of the immediate world is learnt through movement and that this is the basis for all future learning.

Children develop emotional, conceptual and perceptual awareness of the immediate environment through using their hands to explore objects and through body contact with the parents. At this time sensory understanding of surfaces, size and weight, and perceptual concepts of distance, space and orientation of own body weight and movement of limbs into space, are established.

Understanding of self and other interactive skills, such as turn taking, cause and effect and ranges of the primary emotions – for example joy to despair and fear to safety – are established through nonverbal, body movement based interactions during the first year. (For further information on development of communication see Chapter 6.)

Group work based on the Jabadao principles provides an opportunity for participants to explore their moving selves and develop an insight into 'self' and 'other'. Participants can make connections by expressing themselves clearly and by being seen and understood. This is especially important for people with profound physical disability who are dependent on others for all aspects of self care and mobility. As described in Chapter 6, their sensory deprivation, social isolation and inability to access ordinary experience compound difficulties with learning.

Interactive dance/movement can provide this group of people with a range of experiences to

- stimulate
- motivate
- facilitate

natural body movement in interaction with the environment and with forces of gravity.

The direct experiences of the body help to develop recognition of

- space
- shape
- size
- weight
- contrast

Jabadao uses the structure from 'authentic movement' principles to allow each individual to be seen or witnessed in a nonjudgmental way. The individual's unique way of moving/dancing/being in the world is acknowledged in its own right and is possibly reflected in the movements of a partner or the group. Maslow (1962) outlines how growth or learning only occurs when safety is established. Jabadao seeks to provide structures that create safety in which structure and growth can occur.

Place

A room large enough to accommodate equipment and wheelchairs is used.

Participants

The number of participants is dependent on the number of facilitators and the room size. Jabadao is suitable for all levels of learning disability and participants' physical ability level can be at any level on the Hoffer scale or fully independent or entirely dependent. (See Chapter 7.)

Staff

These are usually two therapists from a combination of physiotherapists, occupational therapists speech and language therapists, although more commonly only one is available, plus day centre staff and carers. One therapist or member of day centre staff acts as leader, the others act as facilitators on a ratio of 1:2 or 1:3 therapists to adults with learning disabilities. Students and volunteers to work with participants as directed by facilitators.

Programme: Structure/Process (Hewett 1994)

- Starting point for developing a movement conversation: acknowledgement of each unique individual and his or her particular way of being in the world.
- Structures may be:

- simple games such as individual greeting, discovering the contents of a large box, taking turns to pass under a human arch, changing places under a parachute, mirroring another person's movement
- props such as elasticised rope, scarves, scented balls, parachute, Lycra
- music
• Facilitators must
  - tune in to all the nonverbal body messages being expressed
  - pick up a common theme from all the participants
  - facilitate an appropriate relationship to develop between the group as a whole
  - then intensive interactions can be facilitated within a dance/movement group

It is through relationship that practical therapeutic aims can be fulfilled in every sphere of human potential.

CASE STUDY

• A 20-year-old man with cerebral palsy lives with a foster family and attends a social services 'special care day centre' five days a week.
• He wears a spinal jacket to help to prevent further deterioration of his gross scoliosis and kyphosis of spine, and severe windswept deformity.
• He communicates with facial expression and whole body patterns of mass extension for fear/pain/joy.
• He has a Liberator communicator, which is poorly used by the centre staff due to lack of time, space and insufficient training.
• He has to be hoisted for several changes in position within a 24-hour postural management programme.
• He has regular chest infections
• He is isolated from the rest of the group by a reclining moulded insert in large chair
• He has difficulty with being moved.

This young man participated in a multisensory movement group in which he was positioned on beanbags with others in a circle (following the postural management programme). The use of brightly coloured props facilitated a very visible link between him and other group members.

He was able to feel the movement of others through props and participation in the group. One-to-one work within the context of the group involved him in stretching to touch stimulating props, playing eye contact games, turn taking, feeling the contact of another through feet, hands and trunk and receiving sensory stimulation from different colours and textures. During the session a reduction of muscle tone was achieved through interactions and appropriate touch. He led some sound and rhythm games during which he introduced his own ideas and played with cause-and-effect in interaction.

Overall, this young man became animated beyond normal expectations and expressed sheer delight in the experience he was enjoying.

GROUP ACTIVITIES USED BY THE GENERAL PUBLIC

T'AI CHI GROUP

The ancient Chinese art of T'ai chi is based on movements used for self-defence but is now practised in a slower, gentler form to promote and sustain good health. The philosophical roots of T'ai chi are based in Taoism and the fundamental principles of harmony and balance in nature. Much has been written about its origins and development. To use T'ai chi as a group exercise form it is necessary for the physiotherapist to have some personal knowledge of the basic movements, through attending a club or community group. To learn the basic movements from books alone would be difficult, although reading about underlying principles is to be recommended.

The movement or 'form' consists of slow, gentle postures that flow together and can be suitable for most ability levels. Recent research in the US has demonstrated that regular practice of T'ai chi can reduce the likelihood of falls in the elderly (Wolf et al. 1996; Sattin et al. 2005) and reduce blood pressure measurements in patients recovering from myocardial infarction (Channer et al. 1996). Staff at the Hong Kong Polytechnic University have now begun to investigate the possibility of using a sophisticated gait analysis system to analyse the body's balance during T'ai chi (Kirtley 1999).

As an exercise modality, T'ai chi embraces one of the core skills of the physiotherapist.

Place

This is a day centre room large enough to accommodate participants standing to exercise. No equipment is needed other than music if this is required to create the right atmosphere. The group size may need to be tailored to the space available.

Participants

T'ai chi can encompass diverse ability levels. Although it is useful to aim for some uniformity of ability within the group, this is not necessary, as can be seen in many community groups where people with widely differing ability ranges practise T'ai chi together. It has been described as a journey and all participants are at different stages of the journey, progressing in their own individual way. Participants' physical ability level needs to be 2 or 1 on the Hoffer scale or fully independent.

Staff

These include one physiotherapist plus the number of carers and volunteers required to assist individual participants.

Programme

- Sessions always begin with warm-up and gentle breathing exercises.
- The movement or 'form':
  - joints are moved slowly and rhythmically, within comfortable ranges
  - soft tissue is not overstretched, all movements take place within each individual's own existing ranges; the importance of this must be stressed to the group at the beginning of each session in order to prevent overenthusiastic or competitive movements
  - weight is transferred from one foot to the other throughout the exercises
  - Each limb moves independently and there is heightened awareness of how the individual movements of each part of the body come together to form whole movements, which flow in an uninterrupted sequence
  - T'ai chi requires balance and coordination

There is scope for improvement and development in all these areas as the group progresses.

Clients who are enthusiastic and have gained some confidence may choose to join a community T'ai chi group in order to develop their skills further. The physiotherapist may facilitate this, with continuous support given by family, friends or volunteers. With the recent increase in interest in the martial arts in the West, groups can be found in most areas, local libraries being a good source of information.

Practising T'ai chi is both a calming and relaxing experience and can help to reduce stress. It is said to unify the mind and the body, allowing the *chi* or vital energy to flow freely. It is a highly enjoyable form of group exercise through which many physiotherapy goals can be achieved. It is now used increasingly as an exercise module in falls prevention work with older people in general.

CONCLUSION

Improving physical ability through participating in a group is fun and can improve the participants' ability to communicate and build relationships with others. Participants may learn how to work together, their concentration may improve, their feeling of achievement may be heightened and their skills may develop sufficiently to allow them to participate in a similar group in the community. However, it is important that people who have been referred to therapists for a specific reason should be assessed, assigned to the appropriate group and reassessed at preplanned intervals. This should in no way detract from the enjoyment of the group or from the additional health and social gains.

REFERENCES

Bruce, M. (1988) Occupational therapy in group treatment, in *Occupational Therapy in Mental Health Principles and Practice*, (ed. Scott and Katz), Taylor and Francis Ltd, London.

Channer, K.S., Barrow, D., Barrow, R., Osborne, M. and Ives, G. (1996) Changes in haemodynamic parameters following Tai Chi Chuan and aerobic exercise in patients recovering from myocardial infarction. *Post Graduate Medical Journal*, **72**, 349–51.

Cotton, E. (1970) Integration of treatment and education in cerebral palsy. *Physiotherapy*, April, 143–7.

Crook, P., Stott, R., Rose, M., Peters, S., Salmon, P. and Stanley, I. (1998) Adherence to group exercise: physiotherapist-led experimental programmes. *Physiotherapy*, **84** (8), 366–72.

Gardiner, D. (1971) *The Principles of Exercise Therapy*, reprinted with additions, G. Bell & Sons Ltd, London.

Hewett, D. (1994). *Access to Communication*, David Fulton, London.

Kirtley, C. (1999) East meets West in Hong Kong. *The Standard, Vicon Motion System, 1, 1–2*, Oxford Metrics Limited, Oxford.

Martin, J. (1981) The Halliwick method. *Physiotherapy*, **67** (10), 296–7.

Maslow, A. (1962) *Towards a Psychology of Being*. Van Nostrand Reinhold, Princeton.

Sattin, R.W., Easley, K.A., Wolf, S.L., Chen, Y. and Kutner, M.H. (2005) Reduction in fear of falling through intense tai chi exercise training in older, transitionally frail adults. *Journal of the American Geriatric Society*, **53** (7), 1168–78.

Thow, M. (ed.) (2006) *Exercise Leadership in Cardiac Rehabilitation: An Evidence-based Approach*, John Wiley & Sons Ltd, Chichester.

Wolf, S.L., Barnhart, H.X., Kutner, N.G., McNeely, E., Coogler, C. and Xu, T. (1996) The Atlanta FICST study: reducing frailty and falls in older persons: an investigation of T'ai chi and computerised balance training. *Journal of the American Geriatric Society*, **44** (5), 489–97.

15 Sport and Outdoor Pursuits

ANGELA JOHNSON, JONATHAN GRAY AND
IAN SILKSTONE, UPDATED FOR THE SECOND EDITION
BY JEANETTE RENNIE

INTRODUCTION

This chapter shows how skills learned during the type of group work described in Chapter 14 may be used and developed further in recognised sports and outdoor pursuits, where clients are expected to build on their ability. It explains how new skills must be tailored to fit individual needs and wishes adapting to individual abilities.

Sport as rehabilitation for people with disabilities was introduced by Dr Ludwig Guttman at the National Spinal Injuries Centre, Stoke Mandeville in 1944 (Cashmore 1990). In the 1960s, recreation became recognised as an important element in rehabilitation programmes and in the constructive and creative use of leisure time for people with learning disabilities. Remedial gymnasts began to work in institutions for people with learning disabilities where they encouraged participation in sporting activities, creating opportunities for team work, improved social interaction and increased exercise tolerance (Luckey and Shapiro 1974; Odunmbaku Auty 1991).

The words 'sport', 'outdoor pursuits', 'leisure' and 'recreation' are freely interchanged in conversation meaning one and the same thing to many people. They have been described as follows:

Sport is 'an individual or group activity pursued for exercise or for pleasure, often taking competitive form, any pastime indulged for pleasure, to remove oneself in outdoor recreation' (*Collins English Dictionary and Thesaurus*, 1994 edition).

Leisure is a time in which 'there is opportunity for choice . . . an activity apart from the obligations of work, family and society to which the individual turns at will for either relaxation, diversion or broadening of experience (Honeybourne et al. 1996).

Recreation is 'activity voluntarily engaged in during leisure and motivated by the personal satisfactions which result from it . . . a toll for mental and physical therapy' (Honeybourne et al. 1996).

Learning Disability: Physical Therapy Treatment and Management. Edited by Jeanette Rennie
© 2007 John Wiley & Sons Ltd

The value of sport, outdoor pursuits, leisure and recreation is rarely fully understood or recognised (Malin 1995) and research into its value is neglected. Many people still view recreation as a supplementary pursuit that fills in gaps when an individual is not working or learning. At best it is seen as fun, at worst it is regarded as idle time (Roggenbuck et al. 1990).

OPPORTUNITIES FOR PEOPLE WITH LEARNING DISABILITIES

The professional craft knowledge (Chapter 5 and Higgs and Titchen 1995) of physiotherapists who use recreational therapy daily has shown that sport, outdoor pursuits and games provide an educational experience for people with learning disabilities. They have an impact on sensorimotor systems, cognition and social aspects of an individual's life (see Table 15.1). Organised sport and outdoor pursuits provide opportunities for personal achievement and for constructive use of leisure time allowing opportunity for personal achievement while also helping to channel excess energy and aggression by preventing boredom and loneliness.

According to McConkey et al. (1981) and Kennedy et al. (1991), people with learning disabilities would like to enjoy the same activities pursued by the wider population but rarely have the opportunity to do so (Cheseldine and Jeffree 1981; McConkey et al. 1981; Wertheime 1983). In recent years, opportunities for participation have increased as a result of the recognition of the

Table 15.1. Benefits and development through sport and outdoor pursuits

Physical	Psychological
Improves heart function	Promotes confidence
Improves circulation	Provides motivation to mobilise
Improves muscular and skeletal systems	Improves self image
Improves flexibility	Increases self esteem
Improves balance	Improves listening skills
Improves co-ordination	Improves concentration
Improves fine and gross motor skills	Improves directional sense
Improves exercise tolerance	Increases perception
Improves reflex reactions	Helps to decrease behavioural problems
Improves manual dexterity	
Improves body awareness	**Social**
Improves agility	Provides opportunity for contact with peers
Improves postural awareness	Provides opportunity for social interaction
Improves spatial awareness	Provides opportunity for social interaction
Assists weight reduction	Provides opportunity for community integration
	Provides opportunity for new experiences
	Provides opportunity for fun and enjoyment

rights of disabled people (see Chapter 1) but many are still unaware of what is available and have not learned how to access sporting facilities (Grey, 1996).

Kennedy et al. (1991) believe that the low rate of participation by people with learning disabilities in community recreation is due to both intrinsic and extrinsic barriers.

Intrinsic barriers include:

* social ineffectiveness
* health problems
* physical and psychological difficulties
* lack of skills/knowledge

Extrinsic barriers include:

* Attitudes of others. Despite the Disability Discrimination Acts of 1995 and 2005 there is still widespread apprehension towards people with disabilities (Commission for Healthcare Audit and Inspection 2005). Some sports centres fear that the presence of people with disabilities may discourage nondisabled people from participating in the same social settings.
* lack of appropriate recreational facilities (Cheseldine and Jeffree 1981)
* few qualified instructors (Luckey and Shapiro 1974)
* dependence upon parents and carers, lack of transport
* architectural barriers
* lack of communication, exclusion and omission
* personal economic limitations

THE ROLE OF A PHYSIOTHERAPIST

Professionals in the field of sport and recreation are often unprepared for the challenge associated with learning disabilities. This is where a team of physiotherapists can play a major role in the lives of people with learning disabilities.

Physiotherapists, occupational therapists and speech and language therapists working with people with learning disabilities have embraced the principles of normalisation (Wolfensberger 1972), which provide a guiding philosophy designed to increase individual competence, socialisation and social acceptance (see Chapter 1).

Previously people with disabilities have been critical of the ways in which professionals, especially physiotherapists, have undervalued and underestimated their abilities (Tilstone 1991). They have accused physiotherapists of acting as 'stigma coaches', reinforcing negative stereotypes and focusing on impairment rather than seeking to enable people who are already limited by social and personal attitudes (Rousch 1986) to live independently (Johnson

1993). Professionals are further criticised for taking control and imposing choices once an activity becomes a 'treatment' or 'therapy'. However this should not and need not be the case.

The Chartered Society of Physiotherapy (1991) states that: 'Chartered physiotherapists have an important role to play in the prevention of further disability and in helping disabled people to achieve their maximum potential for mobility and independence.'

Recreation and therapeutic recreation, as two separate entities, do overlap. Therapeutic recreation offers therapy with the accompanying benefit of an enjoyable recreational experience.

Physiotherapists using their knowledge and skills in conjunction with an holistic approach have a vital role to play in maintaining optimum physical function and can provide positive psychological support towards independence.

The selected activities should be within the individual's capabilities and fit into lifestyles within the community. Some people prefer individual pursuits or dislike competition, so activities can be selected that provide support and companionship. Studies have shown that fun and enjoyment are the most important reasons for taking part in recreation and sport and in maintaining involvement (Wankel and Berger 1990).

Group work has been criticised in the past as dehumanising and taking away individual rights and dignity but the disadvantages are usually due to

- faulty selection of clients
- poor communication with individuals
- inappropriate selection of individuals for certain groups
- overcrowding and poor techniques
- low expectations of staff
- lack of appropriate activities (Gardiner 1971; Jahoda and Cattermole 1995)

Experience has shown that teaching in a group allows an opportunity for clients to achieve personal recognition with peers and acquire skills while being provided with help, encouragement and supervision. Well-planned classes can meet individual needs and expectations. Kennedy et al. (1991) suggested that the success of therapeutic recreation is dependent upon the skills, qualities and attributes of the therapist, which include:

- stamina and physical energy
- enthusiasm and a sense of humour
- positive attitude and understanding of societal attitudes
- ingenuity, resourcefulness, creativity, ability to innovate
- capacity to accept limited, slow progress
- commitment
- willingness to experiment

Before selecting a sport or activity it is necessary to assess individual needs, taking into account any medical conditions that may prevent participation – for example, severe heart defects or exercise-induced epilepsy. Goals and objectives are then set. At intervals there must be analysis and evaluation of progress, which will allow modification if necessary.

TEACHING POINTS FOR SUCCESS

- Always follow safety regulations.
- Keep things simple.
- Never underestimate the participant's capability.
- Keep jargon and uncommon words to a minimum; good communication skills are vital, both verbal and nonverbal.
- Break skills down.
- Ensure sequential delivery of skills, allowing plenty of repetition of techniques.
- Provide a variety of activities to prevent boredom.
- Progress skills according to the needs of the group.
- Use voice modulation to motivate and encourage.
- Give good demonstrations.
- Remember that failure to prepare is preparation for failure.
- Adapt to the individual needs of the group.
- Be enthusiastic, positive in approach.
- Observe, give feedback, be consistent.
- Involve participants in the coaching.

The responsibility of the physiotherapist is to rehabilitate individuals to allow them to take their place as independent members of society and not to make them more 'normal' (Appleby and Wright 1980). It is recognised that the Hoffer scale measures physical ability and this has been used to accommodate the variety of chapters in this book. However, in practice, therapists should also consider learning ability, behaviour and psychological state in their assessments and adapt recreation accordingly.

- An individual's level of competence must not be presumed because of a label.
- Capability levels should not be seen as static.

Physiotherapists can provide an increasing range of opportunities and teach skills that allow individuals to be as self-determining as possible. Appropriate dress for sport is very important. It provides a positive image and symbolises to others what the wearer does and enjoys. The positive responses of others through leisure identification reaffirms acceptance of an individual's true self (Haggard and Williams 1992; Samdahl 1992). Interventions must be positive, useful and fulfilling. Practising monotonous skills for hours on end cannot enhance quality of life and, if the skill gained is minimal then time has been wasted that could have been spent in more pleasurable ways.

INDIVIDUAL SPORTS

There are many sports and outdoor pursuits to choose from. A small number of sports that are not normally considered suitable for people with learning disabilities have been selected for this chapter. Some sporting activities and recreational leisure pursuits have their own unique benefits, adaptations and in some cases contraindications. The selected sports are: rambling, volleyball, gymnastics, athletics, circuit training and cycling.

It is recommended that the following summaries are read in conjunction with their source material.

RAMBLING

Hoffer scale suitability: fully ambulant and Hoffer scale 1 to 4 and entirely dependent.

Rambling is one of the most popular outdoor pursuits today (Cotton 1981; Ward and Rippe 1988). It originated in the late eighteenth and early nineteenth centuries during the Industrial Revolution when industrial workers left the smoke-filled towns and cities in search of fresh air and exercise (Channel 4 1994; Honeybourne et al. 1996). Rambling clubs were set up and a nationwide network of public footpaths and bridleways was created. Improvement in transport allowed easier access to the countryside and coastal areas. Few activities can be safer than rambling. It is an outdoor pursuit that can be adapted to suit any lifestyle, age, need and ability. In Australia rambling has been included in the 'programmes for pleasure' for the over-fifties as it combines fitness, activity and pleasure (Wilson 1990).

Unique Features of Rambling (Environ Organisation 1996)

- It can be done anywhere – for example, trails, footpaths, parks, shopping centres.
- There is little risk of injury.
- It is inexpensive and requires little equipment (only shoes, socks and motivation).
- It is quality time allowing communication and time to develop friendships.

- It provides the opportunity to work as part of a group.
- It gives a sense of adventure.
- It is educational.

Adaptations of Rambling

- Making the challenge easy or difficult depending upon the needs and wishes of the ramblers.
- Varying the distance walked.
- Selecting areas of different terrain.
- Backpacking for the more able.

Contraindications

There are no contraindications that are specific to sembling as an activity. Any potential problems will become apparent during their initial assessment.

VOLLEYBALL

Hoffer scale suitability: fully ambulant and Hoffer scale 1 to 4.

In 1895 W.G. Morgan invented volleyball to provide recreation and relaxation for middle-aged man (Bertucci 1987). Since then the game has become popular and it is now an Olympic and Special Olympic sport. Volleyball can be highly competitive requiring high levels of skill, fitness, agility and coordination or it can be relaxing recreation, adapted to any level. It is ideal as a therapeutic exercise as it requires short bursts of energy followed by periods of rest. Physiotherapists do not need special training but it is helpful to have some background knowledge of the game. The aim is to improve individual physical, psychological, and social skills and provide opportunities to participate in a recognised valued sport within a non-threatening environment.

Unique Features of Volleyball

- Simple, clear rules.
- Noncontact sport.
- Played indoors and outdoors.
- Suitable for all ages.
- Suitable for most abilities.
- Requires little space or equipment.
- Twelve players can play at any one time, so it is time and cost effective.
- Allows individual flair even though it is a team sport.
- Disabled players are integrated with those who are not disabled.

Skills to Teach

- The Dig.
- The Volley.
- The Spike.
- The Serve.

Adaptations of Volleyball

- Reducing the size of the court.
- Allowing the ball to bounce before contact.
- Varying the size and weight of the ball.
- Playing mini-volleyball – four per side.
- Lowering the net.
- Playing seated.

Contraindications

Osteoporosis, haemophilia.

GYMNASTICS

Hoffer scale suitability: fully ambulant and Hoffer scale 1 to 4.

Gymnastics has been regarded as a popular and positive sport for many years and is defined as 'practice or training in exercises that develop physical strength and agility or mental capacity' (*Collins English Dictionary and Thesaurus*, 1994 edition).

The primary aim is to develop motor development skills and promote general fitness but the overall philosophy also includes positive psychological, social and emotional development. Gymnastics can be adapted for many individuals and can be used by physiotherapists as an enjoyable, appropriate activity to achieve assessment goals. As a physiotherapy intervention it allows individuals to achieve increasing self-esteem in individual performance by means of movement. It also develops the necessary, appropriate discipline and behaviour involved in taking part in the sport. Sessions can take place within community facilities or within any safe environment that has space to allow movement. All equipment must be of high quality and in excellent condition.

Although gymnastics is suitable for individuals assessed from fully ambulant to Hoffer scale 4, it can be adapted to suit all levels of learning ability. Training in special needs gymnastics is essential and can be arranged through the British Amateur Gymnastics Association. Knowledge of basic gymnastics combined with physiotherapy knowledge allows the therapist to observe movement and break down the acquisition of skills into readily understood stages. When given positive encouragement within an appropriate environment, gymnastics enables individuals to reach their full potential both physically and mentally.

Unique Features of Gymnastics

- Skills can be broken down to allow continuous achievement.
- The gymnast/coach relationship is close.
- The individual is a gymnast throughout the whole session whether performing or awaiting his or her turn.
- Postures and movements have clear simple rules.
- Sessions are focused and involve working together.
- Teaches discipline and set codes of behaviour expected in gymnastics even when not performing.
- Simple specific spoken language and demonstrations.
- Teaches directional sense.

Skills to Teach

- Listening skills.
- To stand like a gymnast.
- To sit like a gymnast.
- Gymnastic postures and terminology – for example, straddle, squat, stretch.
- Names of equipment.
- Concepts of movement and direction.

Gymnasts can be given brief, specific and technically correct hints to correct poor techniques and prevent bad habits from forming. All gymnastics revolves around straight, pike or tucked shapes.

Adaptations for Gymnastics

- Floor work: mats.
- Equipment: beam, box, springboard.
- Planning the position of the equipment.
- Altering the height of the equipment.
- Varying the size of the work area.
- Working in pairs or groups.

Award Schemes

The British Amateur Gymnastics Association runs an award scheme for various grades of gymnastics. Each grade has 10 elements to be completed.

These awards can be adapted by breaking them down further to suit a group's need.

Contraindications

Atlantoaxial instability.

ATHLETICS

Hoffer scale suitability: fully ambulant and Hoffer scale 1 to 4.

The term 'athletics' covers a wide variety of events rather than a single one (Devon County Council 1993). Athletics includes events in both track and field. It can cover road runs, cross country and tug-of-war (North West Council for Sport 1992–6). This variation allows physiotherapists tremendous scope to meet individual needs in a positive and valued way. Some individuals may aim for competitive events but for the majority the physiotherapist can use athletics to meet individually set goals in an enjoyable and fun way.

Athletics can be adapted to suit all levels of physical and learning ability. Special training in athletics coaching is not essential but it is useful to have knowledge of the scope of events available.

Unique Features of Athletics

- It can take place indoors or outdoors within a safe area, in a variety of settings – for example, athletic stadiums, gymnasiums, playing fields.
- It allows natural talent to flourish – for instance, for those who are continually on the move, running may be a suitable pursuit to channel natural skills in a positive and valued way.
- Activities can be simplified.
- Athletics has visual boundaries.
- It creates discipline and control.
- It is inexpensive.
- It has measurable markers for improvement, which provide immediate feedback to the individual and others.

**Skills to Teach (Devon County Council 1993;
North West Council for Sport 1996)**

- Running.
- Jumping.
- Throwing.
- Boundaries.
- Commands – for example, 'go', 'start', 'stop'.

Contraindications

There are no contraindications that are specific to athletics as a sport. Any potential problems for can individual will become apparent during their initial assessment.

CIRCUIT TRAINING

Hoffer scale suitability: fully ambulant and Hoffer scale 1 to 4.

Circuit training was developed in the 1960s by Morgan and Adamson to provide a system of exercise that would maintain and improve fitness levels. A circuit involves a series of exercises (about 10 exercise stations) in sequence, which ensure that the main muscle groups are worked in turn. A circuit can be adapted to suit all ability levels, with the aim of improving progressively endurance, strength, cardiorespiratory efficiency and functional skills (Hart and Hart 1987; Bartlett 1990). Fitness gains are of secondary importance to the psychological, physical and social effects. Exercises in the circuit must be within the capabilities of each individual.

There are a variety of circuits but the following are the two most suitable for people with impaired physical and learning ability.

A General Circuit

Clients can work individually or in pairs. The aim is to achieve all round fitness. Exercises can involve equipment (for example, ball for throwing and catching) or be stationary (for example, running, press-ups, step-ups).

A Functional Circuit

This concentrates upon functional movements encountered in daily activities. It is designed to enhance functional skills by repetition. Exercises may include sitting to standing, rolling, climbing stairs, walking on uneven ground (Latto and Norrice 1987).

Unique Features of Circuit Training

- A circuit follows a definite structure or routine that allows familiarity and decreases uncertainty.
- The exercises are simple and adaptable to all capabilities and fitness levels.
- Circuit allows periods of rest and periods of fitness that can be altered according to fitness levels.
- Working for a set time, for example one minute, at each station prevents the need to count the number of repetitions.
- Everyone exercises and rests at the same time allowing the therapist control and observation of the group.

- Several people with varying ability and fitness levels can work together in the same group.
- A circuit can be designed to fit a variety of settings and room sizes.
- Improvement is measurable.

Teaching Points

- Each exercise must be demonstrated and practised fully.
- Individuals must follow the same sequence of exercise.

Adaptations of Circuits

- Changing the time periods of the rests.
- Counting repetitions.
- Allowing individuals to work at their own pace.
- Increasing or decreasing the number of exercises in a circuit.
- Games circuits, skills circuits and integrated games can be included.
- Equipment can be adapted to suit wheelchair users (for example, sticks shortened in golf and hockey-type exercises).

Contraindications

There are no contraindications that are specific to circuit training as an activity. Any potential problems will become apparent during their initial assessment.

CYCLING

Hoffer scale suitability: fully ambulant, Hoffer scale 1 to 4 and entirely dependent.

Cycling can be a sporting activity, leisure activity or a necessary mode of transport, and can facilitate therapeutically assessed needs. It allows experience, participation and presence within the local community and environment while providing pleasurable exercise on equal terms with nondisabled peers.

Cycles come in all shapes and sizes allowing a greater number of people access to the activity. Static bicycles can be a good starting point for cycling. They require very little space and provide a stable base on which to teach the basic pedalling. Three-wheeled trikes and tricycles allow progression, encouraging balance and posture during movement. Tricycles with two seats side by side allow for one-to-one supervision and physical and psychological support (Bartley 1998). Adapted seating can be attached to some tricycles.

Cycling can be enjoyed in a variety of settings – for example parks, cycle paths and in the countryside. Some clients may in time be able to use public highways but this must be determined by the therapist through continuous assessment and education using the Highway Code.

It is now recognised that cycling has many therapeutic benefits and several therapists have produced literature to support this including Geoff Bartley, Lancaster Hospital and Sybil Williams who was awarded the Front Line Excellence Award and Ann Russell Memorial Award of the ACPPLD for this work in 1998 (see Chapter 16).

Unique Features of Cycling (Bartley 1998)

- Different cycles are available to meet a variety of needs.
- Body weight can be fully supported.
- Little stress is placed on the joints.
- Provides a decrease in muscular tension.
- Allows experience of independent movement.
- Allows experience of movement in the elements – wind, sun, rain.
- Nonsighted clients can experience cycling with unobtrusive one-to-one support.
- Improves bilateral coordination.
- Encourages a controlled pattern of movement.
- Teaches road awareness.

Adaptations of Cycling

- Changing the type of cycle.
- Increasing the distance cycled.
- Increasing or decreasing the amount of one-to-one support.

Contraindications

Overweight clients may be a problem when using two-seated tricycles.

CONCLUSION

Leisure provides freedom, the opportunity to make choices and allows personal growth (Gold 1989). Recreational activities such as sport and outdoor pursuits provide health gains while generating joy and satisfaction, which are crucial for people with learning disabilities who often face boredom, loneliness and isolation. (Emerson et al. 2005). Fulfilling leisure experiences can help to improve quality of life (Johnson 1997). All professionals must realise that people with learning disabilities are as diverse as others in society and have varying interests, attitudes, skills and talents. If people are to be enabled to make an informed choice it is necessary to offer them a variety of experiences in a supportive setting. Physiotherapists should be innovative and creative with their own personal qualities and skills to ensure that they are being effective.

Quality contact must be on an equal status and all individuals should be consulted about what they want and need.

It is vital that all professionals, parents, carers, educators and friends promote a positive image; the ultimate goal of leisure must be towards total integration within community-based leisure experiences. Physiotherapists must encourage, educate, motivate support and defend clients by highlighting ability rather than disability.

REFERENCES

Appleby, K.A. and Wright, A. (1980) The technology of self control. *Physiotherapy*, **66** (12), 403–5.

Bartlett, E.G. (1990) *Weight Training*, David Charles, London.

Bartley, J. (1998) *Cycles for All. A Therapy in Leisure Initiative*, Lancaster Hospital, Lancaster.

Bertucci, B. (1987) *The AVCA Volleyball Handbook*, Master Press, London.

Cashmore, E. (1990) *Making Sense of Sports*, 2nd edn, Routledge, London.

Channel 4 (1994) *Go!* Sports Council, London.

Chartered Society of Physiotherapy (1991) *Disabled People and their Families*, leaflet, Chartered Society of Physiotherapy, London.

Cheseldine, S.E. and Jeffree, D.M. (1981) Mentally handicapped adolescents: their use of leisure time. *Journal of Mental Deficiency*, **25** (49), 49–59.

Commission for Healthcare Audit and Inspection (2005) *Draft Three Year Strategic Plan for Assessing and Encouraging Improvement in the Health and Healthcare of Adults with Learning Disabilities 2006–2009*. Commission for Healthcare Audit and Inspection, London. Available at http://www.healthcarecommission.org.uk/_db/_documents/04021628.pdf.

Cotton, M. (1981) *Out of Doors with Handicapped People,* Souvenir Press Ltd, London.

Devon County Council (1993) *The Devon Approach to Physical Education: Athletics*, Devon County Council, Exeter.

Emerson, E., Malam, S., Davies, I. and Spencer, K. for The Department of Health (2005) *Survey of Adults with Learning Difficulties in England*, Department of Health Publications, London.

Environ Organisation (1996) *Small Steps and Giant Leaps: A Review of the Feet First Project*: Environment and Transport 2000, London.

Gardiner, D. (1971) *The Principles of Exercise Therapy*, reprinted with additions, G. Bell & Sons Ltd, London.

Gold, D. (1989) Putting leisure into life. *Entourage*, **4** (1), 10–11.

Grey, T. (1996) *Forward in Sport and Leisure*, Disability Information Trust, Oxford.

Haggard, L.M. and Williams, D.R. (1992) Identity affirmation through leisure activities: leisure symbols of the self. *National Recreation and Park Association*, **24**, 1–18.

Hart, J. and Hart, L. (1987) *100% Fitness*, Elliot Right Way Books, Surrey.

Higgs, J. and Titchen, A. (1995) Propositional, professional and personal knowledge in clinical reasoning, in *Clinical Reasoning in the Health Professions* (eds J. Higgs and M. Jones), Butterworth Heinemann, Oxford, pp. 129–46.

Honeybourne, J., Hill, M. and Moors, H. (1996) *Advanced Physical Education and Sport*, Stanley Thornes, London.

Jahoda, A. and Cattermole, M. (1995) Activities of people with severe learning disabilities: living with purpose or just killing time? *Disability and Society*, **10**, 2.

Johnson, R. (1993) Attitudes don't just hang in the air . . . disabled peoples' perceptions of physiotherapists. *Physiotherapy*, **79** (9), 619–27.

Johnson, A. (1997) *'Cor I Was Over the Hills': The Benefits of Walking as Viewed Through the Eyes of People with Learning Disabilities*, unpublished dissertation for Master's degree, Sheffield University.

Kennedy, D.W, Smith, R.W. and Austin, D.R. (1991) *Special Recreation: Opportunities for Persons with Disabilities*. W.C. Brown Publishers, Dubuque, Iowa.

Latto, K. and Norrice, B. (1987) *Give Us a Chance*, Disabled Living Foundation, London.

Luckey, R.E. and Shapiro, I.G. (1974) Recreation: an essential aspect of habilitative programming. *Mental Retardation*, October, 33–5.

Malin, N. (1995) *Services for People with Learning Disabilities*, Routledge, London.

McConkey, R., Walsh, J. and Mulcahy, M. (1981) The recreational pursuits of mentally handicapped adults. *International Journal of Rehabilitation Research*, **4** (4), 493–99.

North West Council for Sport (1992–6) *Focus on Sport*. Athletics North West. Warrington.

Odunmbaku Auty, P.M. (1991) *Physiotherapy for People with Learning Disabilities*, Woodhead Faulkener, London.

Roggenbuck, J.W., Loomis, R.J. and Dagostino, J. (1990) Learning the benefits of leisure. *Journal of Leisure Research*, **22** (2), 112–24.

Rousch, S.E. (1986) Health professionals as contributors to attitudes towards persons with disabilities. *Physical Therapy*, **66**, 241.

Samdahl, D.M. (1992) Leisure in our lives: exploring the common leisure occasion. *Journal of Leisure Research*, **24** (1), 19–32.

Tilstone, C. (1991) *Teaching Children with Severe Learning Disabilities*, Fulton, London.

Wankel, L.M. and Berger, B.G. (1990) The psychological and social benefits of sport and physical activity. *Journal of Leisure Research*, **22** (2), 167–82.

Ward, A. and Rippe, J. (1988) *Walking for Health and Fitness*, J.B. Lippincott, London.

Wertheime, A. (1983) *Leisure*, Values into Action, London.

Wilson, C. (1990) Programmes for pleasure: combine fitness with enjoyment in Australia. *Ageing International*, Winter edition.

Wolfensberger, W. (1972) *The Principle of Normalisation in Human Services*, National Institute on Mental Retardation through Leonard Crainford, Toronto.

16 Developing Opportunities for Health Promotion and Fitness Using Standard Local Facilities

JEANETTE RENNIE, MICHAEL CRAVEN, AMANDA LEECH AND SYBIL WILLIAMS

INTRODUCTION

This chapter makes reference to assessments and subsequent treatment methods but concentrates mainly on the mechanics of developing programmes that use local sports and fitness areas. Specific examples are given of two of the activities described in Chapter 15, rambling/walking and cycling, and groups similar to those in Chapter 14. They demonstrate methods that may be used either as 'stepping stones towards independent participation in generally run sports and fitness classes' or 'keeping fit in a local fitness area with long-standing friends and peer group.'

Physiotherapists have always understood the need to promote exercise and general fitness (Barclay 1994) as discussed in Chapter 15. A growing awareness in government circles, however, resulted in a number of UK national and regional initiatives that encouraged all members of the public to take responsibility for living a healthy lifestyle.

The Health Act 1999 instigated local flexible working practices (see Chapter 1). Drawing from a consultative Green Paper, the White Paper *Towards a Healthier Scotland* (Scottish Office 1999) recognised that sporting activities could help to prevent cardiovascular conditions and osteoporosis and that moderate daily exercise such as walking and cycling could contribute to 'positive health and active ageing'.

These policies cascaded down to local level via sports councils, local authority sports centres and a proliferation of private clubs. The aim of tailoring activities for people's needs was strongly promoted by the *Equity Standard for Sport* (see Appendix B); the aims of the document were supported by the Central Council for Physical Recreation (CCPR), the Women's Sports Foundation, the English Federation of Disability Sport, and Sporting Equals.

Learning Disability: Physical Therapy Treatment and Management. Edited by Jeanette Rennie
© 2007 John Wiley & Sons Ltd

Table 16.1. Examples of UK discussion papers and initiatives

UK Westminster Parliament	Northern Ireland	The Welsh Assembly government	1999 Scottish devolution. Health devolved to The Scottish Executive for law making.
White Paper *Choosing Health: making healthier choices easier* (2004). It promised to 'work across government and with other organisations in the voluntary and independent sectors' and produce information regarding health risks that would be 'tailored for people's needs'	Discussions collated and published as *The Cost Benefits of The Physical Activity Strategy for Northern Ireland – A Summary of Key Findings* (Swales 2002).	1. *Well Being in Wales* (2002) 2. *The Healthy and Active Lifestyles Action Plan: a framework for action* (2002) 3. *Health Challenge Wales* (2004) and launch of social action promotion with BBC Wales to promote healthy living and exercising.	1. *Our National Health: a plan of action, a plan for change* (2000) 2. *Building a Better Scotland* (2002) 3. *Improving Health in Scotland* (2003).

It is recognised that people with learning disabilities should have the opportunity to participate with other members of the local community (see Chapters 1 and 15). Anecdotal evidence from support workers and students of various disciplines, however, also shows that they may be more relaxed and consequently achieve higher levels of activity and expertise amongst their peer group, in a similar way to other sectors of society. This is acknowledged by such initiatives as the Special Olympics.

MANCHESTER LEARNING DISABILITY PARTNERSHIP'S FIGHTING FIT PROJECT

Fighting Fit is a service 'strategy' to promote physical activity, healthy eating and weight management. The strategy aims to address all the recommendations to be found in related research. At its core is the fact that 'physical activity is for everybody' and that inactivity and obesity are the most pressing health problems affecting people and ultimately draining the resources of many service providers.

It is important to appreciate the extent of the challenge facing learning disability services. Among all of those people who are in contact with the service approximately four out of every five undertake far too little physical activity and carry too much weight; in some regions two in five are clinically obese. This amounts to well over 1 000 people in Manchester requiring significant and permanent lifestyle changes.

These lifestyle changes must aim to incorporate the recommended 30 minutes minimum of daily 'moderate' physical activity (British Heart Foundation National Centre for Physical Activity and Health) along with all the planning necessary to eat a healthy diet on a daily basis. Bearing in mind the numbers of people involved and the special needs of many, the challenge is enormous. Thus sharing responsibility with all who are in contact with the people who need to change their lifestyle is essential. It is worthwhile listing these key partners based on the following summary:

• Where do the people in need of a changed lifestyle live?
• Who comes in contact with their families and carers?
• Where do they spend their daytime?

In summary, responsibility falls on everybody: day services, all health staff, adult education, the independent sector, carers' groups and people specific to the individual. National service frameworks (see, for example, Department of Health 2005), *Valuing People* (Department of Health 2001) and care standards already state this responsibility but a more detailed and specific 'healthy living service policy' may be required. Incorporating healthy lifestyles within service protocols, for example health action plans, will also ensure that responsibilities are addressed.

Raising awareness of the problem and designating responsibility to all must be combined with offering advice, support, resources, and training to all. (Note: a service 'must do' policy alone will not influence parents and families, or many staff for that matter.) It is an understanding of the need and importance of going for a walk and eating some fruit and the related benefits to health and wellbeing that influence staff and carers.

Numerous training opportunities are available in Manchester and frequently these are tailored to the specific requirements of staff in each location. The impact of inactivity and obesity on the health of people is fully explained. Physical activity is discussed in all of its aspects:

• the amount of physical activity.
• the intensity of activity.
• the different types of activity.
• safety issues.
• risk management.
• accommodation of existing health problems and disabilities.

The importance of planning, how to motivate people and sharing responsibility with all concerned are subjects also addressed.

Staff and carers are more likely to support projects and activity sessions if they themselves were involved in their creation. They are encouraged to initiate their own projects, health events, and activities based on the training received and utilising the resources of which they aware. Staff initiatives may involve improving the health of one person in a residential setting, facilitating a health action plan, developing a walking or dance group, or organising a football session in a leisure centre.

FIGHTING FIT STAFF

One senior physiotherapist has the specific role of coordinating the Fighting Fit project. External funding has enabled the employment of two full-time physiotherapy technicians (FF support workers). Their roles involve staff training, awareness raising, accessing funding, networking, and offering advice and support to staff who are developing activity groups or events. Another form of support to staff is the FF referral process in which a person will receive targeted input resulting in an FF report and action plan.

METHOD OF FUNDING

External support is essential. Direct funding can be an enormous boost to a project. The important point is that learning disability services should be competing for available funding by being visible, networking, and sitting on the appropriate committees. The FF project has received funding from the local primary care trust, local healthy living networks and a significant amount from the neighbourhood regeneration fund, NRF. Partner organisations (Mencap) and parent-run drop-ins have received significant amounts from national lottery funding.

External support in forms other than money can achieve the same end result. The use of facilities for free or at a reduced cost (parks, leisure centres, community halls), the provision of coaches, transport, external trainers, sports equipment, health promotion resources and health equipment have all been acquired from local partner organisations. Many of these organisations have a brief to target high-risk, socially excluded, disabled and unhealthy groups of people. Learning disability services should help these organisations to address their social responsibilities.

Finally, it is important to keep everybody informed. In Manchester the FF directory is regularly updated. Quarterly FF meetings are held with all partner groups being invited to contribute. The minutes of these meetings become the FF newsletter that is cascaded to everybody along with other related leaflets and resources. The FF project has taken six years to achieve the outcomes to date. Similar initiatives will also need to look long term and ensure the backing of service managers.

PEDAL POWER

Cycling is described in Chapter 15 where reference is made to the unique features of cycling (Bartley 1998).

The physiotherapy approach, Pedal Power, was pioneered in Cardiff in 1996 and is run jointly by the Bro Morgannwg Trust and Cardiff City Council.

CRITERIA FOR SELECTING THIS APPROACH TO TREATMENT

- To integrate people with learning disability into the community.
- To increase fitness levels.
- To increase participation in exercise.
- To increase participation in a meaningful activity.
- To increase socialisation.
- To improve mobility.
- To improve balance.
- Enjoyment.

POTENTIALLY INHIBITING FACTORS IN USING THIS APPROACH

- Most participants need support to cycle.
- The weather – some potential participants may dislike the cold and the rain.
- It may be a new experience, and some participants may need time to adapt.

CONTRAINDICATIONS/CAUTION

In the main anybody can participate. A medical questionnaire is filled in for all participants and then their cycling programmes are adapted accordingly. Risk assessments need to be undertaken. Special precautions need to be taken with people who have epilepsy, challenging behaviour, osteoporosis, some heart conditions and people with hip replacements.

SPECIAL PRECAUTIONS TO BE TAKEN

Carers must:

- Know the environment and its hazards.
- Know how to handle the cycle that their client rides.

- Check that the cycle is in working order prior to riding.
- Consider whether the client needs footplates or harness to enable them to cycle safely.
- Know their client – for example, be able to recognise pre-epileptic signs.
- Be firm with clients and insist they follow instruction/warnings.
- Take a telephone with them.

PARTICIPANTS

The programme in Cardiff has been set up for adults aged over 18 – there is no upper age limit. There is no reason why children/young adults cannot participate provided the cycles are of the correct size and that everything else has been taken into consideration.

An award system is in operation; this encourages cyclists to improve their skills, techniques and distance cycled.

Seeking the views of all the users constantly provides feedback, enabling the project to be monitored.

LOCATION

Anyone proposing a similar project should first establish whether anything similar has already been set up in the area. If not, the following should be taken into consideration:

- Safety: a car-free environment.
- Surface for cycling: must be good and firm, not slippery.
- If using trikes/handbikes:
  - camber on pathways should not be too steep
  - pathways should have no large loose stones
  - pathways should be well drained
  - the path must be wide enough for the trike and a pedestrian
- Barriers: can the cycles being used get through them?
- Parking: must be sufficient close to the cycles.
- A disabled toilet is essential.
- Facility to store cycles is essential.

STAFFING

- Initial assessment is undertaken by a physiotherapist.
- A technical instructor will assess correct cycle, need for adaptations, cycling handling skills, fitness levels.
- Technical instructors will facilitate sessions and will progress clients.
- Support staff always accompany their clients – they need to be fit and should have attended the cycle safety awareness course.

PROGRAMME

This depends on goals agreed for the individual. The initial goal could be to get onto the cycle. Further goals could include:

- increase distance cycled
- increase distance covered in a given time
- increase cycle handling skills from totally supported to semisupported, to independent
- increase length of time cycling
- learn to ride a different cycle

SOURCE OF FUNDING

The project is a partnership between the City Council Parks Department and the NHS Trust. Initially the NHS funded the cycles. However, further cycles have been obtained through charitable monies. The cycles are stored and maintained by the Council, with the NHS paying towards maintenance costs. The Council are also responsible for the pathways and cycling areas. The NHS provides staffing to facilitate the sessions.

METHOD OF REFERRAL

All referrals are made through the team physiotherapist and can be made by individuals themselves, day centre staff, support workers or family members.

FURTHER PROPOSALS

There are possibilities to become involved in:

- sport
- long distance cycling
- road cycling and safety-training

And to

- improve the facilities to encourage further socialisation and increase the capacity for more people to benefit from the accessible cycles

BUMS OFF SEATS: SPECIALIST HEALTH WALKS

Bums off Seats is a walking initiative in Fife, Scotland – a part of the Paths to Health Scheme. This initiative aims to promote the benefits of walking through volunteer-led walks, of varying length and terrain. Many clients with learning disabilities are able to participate in the general 'Bums off Seats' walks and receive both the physical health benefits and the social benefits of this. Many others, however, have encountered barriers to accessing the general walks, resulting in the specialist health walks being set up. This section describes the specialist walks for learning disabled clients.

WHY WALKING?

- It is free and requires no special equipment other than appropriate clothing and footwear.
- It is within the physical capabilities of most people and is a realistic goal for inactive people.
- Walking combines all the physical benefits of gentle exercise with an opportunity for social contact and support.
- Walking can easily be incorporated into everyone's daily life.
- It can be enjoyed safely and there is a low risk of injury.

The 'Bums off Seats' specialist health walks are suitable for any client with a learning disability who is either walking independently or a community ambulator on the Hoffer scale (see Chapter 7). There are no other specific criteria; however, those who can access the general 'Bums off Seats' walks without difficulty, should be encouraged to attend them, rather than the specialist walks.

BARRIERS ENCOUNTERED TO ACCESSING
THE GENERAL WALKS BY SOME CLIENTS

- The length of walks was sometimes too great.
- The terrain of walks was sometimes too uneven and hilly.
- Walks were not in appropriate locations for people with some behaviours.
- Volunteer walk leaders were not confident in dealing with and interacting with the client group.
- Other walkers were not keen to interact with clients, so the social aspect of walks was lost.
- Motivation.

THE SPECIALIST HEALTH WALKS

Preparation

- *Initially*. Possible routes are risk assessed with consideration given to clients' abilities, conditions and behaviours. From this information the most appropriate routes and locations are chosen. In general, routes away from busy roads, on relatively flat and even terrain and no further than 1 to 1.5 miles have been found to be most suitable. Consideration was also required in regard to the proximity of appropriate parking and toilet facilities. Leaflets and referral forms were distributed to interested parties.

- *Following referral but before attending the walks.* Our clients are seen for an initial assessment. During this assessment the physiotherapist asks general health questions and determines the clients' current mobility levels. Clients are given symbolised information sheets, which tell them the benefits of walking and what they need to bring with them to the walk in regard to clothing and footwear. The assessment appointment is the only compulsory part of the initiative; following this assessment clients can choose when, where and how often they attend the walks.

CONTRAINDICATIONS

There are no specific contraindications in relation to this walking initiative. The risk assessment of routes and clients' initial assessments should highlight any issues that need to be addressed or which could restrict the suitability for some clients.

COSTS

There are no monetary costs in running this initiative as accessing the countryside is free and there is no specific equipment required. The main cost for the service, is the cost of staffing the walks with a minimum of two people. As the walks are organised three times per week this is a significant commitment. Paths to Health provided training for walk leaders free of charge and as part of the training our staff received waterproof jackets and rucksacks containing first aid kits, to use on the walks.

ORGANISATION OF INDIVIDUAL WALKS

Each walk is organised by two members of staff, one at the front who leads the walk and the other at the back to bring up the rear. All clients walk with their carers at their own pace. The front leader keeps pace with the fastest client and the back leader keeps pace with the slowest. Both walk leaders carry telephones, first aid kits and basic health information about each client so that they can assist with incidents as required. Walks take place in all weathers (except icy conditions) and clients are encouraged to wear appropriate clothing all year round.

MAINTAINING THE MOTIVATION

One of the key elements in initiatives such as this is motivation. Without adequate motivation clients will often attend for a short period of time, then will gradually lose interest. This is overcome by emphasising the social aspect of the walks and an incentive scheme. On the general 'Bums off Seats' walks, participants receive a T-shirt when they have completed 25 walks and a mug when they have completed 50 walks. The same system is used for the specialist health walks, however to take account of their learning disabilities, a visual method of recording the walks is used. Clients receive a sticker at the end of each walk, which they collect in a book. Incentive awards are achieved after 10, 25, 50, 75 and 100 walks.

POSITIVE LINKS AND FUTURE PROPOSALS

The specialist health walks are linked closely with the general 'Bums off Seats' walks with referrals occurring in both directions. Clients who attend general walks but find they encounter the barriers detailed above are referred on to the specialist health walks. Similarly, clients who cope well in the specialist walks and begin to find them less challenging, are advised to progress onto the general walks. This system attempts to recognise the importance of accessing standard community activities, whilst ensuring clients' individual needs are met in the best possible way. It is proposed that some of the volunteer walk leaders from the general walks begin participating in the specialist health walks to increase their confidence in working with the client group. It is hoped that this will allow further integration between the general and specialist walks in the future.

GET FIT AND STAY FIT IN A LOCAL AUTHORITY SPORTS CENTRE

These classes started in response to requests from residents and staff in small group homes and centres to their physiotherapist. Reportedly, their special needs were not being accommodated in general groups in local authority sports centres.

A room is hired in a sports centre in which two classes are run as a private project. The organiser is a physiotherapist who was formerly employed by Learning Disability Services. The classes are advertised through leaflets distributed to staff working in the learning disability service, the local doctor's surgery and agencies that support adults with learning disabilities. Posters are placed on notice boards seen by potential participants. It is made clear that they are for 'People who have difficulty responding quickly to instructions given to a group of people in class form.'

Potential participants may contact the organiser directly at the start of the class or telephone in advance. The most popular method of joining the class, however, has been by referral from physiotherapists, support workers or doctors.

CRITERIA FOR RUNNING THESE CLASSES PRIVATELY IN A PUBLIC SPORTS CENTRE

- Classes will be open to anyone who has difficulty maintaining speed in traditional fitness classes.

- Participants with a learning disability and associated conditions (Chapter 2) will not be excluded
- Classes will not be withdrawn if participating numbers fall, as happens in some local authority classes.

CRITERIA FOR PARTICIPANTS

Participants must

- want to improve their general fitness
- be able to undertake standing and walking exercises
- be willing to learn to use a public sports centre including the concepts of punctuality, paying for a class and meeting and mixing with new people

POTENTIALLY INHIBITING FACTORS IN USING THIS APPROACH

These are the same as for any activity that involves travelling and using different accommodation (see Chapter 15). They include irregular transport and attitudes of support workers, potential participants and some members of the public.

CONTRAINDICATIONS

There are no specific contraindications that would differ from any other sports class.

SPECIAL PRECAUTIONS TO BE TAKEN WHEN RUNNING PRIVATELY FUNDED CLASSES FOR PEOPLE WITH LEARNING DISABILITIES IN A PUBLIC SPORTS CENTRE

- Publicity must outline the general aims of the class.
- Opportunities must be available for support workers to speak to the organiser and accompany the potential member into a class before a final decision is made.
- A health form must be used even though most classes in the sports centre do not require this.
- If concerns over a member's condition arise or a more detailed physiotherapy assessment is required than is possible under the class conditions, the class organiser must contact the appropriate health professional.
- Members' individual aims must be noted.
- Some members may prefer to have a friend or support worker joining in the class; others may require a support worker for safety reasons.

- Risk assessment and standard operating procedure must be used (Figures 16.1 and 16.2).
- A Vulnerable Adults Disclosure Certificate is required for the class organiser.

GET FIT AND STAY FIT CLASSES FOR ANYONE WHO HAS DIFFICULTY RESPONDING QUCKLY TO EXERCISE INSTRUCTIONS.

HELD AT CRAIGLOCKHART SPORTS CENTRE

RISK ASSESSMENT

RISK	TO	MINIMISE BY
1.Fire	• Class members • Leader	1. Class leader read fire instructions 2. Class leader recognise alarm 3. Class leader and members when possible, participate in evacuation practice 4. Class leader ensure fire exits are clear
2. Accidents	• Class members • Leader	1. Class leader read first aid instructions 2. Know how to contact Centre first aider

3. Room / equipment hazards	• Class members	1. Class Leader check floor condition for exercises by people with disabilities
		2. Class Leader check seating for exercises by people with disabilities
		3. Only use equipment which is safe for all members
		  o Theraband must be constantly explained and monitored
		  o Steps must only be used for stepping on to – not running over

4 Dehydration	• Class members • Leader	1. Know where drinking water is available

5 Accident specific to members of these classes	• Class members	1. Health forms must be used
		2. GPs name and address must be included.
		3. Health forms must be taken to the class by leader each day.
		4. Excitability:-
		  o class must start calmly.
		  o If a member is extremely excitable ensure 1:1 with staff known to him/her.
		  o Members must be made aware of the difference between being safely enthusiastic and over competitive.
		5. Wandering: - If a member is known to wander ensure 1:1 of known staff
		6. Members must let leader know reason for leaving room
		7. Exercises must be carried out a safe distance from glass windows

N.B. all instructions may need to be repeated

Figure 16.1. Example of risk assessment form.

**GET FIT AND STAY FIT CLASSES FOR ANYONE WHO HAS DIFFICULTY
RESPONDING QUCKLY TO EXERCISE INSTRUCTIONS.**

HELD AT CRAIGLOCKHART SPORTS CENTRE

One of the aims of these classes is that they should be run on the same lines as any other fitness class and that anyone who can participate in standing exercises should be free to join them.

STANDARD OPERATING PROCEDURE

1. The class leader must be appropriately qualified
2. The class leader will have read all the safety literature in place in the room.
3. The class leader will recognise the sound of the fire alarm
4. The class leader will participate in fire evacuation practice
5. The class leader will know how to contact the Centre first aider
6. The class leader will ensure that health forms are completed and will take them to the classes each week.
7. People who state that they wish to participate in the classes without being accompanied by a friend or carer will be welcome, unless their health form indicates that this may be unwise.
8. People who are liable to become excessively excited, who tend to wander around a building or who are recognised as needing one to one support will be welcome but only when a supporter participates with them.
9. Supporters may only accompany class members in the room if they themselves participate in the class.

Figure 16.2. Example of standard operating procedure.

PARTICIPANTS IN THESE CLASSES

- Between eight and 12 adults aged between 22 and 60 years, plus two to four support workers in each class.
- All have mild to severe learning disability. Their physical ability is level 2 or 1 on the Hoffer scale or fully independent (see Chapter 7).
- Individuals present with: Down syndrome; cerebral palsy; spina bifida; severely limited vision; poor hearing; personality disorders; epilepsy; autistic spectrum disorder; early stage dementia.
- The majority of members in class 1 are more able than class 2 and travel by public bus either independently, with a support worker or in a group with one support worker. Three travel alone by taxi and one walks.

- In class 2, members travel in their support worker's car or their centre bus.
- During class 1, one member is accompanied because of poor balance and another because of erratic behaviour.
- During class 2, one is accompanied because of autistic spectrum disorder and another because of severe learning disability. One support worker accompanies a group from the same centre.

STAFF

The staff are the class organiser, who is a physiotherapist, and support workers who wish to participate. Members of the sports centre staff are on call and organise first aid.

METHOD OF FUNDING

The room is hired by the class organiser and is inclusive of the sports centre equipment.

Individual class members pay their own fee on arrival directly to the class organiser and in return receive a receipt. One group pays en bloc from their Social Work Centre's budget. There is a discount rate for participating friends/ support workers.

PROGRAMME

These classes are similar to the get fit and general fitness groups described in Chapter 14 with the addition of timed balance exercises. Music is used for individual exercises. Additional equipment includes 'resistive exercise bands' steps for aerobic sequence, mats, and light hand weights

PROGRESS AND PROPOSALS

During the three years since these classes started the majority of members have participated in excess of a year, some intermittently. Six chose not to return after two or three weeks. Four members have progressed to participating without their original support workers.

The class programme and music have remained the same but within that programme new exercises and equipment have been introduced and the level and intensity of the exercises has increased. The principle of starting slowly is explained to each new member.

Individual exercise progress is recorded in bar chart format. These are also given to the individual member and, with their permission, to appropriate support workers and health service staff.

Some participants have begun to talk to sports centre staff and other users; it is hoped that they will become confident enough to join classes with a varied composition of membership. However, these classes stand alone as a method of keeping fit in a local sports centre amongst old and new friends.

CONCLUSION

It is accepted that there is need to improve the general health and fitness of the population as a whole. It is also acknowledged that additional support is needed to enable people with learning disabilities to make equal use of, and attain maximum benefit from, standard sporting and fitness facilities. To this end physiotherapists who work with people with learning disabilities are beginning to undertake some of their health promotion and general fitness work in non-health service or social services venues and in conjunction with a range of partners. To accomplish this it is necessary to have the opportunity to manage time and resources appropriately.

REFERENCES

Barclay, J. (1994) *In Good Hands*. Butterworth–Heinemann Ltd, Oxford.

Bartley, J. (1998) '*Cycles for All*.' *A Therapy in Leisure Initiative*, Lancaster Hospital, Lancaster.

Department of Health (2001) *Valuing People – A New Strategy for Learning Disability for the Twenty-first Century*, Stationery Office, London.

Department of Health (2004) *Choosing Health: Making Healthier Choices Easier*, Department of Health Publications, London.

Department of Health (2005) *The National Service Framework for Long-term Conditions*, Department of Health Publications, London.

Scottish Executive (2000) *Our National Health: A Plan for Action, A Plan for Change*, Scottish Executive Health Department, Edinburgh.

Scottish Executive (2002) *Building a Better Scotland Spending Proposals 2003–2006: What the Money Buys*, Scottish Executive Finance and Central Services Department, Edinburgh.

Scottish Executive (2003) *Improving Health in Scotland. The Challenge*, Scottish Executive Health Department, Edinburgh.

Scottish Office (1999) *Towards a Healthier Scotland – A White Paper on Health*, Scottish Office, Department of Health, Edinburgh.

Swales, C. (2002) *The Cost Benefits of The Physical Activity Strategy for Northern Ireland – A Summary of Key Findings*. The Health Promotion Agency for Northern Ireland, Belfast.

The Welsh Assembly Government (2002) *Well Being in Wales*. The Welsh Assembly Government, Cardiff.

The Welsh Assembly Government (2002) *The Healthy and Active Lifestyles Action Plan: A Framework for Action*. The Welsh Assembly Government, Cardiff.

The Welsh Assembly Government (2004) *Health Challenge Wales*. The Welsh Assembly Government, Cardiff.

17 Complementary Therapies

LIBBY DAVIES, JANE BRUCE AND MARIA GUNSTONE

INTRODUCTION

There has been much debate about the definition and interpretation of the term 'complementary therapy', as well as the scope and variety of practices that may be encompassed by the use of such a term.

In the broadest sense, complementary therapy may be thought of as a specific modality applied in its own right or as anything adjunctive to any other given modality. Whether it is a specific entity or an adjunctive practice, one area that is not commonly given an adequate account of is how the therapist sets up the environment physical or nonphysical – for what is to happen. The way the therapist moves and expresses himself or herself and handles any client (both in terms of positioning as well as the more direct therapeutic intervention) will have major effects – positive or negative – and implications for the client and the therapeutic process.

There are many defined complementary therapies. Each tends to have its own concept, philosophy and defined method(s) of delivery, but all are in the main united by a common core philosophy of holistic and systemic healthcare. T'ai chi is described in Chapter 14.

Selection and application of complementary therapies will be governed by certain factors. The knowledge base and experience of the therapist will ultimately be the major screening process. Other screening processes will, of necessity, be client based, in the sense of knowledge and recognition of what is acceptable to any given client, and the likes and dislikes, level of cognition, behaviour and attitude of that client, and social factors.

Many more people are delivering or using defined complementary therapies. This chapter aims to introduce those working with people with learning disabilities to three of them. Aromatherapy and reflexology are particularly beneficial to this client group as they involve a lot of physical contact between therapist and client, thus helping to build trusting relationships. The 'YOU & ME Yoga' system was devised specifically for people with special needs by Maria Gunstone (2001) as a Westernised version of the Yoga that she had studied in Madras whilst on a Churchill Fellowship. Over 2 500 personnel have

Learning Disability: Physical Therapy Treatment and Management. Edited by Jeanette Rennie
© 2007 John Wiley & Sons Ltd

now been trained to use this system. The introduction to each therapy outlines the basic concept; the case studies illustrate ways in which the therapies can be used to benefit the client, and show the valuable part they play in the overall treatment of people with learning disabilities.

REFLEXOLOGY

Like so many complementary therapies, the practice of reflexology has its roots in ancient times. It is a holistic method of treatment concentrating on the whole person and not just an illness or symptom.

As the feet represent a microcosm of the body, all organs, glands and other parts of the body are laid out in a similar arrangement on the feet (Dougans and Ellis 1992). The reflex foot massage is a specific pressure technique that works on precise reflex points on the feet. Using the thumb to 'caterpillar walk' across the foot with even pressure, subtle energy flows are worked on. These energies revitalise the body so that the natural healing mechanisms of the body can do their work. Hence, reflexology can initiate and accelerate healing in the corresponding part of the body and restore homeostasis.

Reflexology cannot diagnose a problem. It may help to confirm what is already known and also alert the therapist and client to imbalances within the body, so helping to bring about an increased sense of wellbeing and relaxation, reduce stress, improve circulation, cleanse the body and balance the system. It is a wonderful, deeply relaxing treatment. It is not a painful therapy, although slight discomfort may be felt as the therapist works on an area of imbalance.

The role of reflexology in the treatment of people with learning disabilities is therefore useful not only for the aforementioned but also in locating imbalances that they are unable to explain and comprehend. It can also be used as an assessment prior to an aromatherapy treatment and help in the selection of oils that will be of most benefit and value to the client.

AROMATHERAPY

Aromatherapy is a natural treatment using essential oils extracted from flowers, leaves, bark, berries, and fruit of a wide variety of aromatic plants. The essential oil is not a single substance, but consists of a number of complex components. It is this that gives each oil a range of therapeutic properties. These oils can be introduced to the body in different ways such as through inhalations, compresses, baths or massage (Price 1983). The oils are highly concentrated and it is important to use the correct concentration and combination of oils to suit the needs of each individual client.

For the purposes of this chapter, the essential oils are used in conjunction with massage and should be diluted with a carrier oil such as almond or grape seed oil. When the oils are used with massage, they help to enhance the physical effect of massage. The oils enter the body through the skin and also through the olfactory system. They can help build up the immune system, calm or lift the spirits, invigorate, or they may be used to treat a specific symptom such as a sore head or stomach. An aromatherapy treatment will balance the body, mind and spirit.

People with learning disabilities can benefit from aromatherapy in many ways. Ideally, the treatment should be carried out in quiet, warm surroundings using a plinth or bed, although this is not always possible in day centres or schools. It can be used to complement other treatments by, for example, helping to relax a client before a physiotherapy session, or by using it along with a behaviour modification programme as seen in case study 3 below. Although it appears that aromatherapy is beneficial, it is usually difficult to receive true and accurate feedback from the clients themselves. The most commonly used method of evaluation is by asking the carers to monitor any physical changes or changes in behaviour following treatment, and the duration of these changes.

The following case studies will help to illustrate the above concepts. The names of clients have been changed to ensure confidentiality.

CASE STUDIES

CASE STUDY 1: LIZ

This study helps to illustrate how the combination of aromatherapy and reflexology can work to treat a particular symptom and how reflexology can confirm the therapist's initial assessment and help in the choice of oils.

Liz is a 24-year-old woman with cerebral palsy and mental impairment. She has a moderate to severe learning disability. Her epilepsy is under control. She is ambulant with a rollator and communicates through signing and using a Walker Talker.

Liz attends sessions approximately once a month, though this can be more frequent if required. She thoroughly enjoys her sessions and is an active participant in her treatment. She enjoys smelling the oils and helps to blend the final mix. She is not able to understand the properties of the oils but knows that they will help her. Liz is able to undress and dress with minimal assistance. She enjoys doing this independently.

Aims of Treatment

- To promote relaxation.
- To treat the presenting problem.

Treatment

Liz has a full body massage during which she is very relaxed and content. At times, towards the end of the session, she can become quite emotional. This can often be linked to her menstrual cycle. The oils used are dependent on how Liz presents on that particular day and through feedback from the centre staff. She has a diary that goes between the centre and the care staff in her flat, which helps with communication. Added to this, a reflexology assessment will help in the choice of oils and will also help to monitor the progress of her treatment.

Treatment Example

Liz has been sneezing and coughing (dry) today. She was not her usual happy self. She was, however, keen to come for treatment. Her foot reflexes showed imbalances in the respiratory and upper lymphatic areas.

Liz was relaxed throughout. She did not sneeze and only coughed at the end when sitting up. She was also a little emotional but was easily calmed.

Outcome

During the afternoon, the staff reported that Liz appeared brighter. At her flat, the staff reported that Liz felt much better.

She was seen again one week later. She had had a good week and the cough and cold were better; the foot reflexes still showed some imbalances. The same mix was chosen and Liz was relaxed throughout her treatment.

Continuing Aims of Treatment

* To promote relaxation.
* To alleviate PMT.

Table 17.1. Oils used case study 1

Oil	Plant origin	Relevant properties
Sandalwood	Santalum album	antiseptic
Niaouli	Melaleuca virdifolia	analgesic, antiseptic, bactericidal, balsamic, expectorant, stimulant (immune system)
Lavendin	Lavandula intermedia	antiviral, antiseptic, decongestant (lymphatic system) – this oil was chosen in preference to Lavender because the properties, though similar, are more penetrating and therefore more suitable for respiratory conditions.
Eucalyptus	Eucalyptus Smithii	analgesic, antiseptic, antiviral, balsamic, decongestant, expectorant

Plan

To continue to see Liz monthly prior to PMT or as necessary.

CASE STUDY 2: DAVID

In this study, the properties and benefits of the oils are brought together to build up the immune system and strengthen the body's resistance to disease.

David is 21 years old and has epilepsy and also a metabolic disease. He lives at home with his mother and stepfather. David is a young man who is multiply handicapped and has severe learning disabilities. He is wheelchair bound, totally dependent and unable to communicate verbally. He can be distressed and tense, which can sometimes be alleviated with a change in position. He is prone to respiratory infections and constipation.

David attends a centre based on the Rudolph Steiner ethos. He is seen weekly for treatment; the session lasts approximately 40 minutes. He always smiles and shows recognition and acceptance of the therapist.

A short reflexology assessment is carried out before the oils are blended. The staff keep the therapist up to date with David's condition, and a diary facilitates communication between his parents and the centre. David enjoys smelling the final blend.

Aims of Treatment

- To promote relaxation.
- To increase circulation.
- To improve and strengthen the immune system.
- To prevent and treat any infection.
- To alleviate constipation.
- To reduce tone.

David has physiotherapy shortly after treatment.

Treatment

The areas massaged are: feet, legs, back, stomach and hands. During the session, David's position is frequently changed. The centre is provided with blends so that massage can continue through the week. Oils are also burnt in the room where David spends some of his day.

Outcome

David has had fewer infections and therefore the need for antibiotics has been less.

Table 17.2. Oils used in case study 2

Oil	Plant origin	Relevant properties
Lavender	Lavandula angustifolia	analgesic, antiseptic, anti-spasmodic, rubefacient.
Tea tree	Melaleuca alternifolia	anti-infectious, anti-inflammatory, antiseptic, antiviral, bactericidal, expectorant, immuno-stimulant.
Eucalyptus	Eucalyptus Smithii	antiseptic, antispasmodic, antiviral, decongestant, expectorant, rubefacient, stimulant.
Sweet marjoram	Origanum margorana	antiseptic, antispasmodic, bactericidal, expectorant, laxative, sedative.
Juniper	Juniperus communis	antiseptic, antispasmodic, rubefacient, sedative.
Black pepper	Piper nigrum	antimicrobial, antiseptic, antispasmodic, laxative, bactericidal, stimulant (nervous, digestive, circulatory).
	Citrus retulata	antiseptic, antispasmodic, mild laxative, sedative, stimulant (digestive and lymphatic).

Plan

To continue to see him weekly and monitor his health as before.

CASE STUDY 3: KEVIN

This case study will help to illustrate how aromatherapy and reflexology can be adapted to include modification programmes and also benefit the client.

Kevin is a 21 year old who has epilepsy and a severe learning disability and short attention span. He is ambulant when using a rollator and assistance. He has an ataxic gait. Kevin has no speech but uses signs for 'please' and 'thank you'. Kevin's moods can fluctuate and he can become frustrated and bite his sleeve and can, on occasions, kick out. He can also become excitable; he will laugh, shriek, clap his hands and bounce up and down.

Aims of Treatment

- To promote relaxation.
- To treat Kevin initially sitting on a chair, progressing to treating him on the floor at the end of the session.

Treatment

Kevin is treated weekly. He is always willing to be treated and can be quite excitable. He is usually very accepting and will interact well with the therapist.

Table 17.3. Oils used in case study 3

Oil	Plant origin	Relevant properties
Geranium	Pelargonium graveolens	relaxing, balancing
Lavender	Lavandula angustifolia	relaxing, balancing
Sandalwood	Santalum album	relaxing, balancing

Kevin has to sit on a chair in the resource centre to be able to participate in activities. This is carried over into the treatment situation, in that the session starts with Kevin in a chair for a reflexology assessment and aromatherapy foot massage. Kevin is then allowed onto the floor for a back massage, which he thoroughly enjoys. For this he must sit up and be still during the first part of the session. Should he lie down, the massage is stopped and Kevin is asked to sit up if he wants the massage to continue. Obviously Kevin's mood and willingness to cooperate is crucial.

Other oils may be introduced should the therapist feel it necessary to treat a specific condition.

Outcome

By incorporating the appropriate element of Keith's behaviour programme, the consistency in handling has made it possible to achieve a good working therapeutic relationship with Keith. On the whole the same level of calmness and control is carried throughout the day.

Plan

To continue seeing Keith as before and instruct the staff on the use of a pre-scribed blend of oil.

CASE STUDY 4: MANDY

The purpose of this study is to convey how the main aim of relaxation may be obtained. Mandy is a 19-year-old woman. She has cerebral palsy with a right-sided hemiparesis and a moderate to severe learning disability. She has no speech but vocalises, uses gross gestures, formal and modified Makaton and some idiosyncratic signs. She generally sits in her wheelchair but can bear weight with a walker. She is always keen to come to her sessions. The first time she was treated was while on holiday with her school. She elected to have her neck and shoulders massaged. During her treatment only Lavender was used and Mandy remained in her wheelchair. She thoroughly enjoyed her treatment and, although she did not totally relax, there was a noticeable reduction in the tone around the shoulder area.

Table 17.4. Oils used in case study 4

Oils	Plant origin	Relevant properties
Sweet marjoram	Origanum margorana	calming, sedative
Lavender	Lavandula angusfolia	astringent sedative
Juniper	Juniperus communis	astringent
Black pepper	Piper nigrum	circulatory stimulant

Mandy now has a place at the centre where aromatherapy and reflexology are available weekly. She attends therapy two to three times a month.

Aims of Treatment

- To promote relaxation.
- To reduce tone.
- To contain hyperexcitability.
- To improve Mandy's balance reactions whilst dressing and undressing.

Treatment

A full body massage is carried out. Mandy's hyperexcitability tends to increase her tone and she does not fully relax. During the massage while in the prone position she insists on leaning on her elbows with her head up but does, however, relax more in the supine position. Alternatively, when a plinth is available, Mandy can be positioned with her arms over the end of the plinth.

Outcome

There is some reduction in Mandy's tone but she does not totally relax yet.

Plan

- To continue treatment with the aim of achieving greater relaxation.
- Mandy suffers from a spotty back and it is planned, in the future after discussion with her parents, to use cleansing oils to try to improve this condition.

YOU & ME YOGA FOR PEOPLE WITH LEARNING DISABILITIES

Yoga means to bring two things together, to meet, to unite. It means to unify fragmented thoughts, to bring about a focusing of attention and to enable the achievement of potential (Desikachar and Jeyachandran 1983).

The YOU & ME Yoga system for people with learning disabilities (Gunstone 1989) has been designed for individual needs to improve quality of life by

- coordinating the activities of mind and body
- reducing the distracted state of mind
- focusing the mind on the present
- developing the adaptive behaviour
- enhancing social behaviour
- increasing self reliance
- improving general health (Desikachar and Jeyachandran 1988)

It is also used to increase students' mobility, physical dexterity, coordination, communication, sensory awareness and self-confidence.

THE COMPETENCE-BASED SYSTEM

This comprises:

- Colour. The colour code assists with the learning process. The body is divided into seven coloured areas easily identifiable on a picture called 'Eddie'. These are related to the appropriate techniques, which are correspondingly coloured (Table 16.5):
  - red area: legs, toes, ankles and knees
  - orange area: pelvic girdle, hips, lower back, eliminatory system
  - yellow area: waist, midback, digestive system
  - green area: chest, upper back, circulatory and respiratory systems
  - blue area: arms, wrists, elbows, shoulders
  - indigo area: coordination of each side
  - violet area: upper and lower (whole) body awareness
- Sound. The audible sound 'ah' is used to help students breathe correctly and in unison.
- Relaxation. This is an integral part of the system.
- Whole-body movement

HEALTH AND SAFETY IN PRACTICE

Information is included in the training materials along with specific precautions required when undertaking this type of Yoga and conditions for which all or some of the 42 techniques are contraindicated.

PROGRAMMES

Programmes are planned in conjunction with the YOU & ME record keeping system, which enables the therapist(s) to see at a glance the condition, limitations and abilities of the student(s). A general health questionnaire is used as appropriate.

Table 17.5. Colours for the body areas, looseners and related postures arranged into a sequence of the whole-body-movement leading to the CAT as the main posture

Colour and body area	Joint Looseners	Postures
Orange Pelvic girdle, hips, lower back. Eliminatory system	Lying, hip flexion	**Warming up for CAT** Ostrich – standing, forward flex at hips. This posture flexes the hips as far as possible then straightens to the standing position. It helps to stretch the structures around the hips in preparation for the CAT.
Blue Arms, wrists, elbows, shoulders	Thumb opposition, abduction and extension	Table – Sitting, putting pressure on hands. In this posture weight is taken through straight arms, helping to strengthen muscles around the joints.
Violet Upper and lower (whole) body awareness	Finger and toes flexion and extension	Thunderbolt – kneeling, bending head towards knees. In this posture attention is shifted downwards increasing both flexibility and awareness of the body as a whole.
Green Chest, upper back. Circulatory and respiratory systems.	Flex and extend arms forwards at shoulder level.	**Main posture** CAT – Kneeling on hands and knees, lifting head, then bringing forehead to floor. This posture helps to protract and retract the shoulder blades and chest wall.
Indigo Coordination of right and left side	Alternate arm swinging.	**Winding down from CAT** Crane – standing take hand to opposite leg. This posture rotates the body to alternate sides while standing, unlike the kneeling CAT posture. It also helps to improve balance and coordination.
Yellow Waist, mid back. Digestive system.	Trunk side flexion – gravity assisted.	Triangle – standing; leaning and flexing sideways. This posture appropriately moves the mid back and waist differently from the CAT and helps to increase flexibility around the waist.
Red Legs, toes, ankles and knees	Stand raise heels then toes.	Palm tree – standing firm and upright. This posture is distinctly different from the kneeling CAT position. It is a very effective grounding posture for winding down from CAT.

The recording charts are used for students' health, safety and welfare and for keeping a record of practice, outcomes and progress. The colour coding of both the body and the related techniques makes record keeping easy enough for most students to complete their own practice record, and indicate their feelings by ticking the column beneath the most appropriate face (for example, smiling or frowning).

This Yoga programme consists of 22 exercises called 'joint looseners' and 20 postures.

The Looseners

These deal with the main joints of the body. The aim of the loosener programme is to stimulate these joints and develop coordination and awareness of the whole body. The student's ability to perform each of the looseners is assessed and the whole body looseners plan is devised by selecting a loosener technique in one of the seven colour areas. (Table 16.5).

Once a trainer has organised an individual's programme plan, the appropriate loosener activity sheets can be duplicated for use in the workplace and/or home to allow for ongoing practice.

When students have developed confidence and ability in practising their personal whole body looseners plan they can progress to the related colour Postures.

The Postures

Programmes of whole body movement are worked out on the basis of the particular part of the body that needs most attention. This becomes the main posture. Each sequence is arranged around the main posture. The sequence starts with warming up movements for the main posture and concludes with winding down movements.

TRAINING MATERIALS FOR PROFESSIONALS, CARERS AND PARENTS

- *Three DVD videos* (originally sponsored by Mencap) showing the system in use with various clients with learning disabilities at 19 different centres in the UK and Eire.
- *Two sets of display cards* for instructing the joint looseners and the Yoga postures.
- *Six books* with over 4000 illustrations showing clients performing their Yoga programmes.
- *CD-audio tutorial* for teaching the basic You & ME Yoga techniques.

EXAMPLE 1: STUDENTS WITH DOWN SYNDROME

Children and young adults with Down syndrome respond very well to YOU & ME Yoga. Many people with Down syndrome are good mimics who can copy the postures quite well. Their generally lax joints enable them to achieve the postures without physical impediment.

Aims

- To improve confidence. Some students are shy although they all enjoy the idea of the social aspect of being in a group. Confidence can be built up using the YOU & ME card system. Students who initially have difficulty recognising the colour of the cards and which parts of the body they represent begin to reply correctly after a few weeks, through repetition of questions and familiarity with the cards. Makaton sign language is sometimes incorporated. When a student is good enough at performing the postures, the YOU & ME system can be used to allow an individual to stand on the teacher's mat and lead the postures – to 'become the teacher'. People with Down syndrome who have participated in these classes have initially tended not to talk spontaneously as they find verbal communication difficult. It is encouraging to see them progress to the point where they are able and willing to teach their peer group.
- To teach body awareness. The students also enjoy using the colours and cards to work out a sequence of Whole-Body-Movement, increasing awareness of their whole body. The regime and consistency of instructions helps to keep members of the yoga group focused. The pattern of using the cards in sequence and reference to the cover with 'Eddie' coloured in the seven spectrum colours also help the group focus. They are asked questions such as 'what is the colour of the body part?' 'Where is that body part?' 'What is the name of the posture?' Once the questions have been answered everyone moves into that posture.
- To improve spatial awareness.
- To improve coordination.
- To improve breath control.
- To improve balance.
- To improve joint stability and muscle strength especially in the trunk, hips, shoulders and ankles.

CASE STUDY 5: JOHN

Background

John, who has Down syndrome is aged 23 years and has attended a college of further education for three years.

John can move quite quickly although he likes to engage in tasks at a slower, more careful pace. He usually chooses not to use his verbal language skills and as a result of this it is hard for staff at the college to identify problems when John is frustrated or unhappy. It was determined that it would be useful for John to engage in some physical activity to use and maintain his physical abilities and to help with weight control. He showed little interest in sport, or adapted sport activities, but was interested in walking, obstacle courses and mat exercises. It was thought that yoga might provide a way for John to express himself. He began the YOU & ME Yoga programme.

Progress

John was keen to participate in the Yoga group from the very beginning. The group is small and each session lasts for 30 minutes. After watching a demonstration he copies the postures quite easily. John chooses the postures he wants to carry out by pointing to the printed cards.

John has practised YOU & ME Yoga at least twice a week for two years and can now complete most of the postures independently. The Yoga session begins by sitting cross-legged on a mat and John will do this without needing to be asked. He has gained the confidence to use his voice during Yoga sessions – he knows the names of the looseners and postures and occasionally says which ones he would like to try.

John's general confidence has grown. He will demonstrate movements to others in the Yoga group – something that he was reluctant to do in the early stages.

EXAMPLE 2: AUTISTIC CHILDREN

Autism or autistic spectrum disorder (ASD) is a very complex condition, which can manifest itself in many different ways (see Chapter 2). However, all children who have an ASD exhibit the same three impairments, which can be summarised as

- severe communication problems
- ritualistic and obsessive behaviours; anxieties and fears
- lack of empathy with others

Lack of motivation to participate in physical exercise can predispose autistic children to be unfit, lethargic and with poor posture and muscle tone.

Yoga provides regular exercise in a controlled stress-free environment where the class feels secure in the structure imposed by the pictures, YOU & ME display cards and familiar routines. Obsessional and ritualistic behaviours are reduced during the session and a general sense of calmness and control seems to prevail. Clients sustain concentration for longer periods than normal and do not wander off or become disruptive. They watch each other and try to work together, as well as making appropriate sounds when asked, and they feel secure.

The Yoga helps to improve their posture and muscle tone as well as giving them control over their breathing, which in turn helps blood circulation and lung function. They also seem better able to coordinate their bodies when performing the movements.

The children's enjoyment is apparent by the frequency with which they smile and laugh.

CASE STUDY 6: JANE WHO HAS CEREBRAL PALSY

Jane is 26 years old and has athetoid cerebral palsy (see Chapter 2). Initially she found it very difficult to control her involuntary movements.

Programme

The YOU & ME teaching pack explains everything very clearly with health and safety in mind. Thus trainers are enabled to select a suitable plan for people with or even without a learning disability.

The colour-coded instruction pack for the postures was essential to give instructions for working out Jane's programme plan of whole-body movement.

Jane's programme was based on the green chest area for her main posture. It followed a similar warming-up, main posture and winding-down procedure to Table 16.5. Hence Jane's programme benefited the whole of her body.

Progress

- Jane can consciously relax completely during the relaxation period, keeping her whole body perfectly still.
- There has been evidence of progress with other members of staff in other learning areas. Jane is more active and confident in the swimming pool; her upright sitting position in her own chair has improved; she has progressed to independent transfers from her wheelchair onto the toilet and back again although assistance to adjust her clothing is still required. Jane has an obvious feeling of achievement and improved dignity.

Whole-body movement is great fun, as well as motivation for learning. Everyone can join in, and anyone can perform the postures regardless of age or ability. Students develop imagination, expression and relationships.

CONCLUSION

The aim of this chapter was to provide an insight into how complementary therapies can be used and adapted to benefit people with learning disabilities using reflexology, aromatherapy and Yoga as examples.

As may be seen from the case studies, all the clients enjoyed and benefited from the therapies. Specific results were noted in some cases. For instance, Liz's and Jane's symptoms improved and there was a reduction in Mandy's tone. In David's and John's case more long-term results were noted. Over two years there was positive evidence that David's general health had improved. John had gained confidence to say which looseners and postures he would like to try and would occasionally demonstrate movements to others. The main aim in the majority of cases was to promote relaxation. A relaxed body is a healthy body, a sound basis for constructive mental and physical activity and for improved quality of life.

Kevin's case, where the behaviour modification programme was carried through to therapy, illustrates the fact that these therapies are complementary and should therefore not be seen in isolation but as part of the ongoing programme.

REFERENCES

Desikachar, T.V.K. and Jeyachandran, P. (1988) *Teaching Yogasana to the Mentally Retarded Person*. Krishnamacharya Yoga Mandiram, Madras.

Dougans, I. and Ellis, S. (1992) *The Art of Reflexology*, Element Books Ltd, Shaftsbury, Dorset.

Gunstone, M. (1989) *Colour-Code Instruction Pack of the Postures*, YOU & ME Publications, Lancaster.

Gunstone, M. (2001) *The Origin of the YOU & ME Yoga System*, YOU & ME Publications, London.

Price, S. (1983) *Practical Aromatherapy*, Thorsous, London.

Appendix A Further Reading

CHAPTER 1

Ainsworth, P. and Baker, P.C. (2004) *Understanding Mental Retardation, A Resource for Parents, Caregivers and Counsellors*, University Press of Mississippi, Mississippi.

Department of Health (2001) *Good Practice in Consent: Achieving the NHS Plan Commitment to Patient-centred Consent Practice*. See http://www.dh.gov.uk/assetRootJ04/01/22/86/04012286.pdf.

Dimond, B. (1995) *Legal Aspects of Nursing*, 4 edn, Longman, London.

Dimond, B. (1998) *Physiotherapy in a Changing Legal Context*, Founder's lecture delivered at the Royal Society of Arts, Chartered Society of Physiotherapy, London.

Dimond, B. (1999) *Legal Aspects of Physiotherapy*, Blackwell Science Limited, Oxford.

Dimond, B. (2005) *Legal Aspects of Occupational Therapy*, 2nd edn, Blackwell, Oxford.

Gates, B. (ed.) (1997) *Learning Disabilities*, 3rd edn, Churchill Livingstone, New York.

Thomas, D. and Woods, H. (2003) *Working with People with Learning Disabilities, Theory and Practice*, Jessica Kingsley Publishers, London and New York.

Zinkin, P. and McConachie, H. (eds) (1995) *Disabled Children and Developing Countries*, MacKeith Press, Blackwell Scientific Publications, Oxford.

CHAPTER 2

Davidson, P.W., Prasher, V.P. and Janicki, M.P. (2003) *Mental Health, Intellectual Disabilities and the Ageing Process*, Blackwell, London.

Deonna, T. and Roulet-Perez, E. (eds) (2005) *Cognitive and Behavioural Disorders of Epileptic Origin in Children*, MacKeith Press, Blackwell Scientific Publications, Oxford.

Portwood, M. (1999) *Developmental Dyspraxia Identification and Intervention: A Manual for Parents and Professionals*, David Fulton, London.

Public Health Institute of Scotland (2001) *National Needs Assessment: Autistic Spectrum Disorder*, Public Health Institute of Scotland, Edinburgh.

Learning Disability: Physical Therapy Treatment and Management. Edited by Jeanette Rennie
© 2007 John Wiley & Sons Ltd

Stanley, F.J., Blair, E., Alberman, E. (2000) *Cerebral Palsies, Epidemiology and Causal Pathways*, MacKeith Press, Blackwell Scientific Publications, Oxford.

CHAPTER 3

Bazire, S. (2001) *Psychotropic Drug Directory*, Quay Brooks Division, Dinton, Wilts.
British Medical Association and the Royal Pharmaceutical Society of Great Britain (2005) *British National Formulary*, 50th edn, BMJ Books and Pharmaceutical Printing, London.
Buck, J.A. and Sprague, R.L. (1989) Psychotropic medications of mentally retarded residents in community long-term care facilities. *American Journal of Mental Retardation*, **936**, 618–23.
Buckley, P., Bird, J. and Harrison, G. (1995) *Psychiatry, a Postgraduate Text*, 3rd edn, Butterworth Heinmann, London.
Deb, S. (1998) Self injurious behaviour as part of genetic syndromes. *British Journal of Psychiatry*, **172**, 385–8.
Fraser, W.I., Nolan, M. (1994) Psychiatric disorders in mental retardation, in *Mental Health in Mental Retardation: Recent Advances and Practices* (ed. N. Bouras), Cambridge University Press, Cambridge.
Gerlach, J. (1991) Current views on tardive dyskinesia. Symposium. Atypical antipsychotics: clinical advantages. *Pharmacopsychiatry*, **24**, 47.
Gilbert, P. (2000) *The A–Z Reference Book of Syndromes and Inherited Disorders*, 3rd edn, Nelson Thornes, Cheltenham.
Kaplan, H.I. and Sadock, B.J. (1993) *Psychotropic Drug Treatment*, Williams & Wilkins, Baltimore.
Linaker, O.M. (1990) Frequency of and determinants for psychotropic drug use in an institution for the mentally retarded, *British Journal of Psychiatry*, **156**, 525–30.
Ryan, M. (1991) Drug use in NSW institutions, innovation for inertia. *Australia and New Zealand Journal of Developmental Disabilities*, **17**, 177.
Thomas, C. and Lewis, S. (1998) Which atypical antipsychotic. *British Journal of Psychiatry*, **172**, 106–10.

CHAPTER 5

Emerson, E. (1998) Working with people with challenging behaviour. In *Clinical Psychology and People with Intellectual Disability*. (eds E. Emerson, A. Caine, C. Hatton and J. Bromley), Wiley, Chichester.
Fripp, S. and Carroll, J. (1997) *Prioritisation and Case Weighting*. Luton and Dunstable Physiotherapy Department: presented as a reviewed poster at The Chartered Society of Physistherapists conference, Edinburgh.
Law, M., Baptiste, S., Carswell, A., McColl, M.A., Polatajlo, H. and Pollock N (1994) *Canadian Occupational Performance Measures*, 2nd edn, Canadian Association of Occupational Therapists Publications, ACE copyright, Toronto.

Ovretueit J. (1993) *Co-ordinating Community Care*, Open University Press, Buckingham.

Spalding, N.J. (1997) Rationing our therapy services: is it rightful and reasonable? *British Journal of Therapy and Rehabilitation*, **4**, 448–53.

CHAPTER 6

Bradley, H. (1991) *Assessing Communication Together*, Mental Handicap Nurses Association, MHNA Publications, York.

Carke-Keahoe, A. (1992) Towards effective communication. In *A Practical Guide to Working with People with Learning Disability* (eds H. Brown and S. Benson), Hawker, London, pp. 31–40.

Goldbart, J., Warner, J. and Mount, H. (1994) *The Development of Early Communication and Feeding for People who have Profound and Multiple Disabilities – A Workshop Training Package for Parents and Carers*, MENCAP PIMD, London.

Knight, C. (1991) Developing communication through interaction, in *Innovatory Practice and Severe Learning Difficulties* (ed. J. Watson), Moray House Publications, Edinburgh, pp. 13–24.

Royal National Institute for the Blind (1993a) *Challenging Behaviour in Visually and Learning Disabled Adults*, RNIB, London.

Royal National Institute for the Blind (1993b) *Stereotypical Behaviour in People with Visually and Learning Disabilities*, RNIB, London.

Royal National Institute for the Blind (1998) *Challenging Behaviour in Visually and Learning Disabled Adults*, Factsheet, RNIB, London

CHAPTER 7

O'Brien, J. and Towell, D. (2004) Building local capacity for person centred approaches. Available from www.bris.ac.uk/deRts/norahfrv/strategy/DaDers.htm.

Routledge, M. and Sanderson, H. (2001) *Towards Person Centred Approaches: Planning with People. Guidance for Implementation Groups*, Department of Health, London.

State University of New York (1994) *Functional Independence Measure (FIM)*, State University of New York at Buffalo, Buffalo NY.

Steiner, D. and Norman, G. (1989) *Health Measurement Scales: A Practical Guide to their Development and Use*, Oxford Medical Publications, Oxford.

Swain, J. and French, S. (1999) *Therapy and Learning Difficulties: Advocacy, Participation and Partnership*, Butterworth-Heinemann, Oxford.

CHAPTER 10

Barnes, M. and Radermacher, H. (2003) *Community Rehabilitation in Neurology*, Cambridge University Press, Cambridge.

Bobath, B. (1978) *Adult Hemiplegia: Evaluation and Treatment*, William Heinemann Medical Books, London.

Bobath, K. (1980) *A Neurophysiological Basis for the Treatment of Cerebral Palsy*, 2nd edn, MacKeith Press, Blackwell Scientific Publications, Oxford.

Broadhurst, M.J., Young, J. and Oliva, B. (2005) Development of a head support system for use during hoist transfer to a swivel walker. *Physiotherapy*, **91**, 257–60.

Caldwell, M., Calder, J., Aitken, S. and Millar, S. (1995) Use of personal passports with deafblind people. *Talking Sense*, Autumn, 9–12.

Fraser, B.A., Hensinger, R.N. and Phelps, J.A. (1987) *Physical Management of Multiple Handicaps. A Professional's Guide*, Paul H. Brookes, Baltimore.

Greenwood, R.J., Barnes, M.P., McMillan, T. and Ward, C.D. (eds) (2003) *Handbook of Neurological Rehabilitation*, 2nd edn, Physiology Press, Hove.

Lacey, P. and Ouvrey, C. (eds) (1998) *People with Profound and Multiple Learning Disorders: A Collaborative Approach to Meeting Complex Needs*, David Fulton, London.

Pope, P.M. (1996) Postural management and special seating, in *Neurological Physiotherapy, A Problem Solving Approach* (ed. S. Edwards), Churchill Livingston, New York.

Scrutton, D., Damiano, D. and Mayston, M. (eds) (2004) *Management of the Motor Disorders of Children with Cerebral Palsey*, MacKeith Press, Blackwell Scientific Publications, Oxford.

CHAPTER 11

Association of Swimming Therapy (1981) *Swimming for the Disabled*, A. & C. Black, London.

Hydrotherapy Association of Chartered Society of Physiotherapy (1993) *Standards of Good Practice*, Chartered Society of Physiotherapy, London.

Reid Campion, M. (ed.) (1997) *Hydrotherapy Principles and Practice*, Butterworth Heinemann, Oxford.

CHAPTER 12

Barnes, T. (1992) Perspective in back riding, in *Therapeutic Riding Programmes* (ed. B. Engel). Barbara Engel Publishing Services, Durango.

Belch, K. (1994) Conductive education with the best of Scottish practice and the horse, in *Proceedings of the Eighth International Riding Conference*, Hamilton, New Zealand, pp. 173–80.

Bertoti, D.B. (1988) Effect of therapeutic horseback riding on posture in children with cerebral palsy. *Physical Therapy*, **68** (10), 1505–12.

Engel, B. (ed.) (1994) *The Horse, the Handicapped and the Riding Team*, Barbara Engel Publishing Services, Durango.

Heipertz, W. (1984) *Therapeutic Riding*, translated by M. Takeuchi, Canadian Equestrian Federation, Ottawa, Canada.

Heipertz-Hengst, C. (1994) Evaluation of outcome in hippotherapy, in *Proceedings of the Eighth International Riding Conference*, Hamilton, New Zealand, pp. 217–21.

Hodge, P. and Barnes, T. (1998) Guidelines for proper backriding. *North American Riding for the Handicapped Association News*, **2**, 4–5.

Quint, C. and Toomey, M. (1998) Powered saddle and pelvic mobility. *Physiotherapy*, **84** (8), 376–84.

Riede, D. (1998) *Physiotherapy with the Horse*, Therapeutic Riding Services MD 21139, USA.

Saywell, S. (1998) The History and Development of Riding for the Disabled, *Physiotherapy Practice*, **4**, 146–54.

Shkedi, A. (1994) Special riding for special needs, in *Proceedings of the Eighth International Riding Conference*, Hamilton, New Zealand, pp. 125–6.

Spink, J. (1992) *Developmental Riding Therapy*, Therapy Skill Builders, Tuscon AZ.

Stewart, I. et al. (1998) Therapeutic riding and self-concept of disabled children, in *Proceedings of the Sixth International Riding Conference*, Toronto, Canada, pp. 181–91.

Strauss, I. (1995) *Hippotherapy, Neurophysiological Therapy on the Horse*, translated by M. Takeuchi, Ontario Therapeutic Riding Association, Ontario, Canada.

Watts, L.M.J. (1994) The design and evaluation of a therapeutic riding programme, in *Proceedings of the Eighth International Riding Conference*, Hamilton, New Zealand, pp. 29–55.

CHAPTER 13

Anderson, E. (1987) Movement education for children with severe disabilities. *British Journal of Physical Education*, **18**, 5.

Hartley, E. and Rushton, C. (1984) The therapeutic use of the trampoline in inhibiting abnormal reflex reactions and facilitating normal patterns of movements in some cerebral palsied children. *Journal of the Society of Remedial Gymnastics and Recreational Therapy*, **113**, 6–11.

Spurling, E. (2002) *The Provision and Perceived Benefits of Rebound Therapy in the United Kingdom*, unpublished dissertation, University of Nottingham.

CHAPTER 14

Houston, G. (1990) *The Red Book of Groups*, Rochester Foundation, Rochester.

Mead, H. (2003) *Use of Rebound Therapy in Adult Learning Disabilities*, University of Nottingham, Nottingham, Chapter 14.

Noorderhaven, N.G. (1999) Intercultural differences – consequences for the physical therapy profession. *Physiotherapy*, **85** (9), 504–10.

FITNESS GROUPS

Hunt, P. and Hillsdon, M. (1996) *Changing Eating and Exercise Behaviour*, Blackwell Science, Oxford.

JABADAO

Adler, J. (1992) Body and soul (authentic movement). *American Journal of Dance Therapy*, **14** (2), 73–94.
Chodrow, J. (1991) *Dance Therapy and Depth Psychology*, Routledge, London.

T'AI CHI

Panter, J. and Davis, R. (1990) *The Art of Taoist Tai Chi (Cultivating Mind and Body)*, Taoist Tai Chi Society of Canada, Toronto.

CHAPTER 16

Chapman, M., Craven, M., Chadwick, D. (2005) Fighting Fit? An evaluation of health practitioner input to improve healthy living and reduce obesity. *Journal of Intellectual Disabilities*, **9** (2), 131–44.
Bouchard, C. (ed.) (2000) *Physical Activity and Obesity*, Human Kinetics Europe Ltd, Champaign.

CHAPTER 17

Gunstone, M. (ed.) (2002) *Learning Difficulties and Associated Conditions Explained with YOGA CASE STUDIES*. YOU & ME Publications, London.
Gunstone, M. (2003a) *YOU & ME Joint Looseners and Variations for Special Needs and Workbook*. YOU & ME Publications, London.
Gunstone, M. (2003b) *YOU & ME Yoga Postures and Variations for Special Needs and Workbook*. YOU & ME Publications, London.
Sanderson, H., Harrison, J., with Price, S. (1991) *Aromatherapy and Massage for People with Learning Disabilities*, Hands on Publishing, Birmingham.

Appendix B Useful Addresses, Telephone Numbers and Websites

CHAPTER 1

Americans with Disabilities Act (1990)
www.dol.gov/odep
Department for Education and Skills. DfES Publications http://www.surestart.gov.
uk/_doc/P0000831.pdf
Department of Health Publications http://www.dh.gov.uk
New Freedom Initiatives: Americans with disabilities www.whitehouse.gov/infocus/
newfreedom
Office of Public Sector Information (OPSI) http://www.opsi.gov.uk/acts
The Stationery Office, London http://www.archive.official-documents.co.uk/document/
cm50/5086/5086.pdf

CHAPTER 2

AUTISM AND ASPERGER'S SYNDROME

The National Autistic Society
393 City Road
London EC1V 1NG   020 7833 2299   www.nas.org.uk

The Scottish Autism Society
Hilton House
Alloa Business Park
The Whinns
Alloa
Clackmannanshire FK10 3SA   01259 720044   www.autism-in-scotland.org.uk

CEREBRAL PALSY

Capability Scotland
Advice Service Capability Scotland (ASCS)

Learning Disability: Physical Therapy Treatment and Management. Edited by Jeanette Rennie
© 2007 John Wiley & Sons Ltd

11 Ellersly Road
Edinburgh
Scotland EH12 6HY   0131 313 5510   www.capability-scotland.org.uk

SCOPE

6 Market Road
London N7 9PW   020 7619 7100   www.scope.org.uk

DOWN SYNDROME

Down Syndrome Association
Langdon Down Centre
2a Langdon Park
Teddington TW11 9PS   0845 230 0372   www.downs-syndrome.org.uk

DYSPRAXIA

The Dyspraxia Foundation
8 West Alley
Hitchin
Herts SG5 1EG   01462 455016   www.dyspraxiafoundation.org.uk

EPILEPSY

The National Society for Epilepsy
Chesham Lane
Chalfont St Peter
Bucks. SL9 0RJ   01494 601300   www.epilepsynse.org.uk

Further   information   on   the   healthcare   commission   is   available   on
www.healthcarecommission.org.uk

CHAPTER 3

RETT SYNDROME

RSAUK
113 Friern Barnet Road
London N11 3EU   National 0870 770 3266   Local 020 8361 5161
www.rettsyndrome.org.uk

CHAPTER 5

Clinical Effectiveness Networks www.nhshealthquality.org/nhsqis/qis

CHAPTER 6

COMMUNICATION PROBLEMS

The Makaton Vocabulary Development Project
31, Firwood Drive
Camberley GU15 3QD   01276 61390   www.makaton.org

LEARNING DISABILITY

MENCAP
123 Golden Lane
London EC1Y 0RT   020 7454 0454   www.mencap.org.uk

ENABLE Scotland
6th Floor
7 Buchanan Street
Glasgow G1 3HL   0141 226 4541   www.enable.org.uk

WORKING WITH PEOPLE WHO HAVE A HEARING PROBLEM

RAD (Royal Association for Deaf People)
18 Westside Centre
London Road
Stanway
Colchester
Essex CO3 8PH   0845 6882525   www.royaldeaf.org.uk

The National Deaf Children's Society
15 Dufferin Street
London EC1Y 8PD   020 7490 8565   www.ndcs.org.uk

The Royal National Institute for Deaf People (RNID)
19–23 Featherstone Street
London EC1Y 8SL   020 7296 8000   www.rnid.org.uk

WORKING WITH PEOPLE WHO HAVE A VISUAL PROBLEM

The Partially Sighted Society
Queen's Road
Doncaster DN1 2NX   01302 323132   www.patient.co.uk

The Royal National Institute for the Blind (RNIB)
105 Judd Street
London WC1H 9NE   020 7388 1266   www.rnib.org.uk

CHAPTER 7

ASSESSMENT

Barthel Index
Stroke Scales and Clinical Assessment Tools
http://www.strokecenter.org/trials/scales/barthel.html

FACE PROFILE LEARNING DISABILITY
WALNUT ASSESSMENT

P I Clifford
British Psychological Society
Centre for outcomes, research and effectiveness
Sub-department of Clinical Health Psychology
UCL
Gower Street
London WC1E 6BT
UK

FUNCTIONAL INDEPENDENCE MEASURE (FIM)

Uniform Data Center for Medical Rehabilitation
270 Northpointe Parkway, Suite 3000
Amherst, New York 14228   (716) 817-7800

www.udsmr.org

The Center for Outcome Measurement in Brain Injury.
http://www.tbims.org/combi/FIM

MARY MARLBOROUGH LODGE ASSESSMENT

Mary Marlborough Disability Centre
Windmill Road
Headington
Oxford
UK   OX3 7LD   01865 741155   www.noc.org.uk

MOBILITY OPPORTUNITIES VIA EDUCATION (MOVE)

MOVE International
1300 17th Street
City Centre
Bakersfield CA93301-4533
USA   move-international@kern.org

MOVE Europe
Wooden Spoon House
5 Dugard Way
London SE11 4TH   020 7414 1494   www.move-europe.org.uk

MOVE Scotland
42 Cammo Grove
Edinburgh EH4 8EX   0131 339 7555   www.moveeurope.org.uk

NOTES FOR CHARTERED PHYSIOTHERAPISTS WORKING WITH PEOPLE WITH LEARNING DISABILITIES

Joyce R Wise
The Stables
College Square
Stokesley TS9 5DN

TELER

A A Le Roux.
TELER Information Pack
TELER PO Box 699
Sheffield   S17 3YG   0114 273 1002   www.teler.com

THE 'OK HEALTH CHECK'

Fairfield Publications
P.O. Box 310
Preston Central   PR1 9GH   www.fairfieldpublications.co.uk

CHAPTER 9

PCSP (UK) Ltd. www.posturalcareskills.com

CHAPTER 10

Equipment is specific to individual clients and several firms may have to be approached before the most appropriate piece is found.

Many areas have a centre where a range of equipment from different firms can be tried by individual clients. The centre staff will know which equipment can be supplied though Health and Social Services and which needs to be privately purchased.

The NAIDEX exhibitions held throughout the UK are a good opportunity to see and compare latest developments from a range of suppliers.

Comprehensive information about independently assessed equipment can be obtained from:

The Disability Information Trust
Mary Marlborough Centre
Windmill Road
Headington
Oxford
UK   OX3 7LD   01865 741155   www.noc.org.uk

UPDATE Scotland's National Disability Information Service
27 Beaverhall Road
Edinburgh EH7 4JE   0131 558 5200   www.update.org.uk

The following is a small selection of well known equipment suppliers.

REHABILITATION EQUIPMENT

Homecraft and Ability One
PO Box 5665
Kirby in Ashfield
Nottinghamshire   NG17 7QX   01623 757555   www.homecraftabilityone.com

Theraplay Limited
32 Welbeck Road
Glasgow G53 7SD   0141 8769177   www.applegate.co.uk

HOISTS AND MOBILITY AIDS

ARJO Ltd
St. Catherine Street
Gloucester GL1 2SL   08702 430430   www.arjo.com

ARJO (Ireland) Ltd
19 Heron Road
Sydenham Industrial Estate
Belfast BT3 9LE   028 9050 2000

Munro Rehab Ltd
8–10 Dunrobin Court
North Avenue
Clydebank Business Park
Clydebank   G81 2QP   0141 952 2323   www.munro.com

Silvalea Ltd
Units 3 and 4

Silverhills Buildings
Silverhills Road
Decoy Industrial Estate
Newton Abbot
Devon   TQ12 5LZ   01626 331655   www.silvalea.com

Sunrise Medical Ltd
High Street
Wollaston
West Midlands   DY8 4PS   01384 446688   www.sunrisemedical.co.uk

Southwest Medical Online
http://www.southwestmedical.com/easy-stand.html

PRESSURE RELIEVING SYSTEMS

Qbitus Products
Units 11 and 12, Victoria Park
Lightower Road
Halifax   HX1 5WD   01422 381188   www.qbitus.co.uk

Spenco Healthcare International Ltd
Brian Royd Mills
Saddleworth Road
Greetland
Halifax
West Yorkshire   HX4 8NF   01422 378569   www.spenco-healthcare.co.uk

SEATING AND POSITIONING

Active Design
68K Wyrley Road
Witton
Birmingham   B6 7BN   0121 326 7506   www.activedesign.co.uk

Edinburgh Harness
The Smart Centre
The Astley Ainslie Hospital
133 Grange Loan
Edinburgh   EH9 2HL   0131 537 9432

JCM Seating Solutions
49 Winsover Road
Spalding
Lincolnshire   PE11 1EG   01775 766664   www.jcmseating.co.uk

James Leckey Design
Kilwee Industrial Park
Dunmurry   BT17 0HD   02890 602277   www.leckey.com

Symmetrikit
Unit 9L
Bromyard Road Trading Estate
Ledbury   HR8 1NS   01531 635388   www.helpinghand.co.uk

SEATING, SENSORY AND POSTURAL

Jenx Ltd also distributors for Rifton Equipment
Wardsend Road
Sheffield S6 1RQ   0114 285 3376   www.jenx.com

The Kirton Health Group Ltd
23 Rookwood Way
Haverhill
Suffolk CB9 8PB   0800 212709   www.kirton-healthcare.co.uk

CHAPTER 11

Aquatic Therapy and Rehabilitation Institute
http://www.atri.org/uk

Halliwick
www.halliwick.org.uk

CHAPTER 12

Hon. Secretary for ACPTR
Miss GM Walker. FCSP.
The Orchard
Broadlands
Lower Paice Lane
Medstead
HANTS. GU34 5PX   01420 562638

CHAPTER 14

JABADAO WORKSHOPS

Jabadao National Centre for Movement, Learning and Health
The Yard
Viaduct Street

Stanningley
Leeds LS28 6AU   0113 236 3311   www.jabadao.org

T'AI CHI

T'ai Chi and Special Needs Video
Linda Chase Broda
Village Hall T'ai Chi
163 Palatine Road
Manchester   M20 2GH   www.taichiandspecialneeds.co.uk

Suitable CDs are available and can be accessed through new age outlets

SENSORY EQUIPMENT

Hope Education Special Needs
Orb Mill
Huddersfield Road
Waterhead
Oldham   OO4 2ST   08451 202055   www.hope-education.co.uk

ROMPA
Goyt Side Road
Chesterfield
Derbyshire   S40 2PH   01246 211777   www.rompa.com

SpaceKraft Limited
Titus House
29 Saltaire Road
Shipley
West Yorkshire   BD18 3HH   01274 581007   www.spacekraft.co.uk

CHAPTER 15

Disability Sport England
Solecast House
13-27 Brunswick Place
London N1 6DX   020 7490 4919   www.euroyellowpages.com/dse/dispengl.html

Special Olympics Great Britain
National Development Office
Ground Floor
123 Golden Lane
London   EC1Y 0RT   0207 696 5569   www.specialolympicsgb.org

Special Olympics Ireland Central Office
4th Floor

Park House
North Circular Road
Dublin 7
Ireland   +353 1 882 3972   www.specialolympics.ie/en

ATHLETICS

UK Athletics Ltd
Athletics House
Central Boulevard
Blythe Valley Park
Solihull
West Midlands   B90 8AJ   0870 998 6800   www.ukathletics.net

OUTDOOR PURSUITS

Calvert Trust
Kielder Water
Hexham
Northumberland NE48 1BS   01434 250 232   www.calvert-trust.org.uk

Badaguish
Cairngorm Outdoor Centre
By Glenmore
Aviemore
Invernesshire PH22 1QU   01479 861285   www.badaguish.org

RAMBLING

The Fieldfare Trust
Volunteer House
69 Crossgate
Cupar
Fife KY15 5AS   www.fieldfare.org.uk

VOLLEYBALL

English Volleyball Association
Suite B
Loughborough Technology Centre
Epinal Way
Loughborough LE11 3GE   01509 631699   www.volleyballengland.org

CHAPTER 16

Sport England
Third Floor
Victoria House
Bloomsbury Square
London   WC1B 4SE   08458 50850   www.sportengland.org

British Heart Foundation National Centre for Physical Activity and Health
www.bhfactive.org.uk

Phab NI Inclusion matters
P.O. Box 780
Belfast   BT15 3YG   www.inclusionmatters.org

Sporting Equals
Fairgate House
King's Road
Tyseley
Birmingham   B11 2AA   0121 707 9340   www.sportingequals.com

English Federation of Disability Sport
Manchester Metropolitan University
Alsager Campus
Hassall Road
Alsager
Stoke on Trent   ST7 2HL   0161 247 5294   www.efds.co.uk

Scottish Disability Sport
Fife Sports Institute
Viewfield Road
Glenrothes   KY6 2RB   01592 415 700   www.scottishdisabilitysport.com

Federation of Disability Sport Wales
Welsh Institute of Sport
Sophia Gardens
Cardiff   CF11 9SW   029 2066 5781   www.fdsw.org.uk

Disability Sports Northern Ireland
Unit 10
Ormeau Business Park
8 Cromac Avenue
Belfast   BT7 2JA   028 9050 8255   www.dsni.co.uk

CYCLING

Cycling project for the North West and Wheels for All – (database of clubs, shops and cycling organisations) www.cycleweb.co.uk, email cpnw@cycling.org.uk www.cycling.org.uk

Sustrans/National cycling Network www.nationalcyclenetwork.org.uk

Cyclists Touring Club CTC www.ctc.org.uk

London Recumbents www.londonrecumbents.co.uk

British Cycling Federation www.bcf.uk.com

CHAPTER 17

IFPA (International Federation of Professional Aromatherapists)
82 Ashby Road,
Hinckley,
Leicestershire LE10 1SN   01455 637987   www.ifparoma.org

Appendix C Relevant Acts of Parliament

Adults with Incapacity (Scotland) Act 2000
Carers Act 2004
Care Standards Act 2000
Chronically Sick and Disabled Persons Act 1970
Community Care and Health (Scotland) Act 2002
County Asylums Act 1808
Disability Discrimination Act 1995
Disability Discrimination Act 2005
Disabled Persons Act 1986
Education Act 1981
Education Act 1981 (Scotland)
Education (Additional Support for Learning) (Scotland) Act 2004
Health Act 1999
Health and Social Care (Community Health and Standards) Act 2003
Human Rights Act 1998
Madhouse Act 1774
Mental Capacity Act 2005
Mental Deficiency Act 1913
Mental Deficiency Act 1914
Mental Deficiency Act 1927
Mental Health Act 1959
Mental Health Act for England and Wales 1983
Mental Health (Scotland) Act 1984
Mental Health (Scotland) Act 2001
Mental Health (Care and Treatment) (Scotland) Act 2003
National Health Service Act 1946
National Health Service Act (as amended) 1948
National Health Service and Community Care Act 1990
National Health Service Reform (Scotland) Act 2004
Race Relations Act 1976
Race Relations (Northern Ireland) Act 1998
Race Relations (Amendment) Act 2000
Vagrancy Act 1713
Vagrancy Act 1714

Learning Disability: Physical Therapy Treatment and Management. Edited by Jeanette Rennie
© 2007 John Wiley & Sons Ltd

Index